THIS IS
WHY

Understanding Human Behavior

**WHY PEOPLE DO
WHAT THEY DO**

ROB ABEL

Published by
We Are Abel LLC

www.iWantToKnowWHY.com

The content provided is for informational purposes only and is not a substitute for professional medical or mental health advice, diagnosis, or treatment. Always seek the guidance of a qualified healthcare provider for any health or mental health concerns.

Copyright © 2026 by Rob Abel

All Rights Reserved. No part of this book may be used or reproduced in any manner whatsoever without written permission, except in the case of brief quotations embodied in critical articles and reviews.

ISBNs:
979-8-9938383-0-4 (Paperback)
979-8-9938383-1-1 (Hardcover)
979-8-9938383-2-8 (Ebook)

Printed in the United States of America

Contents

Introduction 1

Section 100: YOUR WHY NATURE
These are the traits you were born with

Chapter 101: Personality Types 8

Chapter 102: Alphas and Sigmas and Betas, Oh My! 32

Chapter 103: Moving Toward Pleasure People or
    Moving Away From Pain 56

Chapter 104: The Six Basic Human Needs 65

Chapter 105: Capacity 88

Chapter 106: The 5 Love Languages 98

Chapter 107: The 5 WHYs 112

Chapter 108: Bringing YOUR WHY NATURE All Together .. 117

Section 200: YOUR WHY NURTURE
This is what happened to you

Chapter 201: Birth Order 140

Chapter 202: Expectations, Beliefs, and Rules (EBR) 158

Chapter 203: Maslow's Hierarchy of Needs 178

Section 300: YOUR WHY NURTURE
Where you are now

Chapter 301: Balance 182

Chapter 302: Communication 201

Chapter 303: Relationships.....................................225

Chapter 304: Associations, Triggers, and Demons 248

Section 400: YOUR WHY NURTURE
What you might not realize

Chapter 401: Are You Smart Enough to Feel Stupid?...........264

Chapter 402: The Negative Wave 278

Chapter 403: You Are a Slave, Neo............................284

Chapter 404: Tribalism 295

Chapter 405: Good Pride vs. Bad Pride 305

Section 500: YOUR WHY NURTURE
Growing from what we now know

Chapter 501: Being in the Right Environment 310

Chapter 502: Winning 316

Chapter 503: Character..319

Chapter 504: Evolution..333

Chapter 505: Get a Glass of Cold Water Before
You Read This..363

Chapter 506: Being a Good Human 366

Chapter 507: The WHY Bracelet...............................372

Section 600: YOUR WHY NURTURE
Summary

Chapter 601: Bringing It All Together 376

www.iWantToKnowWHY.com

Introduction

Hello! I want to thank you for taking this step towards improving your life. WHY is about WHY you do the things you do and WHY you are who you are, as a person. When I say who you are I mean deep down from the core and to the surface. Everything. I will give you a language to communicate who you are as a person with yourself and other people. There are no frills, no BS, this is not a pump you up session, and there is no judgment, there is just understanding. You finally understanding yourself (and others) and that it is ok to be you. You will realize WHY your life works or WHY it doesn't work. WHY you are happy or not happy. WHY you are "in the right place" or not and how to correctly change that, without guessing.

Do you want to know WHY you are the way you are? WHY you do the things you do? WHY you have the spouse that you do? WHY your relationship is working or not? WHY you have the friends you have? WHY you get along with some family members and not others? WHY you like or dislike your job? WHY you like or dislike yourself? WHY people like or dislike you? WHY other people do the things they do? If yes, then keep reading.

Knowledge is power and this is the power we need to take control of our lives. If your life has felt like a ship without a rudder, then you have come to the right place. If your life has felt like everything has gone right, then this will give you the understanding of WHY that is, so you can better duplicate your success.

I LOVE myself and I LOVE being me. WHY? Because I FINALLY understand myself. I understand my parents, my wife, my kids, my boss, my family members, and new people I meet. I now have a language which allows me to effectively communicate with myself and others. I have spent decades fine tuning this language and now I want to share it with you. Through this understanding, and communication, I can do more or less of the behaviors which serve my happiness. Through this understanding, I have found happiness and peace in my life. Through this understanding, I know which relationships to strengthen and which relationships that need to be cut out of my life. Not that they are bad people, it's just that where they are in their life doesn't serve my happiness. I wish myself well, you well, my family well, my friends well and the people I cut out of my life well (I wrote them in this order for a reason) but now I know WHY, which gives me the understanding and clarity to have a life by design! Does this sound amazing? All I promise you, is the truth. Sometimes you are not going to like what I have to say, and sometimes you are going to have to pause for a major (positive) epiphany, but I promise it will be the truth.

It took me a long time and a lot of soul searching to understand the meaning of life. I am happy to say that I have found the meaning of life! Would you like to know? The answer had to be simple, yet profound. Basic yet complex. Easy to understand yet makes one stop and think. Without further ado…

The meaning of life is: THE WAY YOU FEEL

That's it! Read that many times and it will start to change meaning.

How you feel is directly related to the way you think. The way you think is directly related to your understanding of yourself and other people. Life is about technique. Try to carry five unstacked plates with two hands and you will find that technique doesn't work too well. However, if we stack five plates together on top of one another, you can carry all five with one hand. The quality of your life will be based, in part, on the techniques you use to make your life happen including the techniques you use to effectively communicate. I will explain these techniques and this communication.

WHY else should I read this book? Because we not born with a set of instructions, nor a user manual and we are all somewhat incompatible. The most important reason is because once you understand WHY you do what you do, WHY you behave the way you do, and who you are, then you can finally understand where you fit into the world. You will know who you are sharing with other people. Also, we need to understand one another in order to have connection, compassion and tolerance. Most importantly, once we all understand WHY one does what they do, then we can have tolerance. Through tolerance we can have acceptance. Once we have acceptance, we can have peace.

When you read things that resonate within you, don't fight that feeling. Embrace it, get curious about, and understand it. What feels right to YOU is who you are and that's beautiful.

> *"If you want to clean up the neighborhood, sweep your own doorstep first"*
> ~Earl Nightingale

WHAT TO EXPECT FROM WHY

First, I am going to explain concepts, personality types and behaviors and then tie them all together. This is the blueprint of your life. This is the blueprint of everyone's life. This is WHY we do what we do! The good news is this is not permanent. This is where we are today. Understanding oneself, loved ones, family, friends, coworkers and behavior in general, is the foundation. Understanding behavior from its core is the key to building a life by design. These are the instincts we were born with, traits that were passed down, upbringing, and the learned behaviors we picked up from interaction with others. In these pages you will learn WHY you do what you do. Then you can decide if you want to accentuate certain parts, or eliminate certain behaviors to be the you that you want to be.

Once you understand who you are, it will be like a weight lifted off you that you didn't even know was there. Suddenly, you will understand yourself. You will understand others. You will have a language in which to share your WHY. WHY you do what you do. Through that understanding you will make conscious decisions on whether or not your behavior truly serves your happiness. You will understand you have been subconsciously making those decisions up until this point and you were no different than a ship without control of its rudder. You will also know WHY others are doing what they do and will have the language to articulate what you see. Through this understanding, and those conscious decisions, your life will change for the better, you will become happier, you will become free, you will know who you truly are, and you will know your WHY.

One thing to note about this book. I purposely chose not to have it proof read. Due to this, you will see typos, run on sentences, grammatical errors, and thoughts which may not go together. WHY did I choose this? Because we need to understand that life is not perfect and neither is this book. This book is perfectly imperfect, just like you, and that is beautiful!

Here is the fun part! I spent three years, from 2005—2007, writing the first WHY book. On October 7th, 2007, I finished the book. I gave it to friends, family members and even psychologists to get their opinions and feedback. The feedback was fantastic. I decided not to publish the book. I spent the next 17 years testing the theories and evolving the concepts. I am happy to say, that over the last 17 years, the original book was right on target. Then, in 2024, I began volume 2. Everything didn't flow together so I rewrote them both and combined everything into one. This final version is the combination of theories I have tested to be tried and true over the last 2 decades, along with all of the knowledge and additions I accumulated.

INTRODUCTION

Ever heard of "Nature vs Nurture?" Well, the first 8 chapters, section 100, will explain you. YOUR WHY NATURE. What is inside you, what you were born with, who you are at your core, and WHY. The reason the WHY logo is an upside down triangle is because that is how the first section of the book goes, and what affects your behavior the most. All along uncovering the WHY of your behavior.

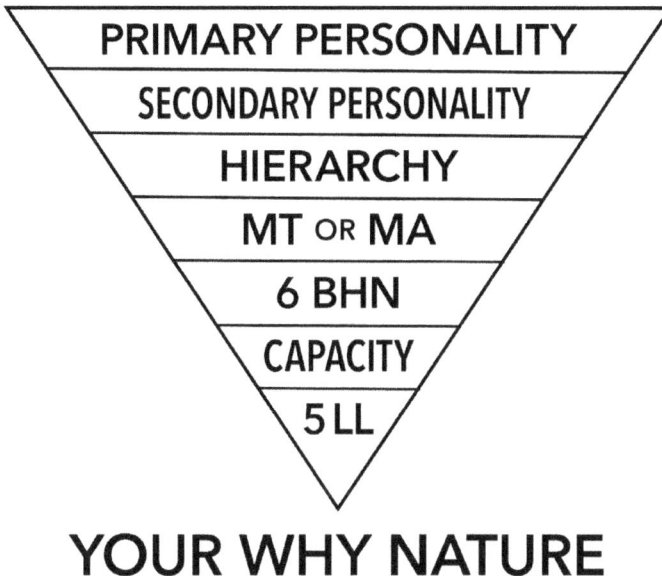

The 200 section starts YOUR WHY NURTURE. These are your experiences, your circumstances, how you were raised, what you currently believe, and WHY. Section 100 is who you are (nature) and section 200 is what happened to you during your life's journey (starting to explain nurture.) Section 300 is where you are now. Section 400 is what we might not realize. Section 500 is growing from what we know. Section 600 is the summary.

Remember, we want to uncover the truth. The truth is not right, the truth is not wrong, it's merely the truth and our WHY. Enjoy!

Google search: The greatest question you can ask is WHY

The statement "the greatest question you can ask is WHY" highlights the importance of critical thinking and exploring underlying causes. It suggests that asking "WHY" encourages deeper understanding, encourages reflection, and helps us move beyond superficial observations.

Here's WHY "WHY" is considered a valuable question:

- **Understanding and Knowledge:** Asking "WHY" prompts us to seek reasons and explanations, leading to a deeper understanding of situations, events, and phenomena.

- **Critical Thinking:** It encourages us to analyze, investigate, and evaluate information, which is crucial for making informed decisions and judgments.

- **Root Cause Analysis:** By repeatedly asking "WHY," we can delve into the underlying causes of problems, leading to more effective solutions.

- **Learning and Growth:** Understanding the reasons behind things allows us to learn from our experiences and make better choices in the future.

- **Personal Reflection:** Asking "WHY" about our own beliefs, behaviors, and motivations can help us understand ourselves better and make positive changes.

- **Motivation and Purpose:** Understanding the "WHY" behind a task or goal can increase motivation and purpose.

SECTION 100:
YOUR WHY NATURE

These are the traits you were born with

CHAPTER 101:
Personality Types

For centuries, different philosophers have had the idea that personality types fit into four categories. As far back as 400 BC, Hippocrates talked about the four temperaments. His philosophy was based on how much, or how little, of certain body fluids one had. Yuck.

In 1921, industrial psychologist David Merrill came up with an alternative. Merrill realized we could usually "type" people by watching their behavior. Merrill called his types, "communication styles," and named them:

- Amiable

- Analytical

- Driver

- Expressive

Only listed this way due to alphabetical order. These are all separate, one is not better than the other, this is not a hierarchy, and not a progression. Let me be perfectly clear here: I am going to pick on everyone. I don't care which personality type you are, some people are going to love it, and some aren't. Some people are going to think you are great and some will think you are difficult. I am only the messenger to tell you WHY and, most importantly, I am here to have fun with it while we learn! Fasten your seat belt.

I can hear some people saying, "Ummm, Rob, you can't just categorize people like this. People are complex and multifaceted and everyone has a unique personality." To those people I say, "You are correct, but so am I. So just read with an open mind and all will be clear."

I have studied this, and lived this, for many years and realized two things:

1. There is a further breakdown of these personality types. They should be broken down into eight categories. It goes like this:

Unevolved Amiable, Evolved Amiable
Unevolved Analytical, Evolved Analytical
Unevolved Expressive, Evolved Expressive
Unevolved Driver, Evolved Driver

People are PRIMARILY one of the four personality types. Start with that. Your personality type is either evolved or unevolved, which is WHY I break it up into eight personality types. Whether or not one knows how to be their personality type makes the difference. Ok Rob, what the hell did you just say? I'm saying, you are (one of those four personality types) who you are. If you don't know WHY you do what you do, then you will just do it in unfiltered and in raw form. Unfiltered and raw = Unevolved.

First, understand (I will define them soon) which one of the four personality types you are: Aimable, Analytical, Driver, or Expressive. Evolved or Unevolved doesn't come into play yet. Then you will begin to know WHY you do what you do. Through understanding, time and training you will get better at being your personality type. I have said several times, and yes I'll say it again, life is all about technique. Employ the wrong ones and you may have a tough road ahead. Employ the right ones and life becomes easier. Try to open a jar with two fingers. You may not be able to. Change the technique and use your entire hand. Now you can open the jar. This change in technique changed the outcome. A small change in technique may achieve the desired outcome in life too. Basically, the difference between Evolved and Unevolved is the Evolved use the right techniques to be good at being an Aimable, Analytical, Driver or Expressive. WHY I am breaking this down into eight categories? Because an Unevolved Driver behaves much differently than an Evolved Driver. Now is where the fun begins!

The second thing I have realized is:

2. Everyone has a secondary behavior type and they toggle back and forth!

Your secondary behavior type is one of the same eight listed above. Example: you could be primarily an Evolved Aimable with a secondary Unevolved Driver or you could be primarily an Unevolved Analytical with a secondary Evolved Expressive. Some combinations are rarer; however, all are possible. Some people, as an example, are primarily a Driver and are secondarily a Driver! Some are primarily an Analytical and are a secondarily an Analytical. If both are the same and both are evolved or both are unevolved, then you may never see the person "toggle" to their secondary.

The secondary behavior type comes out under certain conditions or circumstances. Everyone is different. Sometimes it comes out when one is under stress or needs to focus, maybe when one is scared, or happy, or maybe simply needs to rush to finish a task. Sometimes it can simply come out when the situation calls for it. I will revisit this once I define the personality types.

Hey Rob, wait a minute! Are you saying I chose to have a certain type of job because of my personality type? Yes! Light bulb moment! Que the first epiphany! More correctly it should be said, your job chose you because of your personality type. Now isn't that going to bake your noodle?!

Here is our goal of what we want to figure out, in this order:

1. Which one of the four personality types are you primarily?

2. Which personality type are you secondarily?

3. Is our primary evolved or unevolved?

4. Is our secondary evolved or unevolved?

5. What techniques do I need to learn to become evolved?

6. What makes me toggle back and forth?

7. Do I have a third personality type that I toggle into?

Once you figure these seven questions out, the world will begin to open up to you! This is where a WHY focus group can come in very handy. They can help you diagnose yourself and explain WHY. Misdiagnosing oneself is common, so ask for help to get it right. Once we figure out ourselves then we can move on to figuring out others. If you want to practice figuring out people's personality types, watch kids. Their personality types are completely raw and unfiltered (unevolved.) They will be the purest and most pronounced form of their personality types. It is also easier to see them switch from primary personality to secondary personality.

Once we start to figure out other people's personality types, then we can understand WHY they do what they do. We can also begin to predict behavior. Knowledge is power (said Tony Robbins) right? This knowledge and understanding is one of the keys to Capacity. More on Capacity later. Once we learn who we are and WHY we do what we do we can blend that with other people's personality types and behaviors. WHY is this important? Because these are the people we live with, work with, want to get along with and the ones we have to raise, if we have children. Want to be a better parent or have a better relationship with your child? That is coming if you master this chapter. Once we understand who we are and who they are, we can perfect techniques on how to live with people, work with people, grow with people and get along with people. We will now have a common language we can share and use to create boundaries, explain our behavior, and explain their behavior. Understanding creates tolerance, tolerance creates acceptance, and acceptance creates peace. Understanding these will also make it clear which relationships we should focus on and the people we must wish well while we cut them out of our lives. As I mentioned above, create boundaries.

First, I am going to go over the four personality types in basic form. Just a quick overview so we don't overthink it. Read them and see which one primarily resonates with you. You may say to yourself, I exhibit many of these traits. Sometimes I do this and sometimes I feel this way, or behave that way. Well, spoiler alert, you are an Analytical. Don't get paralysis from analysis! Oh, and remember one thing! This very important thing! One personality type is not better than the other. You are what you are and that is beautiful (as long as you are not hurting yourself or others) or maybe it isn't yet beautiful and we have to work on that a bit. We just want to know who we are and WHY we do what we do. We also want to know WHY our behavior works for our life or WHY it doesn't. What techniques are we employing, or should we be employing, to make it work or what techniques are we employing to make it not work?

Let's scratch the surface…

AMIABLE

Amiables are people pleasers. They themselves are friendly, pleasant, sympathetic and want everyone to be happy. Amiables want other people to be happy so much that they will do what they can to make other people happy, even at their own expense. Many would say Amiables are friendly people; however, many people of each personality type are friendly, so I am not going to list this one. I want to give personality traits more specific to this personality type. Think of all the traits one would exhibit if they wanted you to be happy, and that is an Aimable. Understanding, good natured, not aggressive, rarely assertive, possibly submissive, easy going, and quick to resolve conflict. Those who would cancel their plans to take someone else's shift at work (when they don't need the money) are Amiables. Some people call these people a "giver." They give of themselves to other people and get some to none in return. Unevolved Amiables don't say anything because they want you to be happy. Amiables want the people they please to be mind readers because they never tell you how much effort, or sacrifice, they put into making you happy.

If you have a child who is an Amiable, make sure you teach them self-worth and boundaries. Not just to have boundaries, but when and how to enforce those boundaries. If you are an Amiable and haven't yet learned this in a solid and healthy way, learn them now. You will suffer in one-sided relationships until you do. Capacity suckers will prey on you and appear to be your friend, but really they just need your capacity. I explain this more in the chapter Capacity.

A word about boundaries

In the animal kingdom, there is a pecking order. They push you and nudge you to see if you will stand up for yourself. If you do, they respect you. If you don't, they don't respect you. They will only respect you as much as you respect yourself. People are the same so stand up for yourself and enforce your boundaries. Humans are no more than slightly evolved animals. We can revert back to animalistic behavior very quickly though.

If you think you can self-deprecate and make yourself less important in order to fit in, know that it doesn't work, it doesn't work, IT DOESN'T WORK! You are silently asking people "do you like me?" Their silent answer is "you don't even like you, so WHY would I like you?" When you FINALLY learn this lesson (and you are probably going to learn this the hard way) you will be a happier person. You will also have real and healthier relationships. I love my Aimable friends reading this but you can be your own worst enemy.

ANALYTICAL

Analyticals are information seekers and thinkers. They analyze a situation or experience and then overanalyze it again and again and again. There is a reason this word starts with ANAL, it's because they are a pain in the ass. Hey! I said I was going to pick on everyone. Don't get upset, it's just your turn. They ask a million questions, are slow to make decisions, and can suffer from paralysis from analysis. Because they take a lot of time to make a decision, they are patient or at least appear to be. They are the ones who sit in the front of the class because they want to absorb the information. They crave information and can't get enough of it. They are very good at games and activites which involve strategy. Find me a Chess tournament and I'll find you a room full of Analyticals. They want things neat and orderly. They want facts, figures, statistics, percentages and calculated probabilities. They want to know all of these things, before they make a decision. The good thing about Analyticals is once they have made a decision you can bet your last dollar they are sure of it! If they have decided to be your friend it is because in their mind you have passed a series of tests, questions, and considerations of WHY you should be their friend. They typically have fewer and deeper relationships, rather than a lot of friends they know on a shallow level. You can find them in professions which offer or require a lot of "product knowledge." Many people in the medical field, and legal field, are Analyticals because they read the medical journals, and law books, over and over again. Analyticals can't get enough information. They make good investigators because they love to problem solve.

They are detail oriented and will be notice typos. Yes, Iz be did that on purpose. LOL. If you read "They are detail oriented and will notice typos," chances are you are not an Analytical. If you are still reading and don't know what I am talking about, I purposely put a typo in the first sentence of this paragraph. Since they like details and structure, they are the first to notice when things are out of place.

A high Analytical can be difficult to talk to. They may seemingly not even be able to follow along in a conversation. A conversation with a high Analytical may literally go like this:

Person 1: "Hey Bob, Sally and I are going to go to the store. Do you want to go?"

Analytical Bob: "What store?"

Person 1: "To the mall, they actually have a lot of stores we would like to visit. Do you want to go?"

Analytical Bob: "Go where?"

Person 1: "To the mall Bob, we just talked about it."

Analytical Bob thinking how can I make a decision when you haven't given me enough information: "Yes but which store and at what time are you leaving?"

That is some of the pain in the ass part. All the Analyticals reading this think nothing of that interaction because Analytical Bob is completely in the right. Person 1 didn't give enough information. Analyticals are also frustrated because they want to know who Person 1 is! Yes it's true, I did that on purpose so you can figure out which personality type you are. If "Person 1" didn't bother you, then you are not an Analytical. If you are thinking, whom is Person 1, then you are an Analytical. The more not knowing whom Person 1 is bothered you, because you didn't have enough information, the higher of an Analytical you are.

Analyticals not being able to follow along in some conversations can make others feel like they have to repeat themselves. This can be frustrating. The Analytical truly just hasn't gotten enough information yet and is currently calculating all the variables to what you may be asking them and before they answer they want to clarify your statement so they can consider all the options and articulate their decision effectively and precisely. LOL . . . and exhale.

OMG Bob do you want to go to the damn mall or not?!?!?!

I'm literally laughing out loud right now.

When an Analytical interacts with another Analytical, it is almost heavenly (to them anyway.) What would take two Drivers three minutes to handle, the two Analyticals take their time, give each other all the information they want, answer all the questions they want, don't get frustrated, and weigh all the possible outcomes and variables without being judged. OMG yes! Finally, a person who gets it! Listen, I beat them up but they have a lot of good qualities. This is just a brief overview so you can quickly identify them, or you.

DRIVER

This personality type is for people who like to get in their fancy red sports car and drive really fast. Kidding! Not that type of Driver. Enjoying driving a vehicle or vessel has nothing to do with being a Driver. That is not at all what it means. Drivers are task oriented. They are determined to get the task, agenda or job done and could care less about details. This ask done, that task ask done, another task done, what else needs to be done? If something isn't working, they will use force and sometimes a lot of it. They may skip over details and go right to conclusion. Voted most likely to miss their flight. They will grab the object, forgo the instruction booklet, and try to figure it out. Impatient to highly impatient. A Driver may be able to type 60 words per minute using 4 fingers because they don't see the need for a typing class. Drivers develop skills on their own to better accomplish the task, whatever the task may be. They may memorize their credit card number so they don't have to pull it out of their pocket or so they can complete a transaction even when they didn't bring the card. Sometimes the skills are self-taught and sometimes they will take lessons (preferably from other Drivers.)

They get to the point. Ask a Driver about the "big game" and you are likely to hear "we won." That's it! LOL. Drivers are confident (at least appear that way) and gravitate towards leadership positions.

There is a saying "If you want to get to the moon, hire a Driver. If you want to get back, hire an Analytical." It's so true. A Driver will get the task done. After all, you said you wanted to go to the moon, you didn't say anything about wanting to come back.

They can come across as insensitive or rude because they don't want to hear your story nor explanation. Just get to the point. The more intelligent they are, the less explanation they need. You might be thinking "this person doesn't care about me nor anybody else because they rarely want to know any details." This is not true. Drivers can be misunderstood and not liked because of this. Not to mention when they finish a task that wasn't going smoothly, they used force or barked out orders and made everyone upset.

Also voted most likely to roll their eyes while you are taking too long to explain something. An Unevolved Driver would likely be the person in your audience to say "stop talking." An Evolved Driver would say "please stop talking."

In the Analytical section I wrote this paragraph:

> They are detail oriented and will be notice typos. Yes, Iz be did that on purpose. LOL. If you read "They are detail oriented and will notice typos," chances are you are not an Analytical.

What I didn't write there, because it wasn't time to discuss Drivers, is if you read "They are detail oriented and will notice typos" then you may be a Driver. Seriously, I am adding this line after the chapter was done because when I re-read this chapter, I read that line as "They are detail oriented and will notice typos." My Driver brain blazed through it, not noticing the details. I extracted from that sentence what my mind needed to accomplish the task, and I am the one who wrote it! LOL. I still read it incorrectly. When

I read the next line stating that only an Analytical would notice typos, I surprised myself! I really didn't notice it! That was cool. Ok, not even joking when I read the paragraph again, I did it again. What else have I missed in my life because my Driver brain was going too fast trying to accomplish the task?

Note: this is a short explanation because a Driver has already identified themself. If you haven't snapped your fingers yet and said "yep, that's me!," you are not a Driver. Plus, they want it to be short and to the point.

EXPRESSIVE

Expressives are fun! They are outgoing and are the life of the party. They are loud, love to make an entrance, wear bright colors, and are attention seekers. They are charismatic and make friends easily. They love to be on stage. Many of the people making videos with flamboyant actions on social media, are Expressives. "Look at me" or "watch this" are among their favorite things to say. If there was a room with 100 people in it and a voice came over the loudspeaker saying "free tacos," the 25% of the room that yelled "WOO-HOO!," are the Expressives. They can talk at hurricane speeds and sometimes you will feel like you are caught in a verbal Category 5.

If you are the parent of an Expressive, you have your hands full! You may mistake your child to be "acting out" when in fact, they are not. We have to recognize that we are not born Evolved. A child who is naturally an Expressive is an Unevolved Expressive. Good luck even trying to explain their behavior to them to make them an Evolved Expressive. This won't happen until they are at least teenagers and even then, it may not happen. Some Expressives never become Evolved Expressives.

In their defense, WHY would they want to? From the point of view of an Unevolved Expressive, they have a lot of fun. People are drawn to them. They know a lot of people and are probably popular. They come home on their first day of school and happily report to their family "I made 13 new friends today!" Their extroverted nature gives them the confidence to walk up to complete strangers, introduce themselves and ask someone if they want to be friends. Later we are going to talk about what category a behavior falls into. For now, let's just say if you have an Unevolved Expressive with positive behavior (utilizes their outgoing extrovert nature to make friends, does positive things to get attention like sing, dance or excessive celebrations), then encourage this. WHY? Because they will, they will, they will, continue to do whatever it takes to get attention. There is a chapter coming up called "The Negative Wave" which explains how it is easier to get attention by doing negative things, than positive things. If you have an Unevolved Expressive with negative behavior, you are in for some serious parenting. If your Unevolved Expressive starts having a hard time at school, at home, being understood, being rejected because of their behavior, or simply singing and dancing doesn't get them the attention they need (key word "need"), then they will soon figure out that doing negative things (being destructive, disruptive, shocking behavior, crime, stealing) can get them the attention they need.

PRO TIP: An unevolved Expressive is going to do whatever it takes to get attention.

Expressives came in second in the vote "most likely to roll their eyes while you are talking" because while you are talking, the attention was on you. They want it on them!

Analyticals are saying "what vote was this?" (they need more information)

Light bulb moment!: if you have an employee, or are an employee, where the personality type does not match the job description, you are going to have a tough time! Read that a few more times. It's a life changing piece of advice.

Let's review the free taco situation again. 100 random people are in a room and someone over the loudspeaker says "Free Tacos!" Here are the likely responses:

Aimable: Awww, that's nice. I like Tacos. Umm, yes you can have mine, I guess. (I'm secretly hoping we can use my gesture to bond.)

Analytical: What kind of Tacos? (I need more information)

Driver: Where are they? (Get to the point)

Expressive: WOO-HOO! (Let's take the attention off the tacos and put it back on me, shall we?!)

If you have an Expressive do a speech at your wedding, expect them at some point to take the focus off of you and put it on to them. They can't help it.

Let's revisit when the secondary personality type comes out. They come out under certain conditions or circumstances. Everyone is different. Sometimes it comes out when one is under stress, needs to focus, maybe when one is scared, happy, or maybe simply needs to rush to finish a task. Sometimes it can simply come out when the situation calls for it. Like "when the other part of our job" is needed. Example: Let's say you are a healthcare worker. Part of your job requires you to accomplish tasks like filing, scheduling, and running parts of the office. Let's say the other part is when you have to be "on the floor" talking to patients. If this person is a Driver, with a secondary Analytical, might we see when one personality type is prevalent and when the other one "kicks in?" The Driver is knocking out the tasks of filing the paperwork, making the schedule, and working on the "to do" list to keep the office running well. The Analytical kicks in when a patient is explaining symptoms. The Analytical is trying to diagnose the patient and reflecting on their medical knowledge. If when in Analytical "mode" an employee approached them asking for a schedule change, the response may be "Send me an email as a reminder and I'll get to it asap." What we are really saying is, "the Driver is not available right now but when

I get in Driver mode, I will be checking my email for tasks and will knock it out then."

As far as primary personality type: I have heard that 25% of the population is each personality type; however, I do not know that to be true. Off the top of my head, I would say Analyticals seem to make up more than 25% of the population. I was recently in Atlanta and was very surprised to see such a strong population of Expressives. According to Google, Atlanta is made up of 50% Black/African American, 40% White, 5% Asian and 5% Other. 48% male, 52% female. Median age 36.8. I saw Expressives of every age, gender, sexual orientation, and race. I didn't see a pattern from one particular group. They were just everywhere. WHY are there so many Expressives in Atlanta? Maybe one day I will find out. Wait a second, Rob. You keep telling us you are a Driver. By definition, Drivers don't "see a pattern from one particular group." That is correct! I am a secondary Analytical and my secondary kicks in when I need to figure things out. So, when I said Analyticals are a pain in the ass, I have to check myself when my secondary kicks in because I am guilty of many of the things I mentioned. I told you I was going to pick on everyone!

HELPFUL TIPS

If you are saying, "I think I am a Driver," you're not. A Driver would never say that.

If you are still trying to figure out which one you are, you're an Analytical. You're welcome because I just saved your entire evening thinking about this.

Please do not go through these personality traits and think to yourself, this is the way I want to be so I'm just going to go with that. Find the one that actually resonates with you now and today. Misdiagnosing yourself is a time wasting distraction that will not get you to your goal of understanding yourself.

Embrace your personality type and realize what is special about you!

So! Which one of the four is your primary? Which one is your secondary? What triggers your secondary? Do you have a third? Pay attention here. If you are saying "well sometimes I do this and sometimes I do that, so I think I am all of them," you aren't. There are very very clear toggles from one personality type to another. We just have to know how to see them. If you can't see the toggle in someone you may be missing it or their primary and their secondary may be the same. WHY? Because everyone is different!

Another note: the toggle can happen quickly but being in your other "mode" is not brief, it is for a longer period of time. I am not a Driver for 10 minutes, then I am an Analytical for 20 minutes and then I change back. Like the example of the healthcare worker, they are a Driver, in Driver mode, while doing one part of their job (for hours) and the toggle, to their secondary Analytical, happens when they have to do the other part of their job (for hours.) Again a situation may arise and a toggle may happen. There are no rules.

I will tell you one thing that triggers my toggle. When I am in Analytical mode (I say it this way because I am primarily a Driver and I toggle into my secondary which is Analytical "mode") one thing that can make me toggle back to my primary Driver, is hunger. If I am in a meeting, focused on figuring something out or otherwise distracted and I get hungry, watch out! I start barking out orders. When is lunch? What are we having? Let's go! Let's make it happen! Keep your hands and feet away from my mouth! LOL. Has anyone ordered food or is anyone leaving soon to pick something up? Yes? Great. No? What do we have to eat here and now? Does anyone have a granola bar they don't need? Can you see the toggle here? If we were trying to figure something out and bouncing ideas off of one another and I was intrigued by all this information until all of a sudden I started doing that, one can see the toggle. It is clear when one understands what one is looking for.

Others may see this abrupt change and not know how to explain it. They may think that I am not a very nice person because I started barking out orders at people. Others may try to explain it by saying "he is a nice guy until he gets hangry." When in reality I am a very nice person, but hunger triggers my Unevolved Driver. My Unevolved Driver will accomplish the task quickly, with little patience, and little tolerance for vacillating, delay or error. When I have toggled back to Driver and you ask me a question which requires my Analytical mode, you aren't going to get your question answered. At least not the same way you received an answer when I was in Analytical mode. You may hear something like "I need to eat first and then we can reconvene." Hey Rob, can't you just answer one more question? Rob: "No." Note the one word answer here. There is no commentary, no more explanation, and no room for emotion. "No" was everything you needed to hear.

A Driver will use very few words because they get to the point to accomplish the task and they don't waste time with your feelings. The Driver will have people around him saying "I hate it when he gets like this." The Evolved Driver can accomplish that same task without upsetting everyone. The problem is, this isn't the natural default. Everyone is born into their personality type, raw and Unevolved. Evolved comes from time, age, experience, and circumstances. The Evolved Driver understands more words are needed to soothe other people's feelings. More words means more information for the Analyticals, more words make the Expressives feel important, and more words reassure the Amiables that you don't all of a sudden find fault in their behavior. An Unevolved Driver doesn't care about these things whereas the Evolved Driver understands it's better (and more efficient) not to upset everyone. They don't want to use more words now but they know taking the time to fix everyone's feelings after the fact is more time consuming. I told you in the beginning of the book, you aren't going to like everything I have to say but it will be the truth!

When you understand this about yourself, then you will know WHY you do what you do on a *macro level*. Remember this is an overview, the larger picture, the top of the WHY triangle, and what has the greatest impact on your behavior. Macro behaviors are who you are as a person. This is your Nature. Micro behaviors are the results of what experiences you have had. This is your Nurture. Micro behaviors are situational. Example of micro behavior: if you have abandonment or anxiety issues, they do not stem from being one of the personality types. It probably stems from something in your past/childhood which gave you some level of negative uncertainty. The point I am making is that you will handle these micro behaviors within the scope of your macro behavior. Ok Rob, what the hell did you just say? I'm saying if you are an Analytical with abandonment issues, then you most certainly handle those issues like an Analytical would. You will overthink what happened, justify, rationalize and then think about it some more. Whereas an Expressive may start to act out. Their behavior could become negatively over the top and that could be their form of indicating they need help. An Amiable may try to "sweep it under the rug" and say, "it's ok I forgive them" or "I am going to do my best without making them upset." A Driver may look themselves in the mirror and say, get over it you big pussy, I don't have time for your whiney crap, I have things to do! Personality types are the macro way we will go through life.

There are many behaviors which stem from micro reasons. We are not going to get into micro reasons in this chapter because there are just too many of them. Micro reasons can be caused by a million things but here are some examples: how you were raised, where you were raised, what were the social norms of the time, belief systems, some significant event, some traumatic event, good childhood vs bad childhood, and all other nature vs nurture items. These are just a few of the micro reasons which can affect behavior. If you were punched by someone for the way you spoke to them and now you have more of a diplomatic approach to your speech, that was your micro experience. This chapter is about your macro personality type.

Let's elaborate on that experience and consider how each personality type might react to getting punched by someone for the way they spoke to them.

- **Aimable:** they are upset at themselves for making someone unhappy. They are probably trying deescalate the situation, to make it up to them, and doing what they can to fix the relationship/interaction and/or make the other person happy. They may need advice, perspective and/or consoling.

- **Analytical:** they are analyzing WHY they got punched. Maybe they hit back and are trying to rationalize if that behavior was justified. Once they reach a conclusion, they will share it. Especially if they need closure.

- **Driver:** He hit me because he didn't like what I had to say. I hit him back (or I didn't) and it's over now. Move on.

- **Expressive:** They are thinking they got a lot of attention. The hit may have been worth it for all of the extra attention it is bringing. Examples: they are getting (attention) messages from friends/family asking if they are ok. They get attention by talking about it and maybe even posting it on social media. They may have evolved from this attack and are changing (verbally) the way they express themselves. The need for expression may get shifted into another area like the way they act or dress. Clarification: they may verbally express themselves differently after this experience; however, their need to express will get out one way or another. It's in their DNA.

Again, these personality types are the macro way we handle micro experiences!

Once you have had time to process your personality type and watching yourself doing what your personality type does in real time, it will be like a weight lifted off of you, that you didn't even know was there. Suddenly, you will understand yourself. You will understand loved ones, friends, and co-workers. You now have a language (that you can share with yourself and others) to articulate your WHY. WHY you do what you do. Through that understanding you will make conscious decisions on whether or not your behavior truly serves your happiness. You will understand you may have been subconsciously making those decisions up until this point or making them based on what other people told you. The problem is they didn't fully understand either! You will also know WHY others are doing what they do and be able to articulate what you see in words.

Let's go back to reflect on this light bulb moment: if you have an employee, or are an employee, where the personality type does not match the job description, you are going to have a tough time!

Let's say you want to hire a greeter and that greeter's job has 2 parts. 1. Greet people coming to your place of business and 2. Get their information for future use by the store for marketing, sales announcements, letting clients know when the store has new products and promotions. What type of person would you look to hire? If you said an Expressive with a secondary Analytical, you are correct! The Expressive is going to LOVE being the center of attention, getting to talk to everyone, getting everyone to interact with them even if they don't want to, and (hopefully) will have "thick skin" in case people are not very nice to them. Note: having "thick skin" is not a characteristic of an Expressive but in this situation the Expressive will be so happy, they will take the good with the bad (the pros outweigh the cons) more than another personality type. The secondary Analytical will love making spreadsheets, arranging the names alphabetically, and have already analyzed that uploading this information in real time will be much more useful and beneficial. Even though you didn't ask them to do that, they figured it out for you.

So I ask you: What if you are an Aimable with a Secondary Aimable and this is currently your job? I can already tell you that you are not as good at it as the Expressive/Analytical. WHY? Because when you greet people and they tell you to go away, you do. After all, they told you what will make them happy and that is your primary mission. In contrast, the Expressive would push on with flair, humor or some sort of fun approach to break that person who blew them off, into giving them attention. Once they got the attention, they would capture their information.

Want to know which greeter has results in second place? The Aimable with Secondary Driver. WHY? Because the aimable greets people in a nice and non-intimidating way. They may even greet in a complimentary way because they want people to be happy. They may greet with "Nice sweater" or "OMG where did you get that outfit, it looks amazing on you." Once the aimable has people feeling happy, the Driver kicks in to accomplish the task of getting the necessary information.

So if you are an employer I ask you, how important is this information? Do you want to just keep hiring the pretty girl or good looking guy to greet and hoping they work out? How much time would it save you to hire the best personality type the first time? Would it be good to have happy and productive employees? Would it be good to have employee retention? Because people in the right position stay at their job longer. Learn this information and change your business for the better.

If you are looking for a job, how important is it to understand how your personality type, or types, fit the job description? Crucial right? My sister applied for a job and didn't get it. I called the employer and asked them their opinion of my sister. She has such a happy and bubbly personality they thought she was an Expressive. They knew an Expressive wouldn't fare well in that job. I explained she is actually an Analytical with a secondary Amiable and explained how her personality types were perfect for that role. She got the job and has happily been with that employer for five years.

Now it's time for you to have your own light bulb moment. What is the job description for the job you are currently working in? What personality type would best suit your job? If the personality type that best suits the job is not your personality type, then I can already tell you that you are not happy with your job. It feels wrong. It feels like you are not at your highest and best use. It's because you are in the wrong place. Not the wrong company or store, I mean in the wrong role. Your strengths, and what makes you special, is not being put to good use. If the personality type that best suits your job is the same personality type that you are, then you have been there a long time. Even if you are not happy with your job (because of your boss, the pay, the nepotism, the politics or the commute…separate these things from the job itself), you love it, it feels right, and you wouldn't really want to do anything else. If this is the case, then I am here to tell you the job chose you, not the other way around. You're welcome.

Ok Rob, I've got one for you and I am going to prove you are wrong! I have an amazing singing voice and got offers to perform at venues which got me noticed, opened doors for me and now I am a big star. I sing on stage all the time and I love it, yet I am not an Expressive. I am an Analytical! How do you explain that? Expressives will gravitate more towards the stage; however, this doesn't mean they are the most talented. I will tell you Mr. or Mrs. Analytical who thinks they stumped me, your show is different from that of an Expressive. You may wear black or darker colors because you want the talent to be remembered, not the show. Your shows are more calculated and uniform, whereas an Expressive might not even have a set list. Even though they appear the same, if one peels back the onion one will find they are not. Remember what I said before: you will go through life and handle experiences within the scope of your personality type. Actually I said: Again, these personality types are the macro way we handle micro experiences!

I got a call from a friend the other day who was having issues with her 8-year-old son. She said "he is driving me crazy" and "I am (jokingly) going to kill him." I asked her WHY. She explained that he is very unemotional, can't make up his mind about anything, and asks me a million questions all the time. I give him something to do and he will come back in an hour with questions about how to do it, when he could have just taken that time to do it! She went on to ask, "What is wrong with him?"

My answer was "there is nothing wrong with him, it's you who has the problem." She had the best response one can have. She stopped talking, listened, and asked me what I meant. I commend her for this because it is hard for people to consider they are in the wrong, be vulnerable when instinct is to defend our Pride (more in that chapter later), and listen to what someone has to say about it. What I explained to her is he is an Unevolved Analytical. He is low on emotion, asks a lot of questions because he needs information, gets paralysis from analysis, and is not task oriented like you are (she is a Driver.)

Ok, so now that we have a basic understanding of our primary and secondary personality types, we need to find out if these personality types are Evolved or Unevolved.

Here are some examples of each:

- An **Unevolved Expressive** yells in the middle of a crowded room: I have to pee! They may do negative things to get attention. Love uncertainty. Disorganized, loud, annoying, and may babble incessantly for as long as it keeps your attention.

- An **Unevolved Driver** being forceful may appear to be the have the same behavior as a person being purposely rude or dismissive; however, they are not being this way. Communication and boundaries are needed here to help that Driver evolve; however, if you live with this person, it is important not to take it personally. It is not their intention. It is not uncommon for the Unevolved Driver to have the task complete and everyone is upset with them. Please note: I am not condoning this behavior and it is not ok. I am just letting you know the root of their behavior and WHY they behave this way. Unevolved Drivers can appear flighty or flaky. Drivers are decisive, good or bad, they just make a decision and quickly. It may not be the right decision, but the task is done. Insensitive, harsh, overbearing, and if questioned, sarcastic. As above they will forgo the instruction booklet. If they cannot figure it out they may hand it to someone else and say "do you know how this works?" As a last resort, they will grab the instruction booklet but will put it down the second they find the information they need to accomplish the task. Ask them which way to turn and the Unevolved Driver may quickly say "left" when that may not be correct. They want the task done more than they have the patience to figure it out. We can now see how they can be difficult to interact with.

- **Unevolved Amiables** cannot say no. They have little to no boundaries. They suffer in life because of it. They give from an empty cup, have many one-sided relationships, and even though they bend over backwards to make people happy, they don't always get the results they want. Many times, people are still not happy with them even though the Unevolved Amiable thinks they did their best to make you happy. Unfortunately for them, they cannot figure out WHY. Sweet and merciful Rob will tell you again "it doesn't work, it doesn't work, IT DOESN'T WORK!" You have to have to have to have boundaries and enforce them. The Unevolved Aimable becomes an Evolved Aimable the day they say "never again am I going to feel this way. I try too hard to make people happy and now I need to focus more on myself." This is when they focus more on themselves and redefine the relationships they have.

- **Unevolved Analyticals** think everyone else needs or wants information too. It's so annoying. They will talk you to death with details that non Analyticals find boring. They are constantly being told to "get to the point" by Drivers and Expressives. Amiables are too nice to say that, but they are thinking it. If you have an Aimable tell you to get to the point, you really need to "read the room" and know when it's time to shut up.

That's the test to know if you drive people crazy with all your unwanted details. If you are now defending yourself by saying, "Well who wouldn't want details?!" then I am talking to you.

I will get more into Evolution in that chapter.

So, let's reiterate our goals for this chapter. Our goals were:

1. Which one of the four personality types are you primarily?

2. Which personality type are you secondarily?

3. Is our primary evolved or unevolved?

4. Is our secondary evolved or unevolved?

5. What techniques do I need to learn to become evolved?

6. What makes me toggle back and forth?

7. Do I have a third personality type that I toggle into?

Hopefully now you can answer these questions. If you can, you have taken a giant step into a large and exciting world. If you can't, don't worry, through practice, training and WHY focus groups, it will come.

CHAPTER 102:
Alphas and Sigmas and Betas, Oh My!

Humans, like animals, have a social hierarchy. Think of it as a hierarchy of dominance or "pecking order." Where you are on this pecking order plays a big factor in your life and in the lives of people we want to, or need to, understand. This is another big part of WHY we do what we do.

We need to pause here so we can understand the depth of this chapter (and this whole book for that matter.) Please, please, please start with a clean slate, a blank page, and a clear mind. We have all heard these terms before and we may tend to think we know who we are. Read these descriptions as if it was the first time you have ever heard them and see which one really resonates with you.

Misdiagnosing yourself is the worst thing you can do. When this happens, and I promise you there are people reading this book right now who have misdiagnosed themselves, we are inadvertently living a lie. When we think we are something that we are not, this can be the source of our inner struggles and unhappiness. This is a major reason for anxiety, alcoholism, dependency on chemicals, the need for therapy etc. It is also a major reason that relationships fail. Business relationships, personal relationships, and romantic relationships. This is one of the reasons the divorce rate is so high.

What if what you are about to read is the key to your happiness or the reason for your unhappiness? The goal of this book is to unify people but we cannot do that unless we have understanding.

When you truly understand yourself then you will know what you are sharing with the world. More importantly you will accept that person. You! The real you. I want to eradicate addiction, divorce, war, and the need for therapists. Everyone has to do their part by sweeping their own doorstep first, before we can change the world.

> "Through understanding we can have tolerance.
> Through tolerance we can have acceptance.
> Through acceptance we can have peace."

Now, I want you to read this chapter through this lens and understand the importance of knowing who you are and WHY you do what you do. Let's go…

WHAT IS THE HIERARCHY OF DOMINANCE ORDER?

It goes like this:

Alphas and Sigmas
Betas
Deltas
Gammas
Omegas

They go in this order from top to bottom. Before reading this you may have only thought about people as dominant (Alphas) or submissive (Betas); however, there is so much more! Let's dive in!

First of all, these terms come from the Greek alphabet. Literally the first two letters of the Greek alphabet are "alpha" and "beta" which is where our modern terms alpha and beta derive. Alpha comes first in the alphabet and in the dominance hierarchy. The word alphabet itself derives from the Latin word "Alphabetum" which originated in the 2nd-3rd century. Note: history also helps us understand WHY.

ALPHAS

WHY talk about Alphas first? Because they are first! They are in the lead, they are in control, and they are the most dominant. An Alpha is the top of the food chain. By definition, they are the most dominant, powerful, or assertive person in the group. By that definition the head boss, the president or the chairman is the Alpha; however, that person may not actually have an Alpha personality. Let's separate the two and go beyond the textbook definition because we want to know about human behavior. A Beta personality or Gamma personality (or any other personality type for that matter) may be best suited to "run the show," be in charge, or take care of the business at hand. It is important to understand the difference between a textbook definition and human behavior.

Characteristics of an Alpha personality

- Strong in character
- Assertive
- Decisive
- Dominant (typically active and sometimes passive)
- Bold
- Self-confident / high self-esteem
- Demanding
- Natural born leaders who like to be in charge (The smart ones know they don't have to be. Evolved ones know whom to put in charge and know they can still be an Alpha while the best person for the job runs the show.)
- In control of their behavior and probably their emotions (the more evolved the greater control and restraint they have)

- In control of their environment
- Lacks empathy

Note: There may be other personality types who can "play the role" of an Alpha when needed but this is challenging for them. They are exhausted when they are done because it is not their norm. If I have just described you, sorry for the cold water but, you are not an Alpha. You're just acting like an Alpha when you need, or want, to. The ability to act like an Alpha does not make you an Alpha. A true Alpha does not tire of being an Alpha, nor acting in an Alpha position/role because they are just being themselves. In fact, they don't know how else to be. Read that sentence again.

What do you think happens when you have an Alpha who is an analytical? Alphas are decisive; however, analyticals are slow to make decisions. See the inner struggle here? Remember that when trying to figure out WHY someone does what they do, we need to establish a pattern. We may confuse an Alpha for a different personality type, because they are slow to make decisions. In reality, they are just taking their time to make a decision. If we see an Alpha, who is an analytical with a secondary driver, in driver mode, we may easily misunderstand this person. We must see the patterns and not be quick to judge.

Are all Alphas the same? No!

There are different levels of Alphas within the Alpha group. Active but quiet dominance is a characteristic of a top Alpha. What do I mean by that? When a true top Alpha walks in the room, people just know it. Once evolved, and accepting of their personality type, he/she doesn't have to yell and beat on their chest to exert their dominance. They don't have to. The person who does that is a paper tiger emulating an Alpha. The loud people have no real substance to their character and they will fold in the face of a top Alpha. Weaker Alphas (I am not talking about other personality types who misdiagnose themselves and think they are an Alpha) will size up other Alphas to see who is stronger. Unevolved Alphas (more on this in the chapter "Evolution") will use force, intimidation, or may be physically threatening. True top Alphas don't ever initiate any of these (because they don't have to); however, they may respond with it.

Evolved top Alpha tip: if you are the person in charge, the head cheese, the one who calls the shots, or the person where "the buck stops here," then don't say it. There is an old saying "when you are good, you tell everyone. When you are great, people tell you." The times I have been the most impressed is when I was speaking with someone, who just introduced themselves by their first name, to later find out they were the owner, or the president, or the person who calls the shots. When people find out later you are "the person" and you didn't introduce yourself that way, it is much more impactful.

"In control of their environment"

When two Alphas meet, or interact, one has to be submissive to the other or they have to agree to coexist in that environment/situation. Read that sentence again. If they do not, a clash will happen. This reminds me of the movie *Highlander*. The famous line "There can be only one!" I digress. When Alphas clash it may be verbal, physical, threatening, manipulative, and/or undermining. It is designed to be, in one way or another, damaging to the other Alpha's dominance.

Two Alphas may meet, exchange glances and simply nod at one another. This means I see you, I acknowledge you, and I'm fine with you being in, or near, my space. I am showing respect and am willing to coexist. One of the first things males do in any situation and regardless of dominance hierarchy status, is threat assessment. This nod alleviates that concern. If one were to nod and the other one continues to look but doesn't nod, a new level of concern arises. If one man nods and the other looks down, we have established dominance.

Another scenario may be two Alphas may see one another in the same room or proximity and then one may simply look away. Notice I didn't say look down. An Alpha wouldn't do that. Looking away without a nod or acknowledgement is basically an indifference to that person. I am not interested in you and I have not considered you to be a threat, but I have determined we can be in the same room without incident.

Note: the male threat assessment primarily has to do with environment and circumstances. He doesn't sit with his back to the door, in case someone threatening comes in. He also walks closest to the road while his loved one(s) walk further in, on the sidewalk. He literally puts himself at greater risk since he is concerned with the safety of his loved ones. Females will also do threat assessment; however, it is geared more towards their personal safety (or family/friends safety if she is with someone she cares about) and the threat of another female's ability to attract their male.

Females, in general, have a physical disadvantage. As such, females need to assess personality, intentions, and truthfulness to ensure their personal safety, more than a man does. Once a woman becomes a mother she will develop a sixth sense about her offspring's safety, which may not be as evident to others, including the father. A female will size up another female and calculate whether she has the ability to take her throne. She will react to this female based on the results of her assessment. In contrast to this, a male (who hasn't seen his belt buckle in years and possibly not even his feet when standing) could literally have a super handsome and fit male walk in the room, look at that male and dismiss him as not being a threat. While rubbing his belly, which has welcomed the last hole on his belt, he is thinking to himself, "she isn't going anywhere while she's got a man like me!" I crack myself up, but it's true!

Alpha females can be their own worst enemy. Since she has a strong personality, is confident , decisive, assertive, and dominant, she can be a challenge in a romantic relationship. She may gravitate towards a non-Alpha male; however, she may not respect him and this can be a major problem. WHY? Because men need respect and women crave the need to respect their man. It is possible for these relationships to be successful; however, many times she runs him over, disrespects him (even publicly), and would prefer a different dynamic in her relationship. The good news is many Alpha females are happy portraying these traits when they are at work, teaching their class, or running the show outside of the home; however, when they come home they are happy to be submissive towards their Alpha or Sigma partner. The problem with the Alpha female is when they want to relinquish power, they want someone to clearly take the reins and be in power. The indecisiveness of some of the other personality traits annoys her. If you have ever heard the term "power couple," they are both Alphas. Alpha females are confident. If she is attractive, she may use her beauty and confidence to get what she wants. If she abuses this power, then any romantic partner has their hands full. If her Alpha male counterparts are not good providers, this will be a problem for her.

Alpha females take note: an Alpha male will (politely) put you in your place. This is not a negative thing. Your place is in your feminine power, not challenging for dominance of the Alpha male. If you have ever seen a man and a woman who constantly argue, maybe throw things when they get angry at one another or constantly power struggle, it is likely these are two Alphas, and she is not relinquishing power. The worst part is, if the Alpha male relinquishes power, she will not respect him and the relationship will take a downward turn. Once she doesn't respect him, her behavior will continue to deteriorate. On another note: the woman who behaves this way most certainly came from a broken home and/or a home full of chaos. She has a strong need for uncertainty (more on this in that chapter) or, even worse, her need for certainty is filled by chaos because that is all she knows. There may also be past trauma from being treated "less than" because of her gender and she is out of balance.

If an Alpha female is in a relationship with a Sigma male, he will not tolerate challenging nor poor behavior. He will be clear where his place is and where your place is. Where an Alpha male may continue to power struggle you, a Sigma male will not. If you do not relinquish power, constantly challenge him, or behave poorly inconsistent with his values, he will simply show you the door. WHY? Because he made his boundaries clear from the beginning and you are violating them.

If an Alpha female refuses to relinquish power, and is tired of chaotic relationships with other Alphas, then she may choose a relationship with a male who is not an Alpha nor Sigma. The problem with this is she won't respect him, which typically makes these relationships unhealthy. Typically, these are relationships of convenience. He wants a woman who handles everything and makes the decisions. She just wants a man in her life who doesn't challenge her (nor kicks her out the door) while she is driven and focused on building her business or obtaining her goals. I say unhealthy because many times she will emasculate him (even in public) and he will not be respected by other men. This will, in turn, make him resentful toward her. These relationships are at high risk of infidelity. Again, Alpha females can be their own worst enemy.

A female, who is a Beta or Delta, will be the most grateful to have an Alpha or Sigma male. WHY? Because she is not decisive nor a natural leader. She wants him to take the lead in the relationship and if she trusts his judgment through his good decision making, she will be highly grateful to have that man in her life. If you are an Alpha male or Sigma male (you are a good man that makes good choices) who craves gratitude and respect, these female personality types may be the best match for you.

SIGMAS (THE LONE WOLF)

Sigmas share a lot of the same characteristics as Alphas, so they may be hard to tell apart. They may be easily misinterpreted. Sigmas share the same interests of being in charge, being in control, and being successful; however, they do it differently. Alphas want to run the group, climb the corporate ladder, have the title, and be dominant over others. Think of an Alpha as more aggressive, social, and an extrovert.

In contrast, Sigmas want to be in charge but are more likely to leave the corporate structure and start a small business. They are off the beaten path. They are content being in the background while knowing they are still dominant. Just knowing they are strong willed is enough for them. They are strong in character but more laid back at the same time. They measure success through personal fulfillment, rather than wealth or status. Think of a Sigma as unrecognized determination, preferring solitude, and being an introvert rather than being the center of attention. Some would say they are outside the social hierarchy.

Characteristics of a Sigma

- Independent (they don't follow the pack nor acquiesce to social norms)
- A bit of an enigma which can make them interesting / fascinating
- Clever
- Intuitive (they pick up on the difference between what you said/what you did/how you reacted)
- Work outside the system
- Charismatic
- Persuasive
- Calculated
- Not likely to be an Expressive
- Solitary

- Appear relaxed
- They need their space
- Value authenticity
- Intolerant of people who are "victims" or narcissists
- Not interested in their social status
- Establish clear boundaries

Some people move their boundaries depending on who they are with. Some people may bend their rules for romantic partners and compromise when in a business situation. Not Sigmas. Sigmas establish their boundaries and stick to them. Violate their boundaries and they will most likely cut you out of their life. Clear and decisive without debate. Disrespect a Sigma and get ready for a response like a bull showing you his horns. Even if you are kidding or disguising disrespect with humor. Where most people would laugh this off, even if your comments hurt them, it doesn't matter to a Sigma. You have crossed a boundary, and they will enforce it. If you have ever asked someone "can't you take a joke?" and they replied "no," that person is a Sigma. Oh and by the way, the answer really is "no." You putting them down and disguising it as humor is unacceptable. You may get one warning but just know, in the Sigma's mind, you now have a red flag on you. You will not get a second warning. You will just decisively be cut out of their life.

Amiables listen up!

Important note here: when someone puts you down and disguises it with humor, listen for the truth hidden in their joke. This is how they really feel. They may be jealous, envious, insecure, passive aggressive, judgmental about your decisions, and even have a true disrespect/hostility towards you. Tolerating this is emotional abuse and even gaslighting. Sigmas easily pick up on small cues and know these people are saboteurs. Sigmas have too much self-respect to allow this in their lives (and neither should you, regardless of your personality type) because eventually these people will show their true colors. If you need a friend that badly, get a dog but cut these people out of your life.

If you want to successfully interact with a Sigma, be genuine. If you are, they will know and will gravitate towards you. If you are not (and they need you) they will red flag you, adjust inside how they feel about you, will watch you like a hawk, and won't ever say anything about it until they either trust you again or cut you out of their life.

Sigma females can be intimidating. She will command attention when she walks into a room. She is more likely to get attached to a romantic partner than an Alpha female and, unlike her Sigma male counterparts, she will have a harder time breaking off a relationship. She is confident. If she is attractive, then she may use her beauty and confidence to get what she wants. Sigma females can be in the spotlight but are more approachable than an Alpha female. A Sigma female will be a loyal friend.

BETAS

This is a tough personality type. Beta males typically get frustrated with themselves because they want to be Alphas. WHY? Because they want the spotlight that the Alpha keeps getting, and they want the respect that the Sigma has. Beta males think women want a strong, decisive, and confident man, and they just cannot be that way.

We have all seen large and muscular men saying "you have to be big and strong or you are not a man!" This may be followed with sayings like "don't be a pussy" and "stop acting like a girl." Ask the person saying this to describe what it means to be a man and they may tell you "if you can't crush a person's skull with one hand then you are not a real man!" Ummm, ok. You are certainly entitled to your opinion but not everyone agrees with that description. The problem with this is Betas (as well as Deltas and Gammas) hear this and it confuses them. They think they have to be this way in order to get respect.

Characteristics of a Beta

- They are usually nice people!
- Unclear boundaries
- Lack confidence
- Probably Amiables, less likely to be a Driver because Drivers are decisive
- Frustrated with themselves and want to be Alphas
- Anxious
- Good social skills and uses those skills to work well in groups or collaborations
- Laid back
- Craves external validation
- Submissive rather than assertive
- In touch with their emotions and probably an average to high EQ (did you read IQ there?)
- Easily manipulated and more likely to agree to things they don't really want to do
- Doesn't like conflict so they avoid confrontation and dominance
- Loyal—many times because they feel as if they have a lack of options
- More prone to feeling awkward, depressed or not knowing where they fit in

- Desperate to be respected—tend to brag in an effort to gain respect
- Fades into the background but doesn't want to
- Envious/Jealous
- Tend to go on power trips to emulate an Alpha
- Struggle with rejection
- Indecisive (did I say indecisive enough? I can't decide)
- Feels inferior
- Tend to fall apart when it's their turn to show what they can do and then they are mad at themself
- Try too hard to be impressive or confident—again trying to give the appearance of an Alpha
- Cooperative and diplomatic
- Likely to give more than they take in a relationship

The movie *Back to the Future* comes to mind where Biff, the seemingly Alpha male, is a bully to George McFly, the Beta male. In the movie, George is physically threatened, emotionally abused, put down, and made to do Biff's homework out of fear. A Beta may have their food taken, literally get pushed around, and may get taken advantage of due to their kindness and good nature. By the way, do these traits sound like another personality we have discussed? Amiables maybe? Hmm, maybe there is a connection here. I think a Beta is much more likely to be an Amiable, next an Analytical, next a Driver, and rarely an Expressive.

One of the reasons romantic relationships fall apart is because the Beta male tends to emulate an Alpha. If a Beta was acting like an Alpha and confused the female who wants an Alpha, this relationship has a bomb in the building. WHY? Because she will, at some point, figure out the man is actually a Beta. Women are intuitive and always discover the truth. The Beta male cannot keep up the façade forever. He is hoping he can attract her and get her vested in the relationship so she won't leave after discovering the truth. In his mind he really really wants to be an Alpha, he just can't do it. Have you ever heard of "the friend zone?" It is full of Betas who think if they hang around long enough, she will eventually love him.

My suggestion is, if you are a Beta male, own it and see what is special about you. No one should be something they are not. Tell a potential romantic partner this is who I am (nice, supportive and respectful), and this is who I am not (insert Alpha characteristics here.) Remember you have qualities that people value. Just be clear, accept yourself and be yourself. Don't get into a relationship under false pretenses. It doesn't work. When a potential romantic partner accepts you for you, the chances of the relationship succeeding go way up!

Beta females are most likely to get looked down upon, like their male counterparts. They are submissive, kind and passive, in an effort to avoid conflict. She is quiet and not direct. She may feel like she is not good enough. Beta females, who are amiables, are most likely to get taken advantage of. Beta females who are analyticals are very likely to have anxiety because they will think about a situation, think about it some more, over think it, and then have a hard time making decisions.

Beta females take note: Capacity suckers will prey on you! More on that in the chapter "Capacity." Your kind nature and willingness to help will be attractive to the wrong people. You are very likely to have one-sided relationships while you struggle with enforcing your boundaries. You will "feel bad" when someone tells you that you are not doing enough and this is the emotional control they need to take your capacity. You will attract gaslighters and people who want to take advantage of you. Until you establish, define, and enforce your boundaries, you will struggle to "find your place in the world."

Every personality type can find happiness and peace but, as I keep saying, it first comes from understanding, then tolerance, and then acceptance. Accept when you have a hard time making decisions and convey that to people close to you. If you don't think you will be accepted because of this, then they aren't your friends. You're welcome.

DELTAS

Known as "the average man." This is the most common personality type. Think of Deltas as "the worker bees." They are often considered to be resigned to their role in society. They may have a fear of failure contributing to an overall sense of disillusionment.

Characteristics of a Delta

- Reserved
- Introverted
- Hard worker—wants a paycheck for an honest day's work
- Less likely to take financial risks
- Happy not to be in charge
- Seem to lack drive and ambition
- Likes balance in life (more in the chapter Balance)
- They blend in with the crowd and conform
- Doesn't share with the world
- Realistic
- Crave respect and recognition
- Crave normalcy
- Competent

- Lack confidence and will be attracted to females with a lack of confidence. The problem is many Delta females are attracted to confidence, position, decisiveness, and power that Alphas and Sigmas have.
- May seem boring
- Typically average people
- Satisfied with their lives
- Doesn't need to be in charge
- Doesn't desire to be, nor emulate, an Alpha but they can be resentful of them

Women may be attracted to this personality type because Delta males are no frills solid people. If you don't want too many highs nor lows in your life, a Delta man is for you. Delta males are competent, they do good work and are very likely to stay employed. Women may see a Delta male as a project (for what he could be) and some women love a good project. A woman may enter into a relationship with a Delta male because of who this man has the potential to be, rather than who he is today. Now you know what's coming! If the Delta male does not become an Alpha male, and he won't, the female may leave to find someone stronger or more ambitious. She may grow tired of his lack of excitement, his resentfulness towards the personality type she is trying to get him to be, and how normal/average he is (aka boring.)

The woman who wants a stable, reliable, and uneventful relationship will be attracted to Delta males. A woman exiting a relationship with an Alpha male who was too dominate, or a Sigma entrepreneur, who took them on a financial roller coaster, will be out of balance (more on this in the chapter Balance) and may look for a sensible and stable relationship the Delta male offers. The Delta male should ask their romantic partner, are you in love with who I am now or with what you think you can change me to be? If they are not in love with who you are today, then the relationship has a higher chance of failure.

Delta females can be difficult partners for Alphas and Sigmas unless the Delta female completely relinquishes financial control. Because Delta females are adverse to risk, she will not be supportive when her partner wants to do something (like start a business, invest in a new stock, or buy an investment property) outside of the worker bee norm. Delta females like a small friend group so she may struggle with extrovert Alpha males and expressives (regardless of the expressive's hierarchy.) She may think she will match well with a Sigma; however, Delta females are realistic (which can sound pessimistic), grounded, practical, and patient. These characteristics make her a challenge for Sigmas who have chosen to be entrepreneurs, like to think outside the box, and don't like to be questioned. Younger Delta females may be insecure and self-conscious, so she may seek out a confident partner. Older Deta females may have started out life as Alpha females. Now that her drive has subsided and she has accomplished everything she set out to accomplish, she may just exhale and become a Delta.

GAMMAS

Gammas do not possess dominant Alpha traits, nor do they possess the submissive Beta traits. Some would say they don't belong on this hierarchy because they operate outside of it. Gammas can be described as rebels, non-conformists, creative, high EQ, high IQ, and romantic. Sounds good? Hear the rest before you answer because Gammas can be bitter that they are not the personality type they want to be. They can be a difficult romantic partner for many reasons including they don't like to admit when they are wrong, and they lack the ability to compromise.

Voted most likely to say, "you think you are better than everyone else, don't you?"

They may initiate conflict with Alphas because they feel entitled. When they encounter or clash with Alphas, they feel jealous or insecure. It may not even be the Gammas fault; he or she may legitimately mistake themselves for an Alpha and try to act like one. Even to the point of being delusional. They may think they are an Alpha, when everyone else knows they are not. See where the bitterness comes from? How do we know the difference? A Gamma often feels insecure or jealous. An Alpha rarely, if ever, feels insecure. Gammas may be the people who beat on their chest, yell, and intimidate others, so everyone thinks they are an Alpha. Then again, an unevolved (young or mentally young) Alpha may do the same thing. See how it can be confusing?

Characteristics of a Gamma

- Rebellious
- Interesting
- Adventerous
- Loves to move around and explore (may have a strong need for uncertainty)
- Independent and may seem like an outsider
- Aware of their own value even to the point of delusional
- Organized and Consistent and will be a good friend inspiring you to be the same way
- Can have drive and may be misunderstood to be an Alpha
- Inability to compromise—which makes for a difficult partner
- Avoids conflict
- Leans towards calculated risks
- Insecure

- Jealous
- Rejects social norms
- Questions authority

OMEGAS

Omegas are at the bottom of the hierarchy. Unlike Alphas or Betas, the Omega is often characterized by traits that set them apart from the conventional hierarchy. They have a detachment from traditional social standings and roles. Regarded as social outsiders or loners, they are focused on independence, non-conformity, and quiet creativity. The easiest way to say it is the nerds in the movie "Revenge of the Nerds" were Omegas.

Characteristics of an Omega

- Nerdy
- Self-aware
- Sure of themselves
- Introspective
- Not confrontational
- Curious (I don't mean sexually)
- Know their self-worth
- Don't need feedback about themselves
- Successful
- Shy
- Reserved on the surface but has strong emotions
- Introverts

- Quiet and keep to themselves
- Supportive
- Likely to read romance novels or watch romance movies to live vicariously through them
- Lack social skills and struggle with social interaction, which can make them unpopular
- Prefers solitude and their own hobbies
- May excel in specialized skills
- Capable of extraordinary things when they are passionate about it

HOW TO QUICKLY IDENTIFY THESE PERSONALITIES, AT A GLANCE:

1. Determine if the person is dominant or submissive
2. Ask yourself "is that person a natural leader or not?"
3. What do they do for a living, do they like it, and what social groups are they involved in?

Here are the answers to these questions for each hierarchy:

■ Alphas

1. Dominant—actively dominant—they may remind you of it but probably don't need to.
2. Natural Leader.
3. Involved in big companies. They will either like it or are frustrated they haven't taken over yet. Involved in large group(s) and excel within the group.

(Alphas may be the most obvious except for people trying to emulate them)

- **Sigmas**

    1. Dominant—passively dominant, think of it as quiet confidence.

    2. Natural Leader but typically only leads when they want to or if called upon.

    3. Involved in smaller companies, self-employed, Lone Wolf personality, involved in something "off the beaten path." They like all of these. If involved in large company, they are not a big fan.

(Easily mistaken for Alphas but once you understand them, they are obviously different from Alphas)

- **Betas**

    1. Submissive and lacking confidence, may occasionally try to act dominant but it appears awkward.

    2. Not a natural leader, they may be in a leadership position but it doesn't feel natural to them nor you (trouble making decisions or wishy washy.)

    3. Whatever they do for a living, they are typically in the background or in a supportive role.

- **Deltas**

    1. Submissive but don't call them submissive nor challenge their beliefs.

    2. Not a natural leader and doesn't prefer a leadership role.

3. Works in a solid job or trade. Has been working in job/trade for a long time (or was at last job for a long time if recently changed.) Ask them if they like it or not and they may say "it's a job" or "it pays the bills."

■ Gammas

1. If you are thinking, "I am not sure if this person is dominant or submissive," they are probably Gammas. They are tougher to determine because they may initiate conflict with dominant personalities. Onlookers may perceive this as dominant, but ultimately Gammas are submissive and rebellious towards leadership.

2. May seem to be a leader but typically just leading towards rebellion with behaviors typically laced with jealousy or insecurity.

3. What they do for a living may vary greatly. If they started a business, it was probably to go against the grain, be rebellious, prove a point, or to make change.

■ Omegas

1. Submissive and nerdy

2. Ish. Omegas are sure of themselves and self-aware so Omegas may seem to have natural leadership skills, but it's not the same quality as Alpha, nor Sigma, leadership.

3. Whether employed or self-employed, Omegas will typically have a specialty and may be very passionate about it. Most typically it will be in a supportive role. They will be happy if they feel valued.

Let's go through the questions again:

1. Determine if the person is dominant or submissive

If they are dominant, then you only have 2 choices to pick from: Alpha or Sigma.

If they are Submissive, then you have to identify from 4 choices: Beta, Delta, Gamma, or Omega. If you are unsure which submissive they are, see if you can eliminate 2 of the choices, so you are debating between the remaining 2 choices. Example: if they are not nerdy (Omega) nor rebellious and challenging (Gamma) then you just narrowed it down to Beta or Delta.

If you are confused between dominant or submissive, look for the rebellious Gamma.

2. Ask yourself "is that person a natural leader or not?"

If you answered question 1 as dominant and you think they are a natural leader, then you are correct: they are a dominant hierarchy.

If you answered question 1 as dominant, yet they are not a natural leader, then you got question 1 wrong: they are a submissive hierarchy emulating an Alpha. Getting this one wrong is a big relationship killer. If a woman wants a dominant personality and a submissive hierarchy tries to be dominant, the woman will one day realize the submissive was emulating a dominant personality. Important tip: women always figure out the truth.

3. What do they do for a living, do they like it, and what social groups are they involved in?

If dominant hierarchy then this question will separate Alpha from Sigma.

If submissive hierarchy:

- Beta: will be in the background or a supportive role
- Delta: trades an honest days work for a paycheck. Is a realist.
- Gamma: what they do for a living won't be conclusive. Ask

them if they like it and you will hear the rebellious nature. Same with social groups.

- Omega: typically a specialized career. Probably an intellectual job which required education. Happy if they feel valued, because they know their worth.

Once you have determined what you think the personality type is, look at the other traits of that personality. If the person has those other traits, chances are your analysis is correct. Once we know the personality type, the behaviors will make sense. Once everything makes sense, we can begin to predict behavior! Once we begin to predict behavior we will no longer be surprised by actions nor reactions. That is where your life gets easier and the fun begins! Then we get closer to our goal…

> **"Through understanding we can have tolerance.**
> **Through tolerance we can have acceptance.**
> **Through acceptance we can have peace."**

CHAPTER 103:
Moving Toward Pleasure People *or* Moving Away From Pain

Sigmund Freud introduced a concept that all human behavior is based on the principle that people make choices to avoid/decrease pain or to increase pleasure. Here is my take on it: I think these are actually a personality type. This is WHY one person has motivation, or is motivated, and another seemingly does not have motivation. If you want to understand what motivates someone (including yourself), or if you want to properly motivate someone else, then understanding this concept is one of the keys to creating motivation. It's important to understand one is born with this personality type as part of their DNA. This is your Nature. Let's review...

MOVING TOWARDS PLEASURE (MT'S) PERSONALITY TYPE

MT's are ambitious and self motivated. This is the easier of the two personality types. These people are easier on themselves, easier on relationships, and require much less external motivation. If one tells an MT: if you do A, B, and C, then you can have this reward, this pleasure or this status, that is all they need to hear. They will Move Toward getting that reward, pleasure, or status. High achievers are typically MT's. If you see someone who is a "go getter," who is motivated, who is "hungry," and seems to accomplish things easily, they are most likely an MT personality.

Note: the MT has to want the reward, pleasure or status in order to be motivated. A conversation with an MT may go like this:

Employer: Hey MT, if you do X, Y and Z, I will give you a paid day off from work.

MT: No thanks, that is too much extra work for only one day off. Make it 2 days off and you've got a deal.

Employer: Deal!

Now that the MT wants the reward. No extra motivation is required. They will Move Towards (the reward) pleasure.

MOVING AWAY FROM PAIN (MA'S) PERSONALITY TYPE

What do I mean by Moving Away from pain? People in this category typically do not do something unless the alternative is more painful than the action. WHY? That is just the way they are wired. Again, this is in their DNA, their Nature. They appear to be lazy. Other people feel like they constantly have to kick them in the butt or threaten them (with something painful) to get them to do something. If you are in a relationship (romantic, employment, contractual, or otherwise) with an MA or have one in your family, you know exactly what I mean. There is seemingly no limit to how much pain they will justify, rationalize and adapt to, so they don't have to take action. It is a difficult relationship for people who need them or count on them, and it is a difficult life for the MA because they are constantly being threatened with pain.

Note: when I say pain I don't mean literal pain (although it could be.) I mean something painful to their lifestyle. To a child it may be taking away their games or taking away their privileges. To an adult it may be getting fired from a job or getting a car repossessed by the bank.

If you hear someone say "I just want to be left alone," they are probably an MA. They are tired of all the painful threats and people barking at them for all the tasks left undone. MA's are more likely to live in an unkept home because getting the motivation to clean the house is much more painful. MA's may actually buy more clothes rather than do laundry. Being homeless may be less painful to them, than holding a job. Again, whichever is less painful in their opinion. Key phrase "in their opinion."

MA's are the people who have a lot of college degrees or accolades but didn't maximize them. They didn't take their doctorate level learning, start a business and make tons of money. An MA did all the heavy lifting early in life and got their college degrees, so they could get the teaching job they wanted. Once tenured and they cannot be fired, they are on "easy street." No stress and no worries. Disclaimer: I am not bashing college professors nor am I saying all tenured professors sought out their job with ulterior motives. Many professors seek that job because they love to teach and teaching fills their needs for Growth/Contribution, Significance, Connection, and Certainty. The same way I gave the example that an Analytical is likely to be drawn to being a Lawyer, an MA is likely to gravitate towards being a tenured professor. The professor who takes their job seriously, cares about their students and puts effort into their job should be commended. The professor who doesn't care, doesn't engage their students and just tells everyone in class to "read chapter 7 and don't bother me," is likely an MA.

REAL LIFE SITUATIONS

If you are a boss, teacher or parent of multiple children, think of your employees, students or your children and how much you have to do to get them to finish their tasks. You may have Jennifer (MT) and Tom (MT) where all you have to do is ask them to finish/

accomplish these things and they will get the day off tomorrow and that is all you have to say! In fact, don't get in their way nor inhibit their ability to accomplish the task because they will run over obstacles. This sounds like I am describing a Driver personality but this applies to all four personality types. The MT wants that day off (reward) and they will put in the extra effort (Move Towards) it takes to get it. This is an easy relationship for all parties involved. MT's typically get promoted quicker, have more (money, resources, fun) and are more likely to lead a happier life.

On the other hand, you have Sally (MA) and Larry (MA.) You told them the same thing and they didn't do it. The thought of having the day off wasn't a big deal to them. You asked them if they would do it with two days off and they said they didn't want to do it at all. The next thing you try is telling them they are going to get in trouble if they don't accomplish the things you asked them to do, by tomorrow. Sally and Larry ask you "how much trouble?" or "what kind of trouble?" They are trying to access if accomplishing the task is more painful than the trouble, in their opinion. Again, huge key phrase: "in their opinion." Because what may be painful for you and me, may not be painful for them. Oh and you will be surprised how much pain they can tolerate.

Tomorrow comes and you find out, even after being threatened with "getting in trouble," they still didn't do it. Now you are "the bad guy" and have to give them the punishment you threatened. Sally and Larry take the punishment. Then you tell Sally and Larry if they don't do the tasks today, they will get their pay cut. Both ask "by how much?" Again, they want to access if the pay cut is more painful than doing the work. You are thinking "WHY does it matter?! Isn't any pay cut painful enough?!" Apparently not, so you tell them how much you are going to cut their pay if the required tasks are not completed by the end of the day.

Tomorrow comes and you are dreading having to deal with Sally and Larry. The whole drive over you are thinking about this. You get into the office to find out Larry did the task, maybe a bit sloppy and with half effort, but he met the minimum requirements of what you asked him to do. He may have even interpreted what you told him to do "a certain way" just so he could cut corners. You argue with Larry that is not what you told him to do and he argues back that is how he understood it. He continues by saying "you should have been more clear." This is a quintessential interaction with an MA personality type. If an MA is an analytical, which many seem to be, they have figured out how to debate this.

This is painful for you because you don't want to be in the position where you constantly have to be threatening, nor be the "bad guy," but they are putting you in this position. As the employer, teacher or parent it is your job to get them to do their work. This might even make you resentful towards them. If this person is an employee, you want to fire them. If this person is a student, you want to strangle them and can't wait until they move on out of your class. You might even pass them/graduate them just so you don't have to deal with them again. If this is one of your children… well…good luck. You may feel trapped. You may feel like you are pleading with them to change all the time, so you don't have to fight about it anymore, and maybe even regret parenthood. All I can say is, now at least you know you know WHY. This is particularly obvious when you have two children where one is an MT, and the other is an MA. Part of the conversation with the MA may include, "WHY can't you be more like your sibling?" This comparison may cause resentment amongst the siblings. It may feel like favoritism to all the family members. It makes for an unhealthy household and everyone just wants it to stop; however, this is not painful enough for the MA to make a change, so the MA just pleads to be left alone.

But what about Sally?

Oh no. I forgot about Sally. Now I have to walk over there and ask Sally if she did her work. I know she didn't, I just know it. If she did, I know she did it with half effort, just like Tom. OMG I hate being a manager. Maybe I should rethink my life. I am dreading this. This is triggering my anxiety. I am not ready to deal with this now. I am going to do my morning reports, call a few people and wish them happy birthday to I get myself in a good mood, have lunch, and then bite the bullet and deal with Sally.

After lunch I get back to my office and plan my afternoon. I am going to do this at 2pm, that at 3pm and oh no, I forgot about Sally. Aww man! Come on! I don't want to have to deal with this today. Uggghhh, fine! Let me just go over there and get this over with. You, the manager, marches over to Sally. As it turns out, Sally didn't do her work, again. You let out a big sigh, shake your head and ask her WHY. You plead with her to do her work. You try to counsel her on WHY getting her work done makes everything so much easier. You ask her if she wants her job and she nods her head yes. You remind her that doing her work is imperative if she wants to keep her job. She nods her head again indicating she understands and agrees with you. You politely ask her to do her work and go back to your office.

The next day you are optimistic because you know that you connected with Sally during yesterday's conversation. You start thinking "that was a good intervention and maybe I am a good manager after all!" She just needed a heart to heart conversation to give her the motivation to do her work. Yeah, that's it! I just know Sally did her work! As soon as you get into the office you walk over to Sally with a smile on your face and optimistically ask her if she did her work, expecting good news. Sally tells you she did some of it but didn't understand everything, so she stopped. You ask her WHY she didn't message you to get clarification and she replies that she didn't want to bother you. This makes you fed up so you give Sally a final ultimatum that she better get her work done before she goes home, or she needs to find another job. Many people heard you say this, don't know the back story, and jump to conclusion that you are not being very nice to Sally. The next day you come into the office dreading your interaction with Sally. You walk over to her and ask her if she did her work, and she replies "yes."

What do we learn from this? What was painful enough for Larry to do his work wasn't painful enough for Sally to do her work. Sally kept Moving Away from more and more pain. She took the reprimand, the pay cut, and your long boring conversation (which she has heard many times before from other people who were also wasting their breath) about everything being easier if she just did her work. All of those were less painful to her (again key phrase since what she interprets to be enough pain is her motivating factor) than doing her work. To Sally, getting fired was more painful than doing her work, so she finally found the motivation to pick the less painful one. Do you see how both parties are enduring this unpleasant relationship?

This happens across all four personality types but I have seen it more prevalent in Analyticals. Maybe it's the characteristically low emotion or the ability to calculate, justify and rationalize which is more painful, I am not sure. Drivers and Expressives are the next likely to be an MA. The least likely to be an MA are Amiables (because they want you to be happy and accomplishing the tasks will make you happy.)

Deltas, who are an MA personality, are voted most likely to say "that's not my job."

The only time an MA can be mistaken for an MT is when they have had their pain, and that motivation is lasting. Example: an MA grew up in poverty, which was painful for them (key phrase), and consequently they worked their tail off to become rich and successful. That person may appear to be an MT but may actually be an MA using their pain as motivation. They have effectively converted to an MT, but they will always think like an MA.

PRO TIP: All the external conversations in the world won't create the motivation to act like a MT, it has to come from within. All you rescuers read that line again because you can't help someone who won't help themselves.

I paused for a moment to consider if an MT would ever convert to an MA. It is unlikely but it would only happen if they were rich enough (in their opinion) that they didn't need to Move Towards pleasure anymore, they can just buy their reward, pleasure, or status.

So Rob, how do we know if someone is an MT or an MA without straight up asking them? Simple. Ask one question: "If you won a million dollars, what would you do with it?"

MT response: I would buy a bigger house, start the business I have been dreaming of and give my parents enough money so they can finally retire. Translation: I would make happen all the rewards, goals, and accomplishments I have been trying to achieve.

MA response: I would pay off my house, pay off my car, quit my job and probably do something less stressful with my life. Translation: my mortgage payment is painful, my car payment is painful, my job is painful, and what I do for work is painful, so I would relieve my pain.

MA who appears to be an MT: I would invest it in something that makes me more money because I have been poor and I vowed I would never be poor again. Translation: I am still moving away from pain. An MT would never say it this way. An MT would say: when I was young, my whole family was poor and I wanted to be the first one to break away from that. Do you hear the word choice of an MT in comparison? The MT didn't like being poor and wanted to Move Towards (status) pleasure.

How does one motivate a room full of people when half are MT's and half are MA's? Easy. Sell both personality types from their point of view.

Every good salesperson knows that selling is based on features and benefits. You cannot sell based on just features, you have to explain what benefits those features provide.

Feature:

If I said to a room full of people that if you were to acquire X,Y and Z skills, you would make a pile of money. No one is motivated yet until I cement the suggestion with Benefits.

Then I continue with the Benefits:

With that pile of money, you could buy a brand new Porsche or take a dream vacation. With that pile of money, you could pay off your house, be debt free, quit your job, retire, and take stress out of your life.

Here is the amazing WHY part: the MT's never even heard me say "pay off your house," "be debt free," or "quit your job, retire, and take stress out of your life." MT's are not motivated by that! The MA's heard that though. WHY? Because those are Moving Away from pain benefits and the brain naturally filters out what we train it to look for. An MT only heard "buy a new Porsche" and "take a dream vacation" because those are pleasure!

The MT people who are primary Drivers have already asked where/how they can learn X,Y and Z. The MT Analyticals are currently gathering more information and considering the risks and rewards. The MT Expressives are thinking how good they will look in that new Porsche. The MT Amiables are politely asking where they can get the X,Y, and Z material.

CHAPTER 104:
The Six Basic Human Needs

I want to thank the great Tony Robbins for his work and give him credit for the creation of this list. I am going to explain these Needs as I understand them and most importantly, apply the list to WHY.

Many actions can be traced back to these Needs. The most important thing to understand is, these are Needs. These are not wants, desires, nor preferences. Every human on the face of the earth has these Needs. We should understand many of our behaviors are derived from the need to fulfill these Needs. The stronger the Need, the greater the behavior to fulfill that Need. For example, if you have a strong Need for Significance, then you have strong behaviors that you designed (key phrase "that you designed") to fulfill your strong Need. If the Need for Significance is not very important to you, then you have designed behaviors for yourself, so you don't feel overly Significant. It goes both ways.

Think of these first few chapters as the center of the onion (if you were an onion.) This is your nature. It is who you are on the inside. The good news is: this chapter is the easiest category to change. If while you are reading this you realize your Need level is a "9" and then you realize the behaviors you designed (to fill your "9" Need level) don't make you happy, then you can make conscious decisions to change your Need level. Correspondingly you can consciously change our behavior. This is one of the quickest ways you can take control of your life and make immediate impact on having a life by design. After all, we don't want to be a slave to our Needs, we want to design our life.

Goals of this chapter

1. Understand your current need levels (let's use a 1-10 scale with 10 being the strongest)
2. Decide if this level makes you happy and fulfilled
3. Figure out what actions you have created to fulfill or maintain your current Need levels
4. Make conscious decisions if changes in your levels and actions will improve your happiness and quality of life.

In no certain order, this is not a hierarchy nor tier system, here is Tony Robbins' list of The Six Basic Human Needs:

1. Significance

2. Connection

3. Certainty

4. Uncertainty

5. Love

6. Growth and Contribution

Just like the four personality types these are not a progression, and one is not better than the other. What they mean to you is exactly that, it what they mean to you. How strong your Need is for each one is directly related to the actions you take, and the behaviors you have, to fulfill that Need.

Let's dive in…

1. THE NEED FOR SIGNIFICANCE

Everyone loves to feel Significant. When I say Significant I mean:

- Important
- Substantial
- Meaningful
- Distinguished
- Great
- Impressive
- Famous
- Essential
- Outstanding
- Noteworthy

Whether it is getting an award, being recognized for your great work, being told you look attractive today, being a person others look up to, or just simply being special in someone else's life, everyone likes to feel Significant. The question to ask yourself is: how important is this Need for me? What is my Need for this? Again, we want to assign a number to what we think is our own Need level. If your Need level is a "2" in this category, then your behavior is influenced to fulfill your "2" Need level. If your Need for Significance is a "10" (yes there are plenty of people out there who are "10's") then many of your actions are strongly influenced by fulfilling this Need.

By the way, I am not encouraging you to raise your Need level from a "2," to a "5" or "10." Quite the contrary. People who are "10" in Need for Significance are typically tough people to be around. They are full of themselves and their behaviors can be selfish, self-centered, and annoying. I am asking you to make conscious decisions to see if raising or lowering your Need level, in each category, would be better for you.

Let's ask ourselves: are there actions we take in order to feel Significant? I assure you that you have at least one action you do on a daily, or weekly, basis that satisfies or attempts to satisfy your Need for Significance. I also assure you there are some people reading this that spend their entire day trying to fulfill this Need. I want you to be able to control your life, not have life control you. Here are some example questions you can ask yourself:

Do I find Significance in:

- The way I dress

- The position I hold at work

- The team I root for

- The way I speak (unique accent, authoritative, loud, swear a lot, eloquent, brag a lot, use vocabulary others may not understand to show we are educated, use technical jargon others may not understand)

- The house I live in

- Making people aware of my position or status

- My spouse (you are the spouse of an important person, highly attractive person, or accomplished person)

- My children (brag they are best in their class, or you let people know you are the parent of an accomplished child)

- My parent(s) (Dad or Mom own the company I work for, is a celebrity, is in politics, is famous)

- The car I drive

- The amount of money I have or don't have (oh woe is me… crying poor to get attention)

- Who I make fun of

- Who I am friends with or associate with (maybe you are a namedropper)

- The position I hold, at work, in a group, or social club that I am a member of (hello Alphas)

- Being rude to people

- Being nice or helpful to people
- My drive to be the best at something
- My appearance (beautiful hair, manicured nails, healthy skin, make-up or you purposely dress unusual for attention)
- Altering my appearance (changing yourself through plastic surgery may finally allow you to feel Significant)
- Work out to stay in shape
- Smoke (thinking it's cool)
- Being unique
- Acting disinterested
- Committing crime
- Getting a tattoo
- Being annoying
- Being entitled
- The sport you play
- How tall you are (If you are really tall then you literally look down at people which can make one feel Significant. On the other hand, if you are really short (especially for short males) looking up at people can make you feel less Significant. This feeling may lead to other actions designed to try and offset it.) Remember this when you read the Andre the Giant story below.

Take a moment and ask yourself how important is it to feel Significant? Expressives are yelling "10!" and "Am I allowed to say 11?" LOL. Alphas may also be saying "10." Amiables probably have a lower Need for Significance.

So where do you think you are on a scale of 1-10? Just answer without thinking. Are you a "2"?, a "6"?, maybe a "9"? How important is feeling Significant to you? There is no right nor wrong answer. This is the way you feel about yourself and how important it is for you to feel Significant.

What does a person who has a "2" Need for Significance do to fulfill their need?

Well, Significance is not very important to them, so they are probably quiet and like to be in the background. They may take pride in knowing they have "this degree" or "that level in their job" but they don't flaunt it. If someone wanted to recognize their achievements, the "2" might reject the award. They might suggest someone else deserves it more or might say they are flattered to receive it but please don't make a big deal out of it and single me out. Just knowing someone thought they should get an award might fill their "2" Need for Significance. Who fits this description? Amiables, Analyticals, and Sigmas may be typical here. WHY didn't I say "Betas?" Remember Betas are in the background, but they don't want to be. Beta males will typically have a stronger Need for Significance because they want to be Alphas. What behaviors have Betas chosen to accomplish this? They learn and emulate Alpha type behavior.

What does a "6" do?

A "6" has a stronger Need for Significance, than a "2." A "6" wants to be recognized but maybe in a passive way. A "6" may not ask if there is an award for this achievement but if there is, the "6" wants their award. Who might the "6's" be? Analyticals, Drivers, Deltas, Betas, and Omegas may be typical here.

What does a "10" do?

"10's" may ask a question they already know the answer to, so when everyone answers the question it makes them Significant.

Sally asks: "who was the champion last year?" Answer: "It was you, Sally!" Sally smiles and revels in her Significance. Don't mistake this for insecurity because insecure people rarely call attention to themselves. The reason people have a strong Need for Significance will vary greatly so don't assume everyone has the same reason, like insecurity.

What else does a "10" do? This can best be told with a fun story! Yay, story time!

Once upon a time I was working in the diamond business. At the time, I was the #2 salesman in the country with about 5 or 6 years working in that industry. I am saying this because high producing salesmen (in any industry) are valued, and typically treated with respect because the company does not want them to leave. On this particular day, the boss's, boss's, boss (the VP of the company) was in our store. I was dressed in a nice suit, as I always was. I was standing just outside the store, minding my own business, when the VP walked over to me. I waited for him to speak first. He began telling me his impression of the couple inside the store, buying a diamond. He shared his guess of what he thought the man did for a living, what the woman did for a living, what size diamond they might buy, and the price range he anticipated them to be in. I listened to his soliloquy silently and intently. When he finished speaking, and I felt it was my turn to speak, I smiled, nodded my head and simply said "that sounds about right." The VP immediately changed his tone and snapped at me saying "I didn't ask you" and walked away. That was 30 years ago.

I still remember this interaction because it was so ridiculous. The VP came over to where I was standing and shared his thoughts with me. It would have been rude of me to say nothing. There was no win here. After watching patterns of his behavior, I can tell you his Need for Significance was a "10." It was his intention to walk over to me and use his position to engage me in a "no win situation" so he could flex on me and feel significant.

The problem with "10's" is they can never fill this void. It doesn't work. The VP might have walked away saying to himself "I really showed him"; however, the people he does that to do not think he is Significant. They think he is a real jerk. There is a chapter coming up called "The Negative Wave" where I discuss my philosophy that it is so much easier to do negative things to get attention, or feel Significant, than it is to do positive things to get attention and feel Significant. Remember this story during that chapter and it will make more sense.

So who makes up our potential "10's?"

- Alphas—they will give you their resume, accolades, achievements, or just tell you how awesome they are.

- Gammas—their "Alpha like" drive, rebellious nature, and adventurous nature screams Need for Significance.

- Expressives—they can't help it. It's in their DNA to be the center of attention and crave Significance.

What about an Alpha or Gamma who is an Expressive? OMG. They have probably designed a lot of negative behaviors to fill their strong Need.

This next group of potential 10's exhibits poor behavior in order to fulfill their "10" need level

- Betas/Gammas—who crave respect very badly (like the VP)

- People affected by Birth Order

- Adults who were neglected/ignored as children

- Someone divorced—who was treated poorly/emotionally abused or gaslighted by their spouse

- People who are out of balance in life, like someone who has been in a supportive role too long

(See a pattern here? Many times, 10's come from negative situations)

If you want to understand a person's Need for Significance visit them, or video call them, on their birthday and sing happy birthday to them. The larger they smile, the stronger their Need for Significance. If they assist the gesture by cooperating (like waving their hands like an orchestra conductor) they have a very strong Need and/or they are an expressive. If they simply blush, they may have a medium Need. If they try to interrupt you to get you to stop, they have a very low Need.

Take a moment and think about what you do or what actions you do to fill your Need for Significance. If you are honest with yourself, you may be surprised at the things you do to fulfill this need. The goal here is to understand WHY you do the things you do. Then you can assess if they are really important to you, if they serve your happiness (as Mr. Robbins would say), or if you are a slave to them (like the VP.)

One of the problems with a strong Need for Significance is that you usually have to separate yourself from others, in order to achieve it. What do I mean by that? If you are better than someone *at something* and you separate yourself then you will be more Significant. Notice I said "better than someone 'at something.'" If you read "if you think you are better than someone" then you have a whole different level of self-reflection ahead. Seriously because I even *italicized* "at something" the first time I wrote it, yet you still missed it. If you fill your Need for Significance through selfishness and separation, you have a lonely road ahead.

The behaviors we employ to fill our Need for Significance are typically rewarded by a short-term dopamine hit. Dopamine is a chemical our body releases which gives one a feeling of reward and provides a motivation to continue. Do you see WHY we might get addicted to this?

I heard something amazing the other day. Andre the Giant, who was an extremely imposing 7' 6" tall and weighed 520 pounds, starred in a movie called *The Princess Bride*. After the movie someone asked Andre "what did you like most about making the movie." Andre replied that the thing he liked most was that, for the first time, he felt like he was treated like an equal without the usual stares and attention due to his size. He felt like he belonged much like he did in a wrestling locker room, which he considered a sanctuary. He also appreciated being able to defer to others and call them "boss," even though they were often much shorter than him. This was his way of showing respect and making them feel comfortable around him. OMG. I immediately knew his Need for Significance was much lower than all the Significance he received from being such a large man! This may also be the reason famous people do not handle fame well. They get recognized, besieged by fans, and chased by paparazzi much more than they want to. WHY? Because their Need for Significance is much lower than the Significance they receive. Kurt Cobain, of the band Nirvana, wanted to make great music and those who knew him have said he wanted his music to be recognized; however, he felt a deep discomfort with the fame commensurate with that recognition.

If you just said to yourself "I would love to have that much fame, recognition, and Significance" then your Need for Significance is much higher than the Significance you receive. What you really want to reflect on is what behaviors have you developed to compensate?

So what happens when we have a strong Need for Significance and separate ourselves from others? We sacrifice our Need for Connection...

2. THE NEED FOR CONNECTION

"True connection is achieved through gratitude"

The Need for Connection is exactly like it sounds. Connecting with people, animals, beliefs, and places is something we Need. In this heightened sense of emotion our bodies release endorphins. A chemical which is a natural pain reliever that creates a sense of well-being. Have you ever hugged a loved one, felt your heart rate slow and let out a big sigh? Maybe just hugging this person felt like "home" and "safety." Hello endorphins! See how we might get addicted to this?

What would you want your loved ones to say at your funeral? Would you want them to say "she looked really good in a bikini?" or "he really thought he was an important guy?" Maybe not. Would you prefer your loved ones to say "she had a big heart and a caring nature?" or maybe "he was such a generous and loving man?" I think I would prefer the latter in my eulogy.

We should understand "looking good in a bikini" and "he was an important guy" are what we might do to fulfill our Need for Significance. "She had a big heart" and "he was such a generous and loving man" are the result of actions we took to fill our Need for Connection.

Let's drive this point home

If you were lying there dying in someone's arms would you say, "Tell me I'm smart," and fill your Need for Significance or would you say, "Tell my family I love them very much"? If the latter, then let's focus on our Need for Connection in our lives.

Connection starts with you. One of the most important Connections we can have is Connection with ourselves. Know yourself, understand yourself, be yourself, and love yourself. After all, if you outlive your life partner and your friends, the only Connection you may have is with yourself, so learn to like yourself, date yourself, and love spending time with you. Once you do that then you will know whom you are sharing with the world and your Connections with others will deepen.

We have to watch when we Connect with negativity. Sometimes when we feel excluded, we can emotionally go to that dark and secluded place of isolation because this is a familiar place. If we do this, we have to break those patterns and stay in a mentally healthy place. If you have these issues, talk to someone about it and seek help. Whether it is with a wise friend or a paid professional, there is never shame in getting help!

Sometimes we crave the Need for Connection because we are Certain we are going to feel a Certain way…

3. THE NEED FOR CERTAINTY

The Need to feel Certain is strong in many people. Tony Robbins describes Certainty as the Need for safety, security, comfort, and the Need to avoid pain. Certainty can be achieved in many ways therefore it can be found in many actions.

What do you do to create Certainty?

- Rules
- Laws
- Schedules
- Routines
- Habits
- Hobbies
- Traditions
- Stay in a relationship (whether good or not)
- Live in the same home for a long time
- Drive the same car for a long time
- Apply make-up (because you are Certain you will look good)
- Eat at the same restaurant
- Go to the same chain restaurant you go to at home, when you are out of town = stronger Need

- Order the same dish at different restaurants
- Order the same thing at the same restaurant all the time (very strong Need)
- Keep the same job
- Have a fear of the unknown
- Fear change
- Like being in control
- Have anxiety about things you cannot control
- Watch a movie more than once (if you liked it the first time, you're certain you're going to like it again)
- Buy the same product again after the last one wore out
- Listen to the same songs over and over again
- Vacation at the same place—buying a vacation home there = strong Need
- Rarely, if ever, redecorate your house
- Keep the same hairstyle
- Lock your doors
- Avoid variety and trying new things
- Stay in your comfort zone

The list goes on and on…

PRO TIP: Certainty and Uncertainty conflict with one another. You have to find your balance between the two.

If you have a "9" Need for Certainty and you become out of balance (usually from monotony and boredom) you will feel the

Need for something new. A new car, a new job, try a new restaurant, or maybe a new hairstyle. New = Uncertainty through change. If Certainty is a strong Need for you, once you have acquired your new item(s) you will eventually settle back into Certainty (through routines and habits.) That is, until the process repeats and you become out of balance again. Analyticals are at risk for monotony and boredom through their Need for Certainty. WHY? Because Analyticals figure out the best way to do something and then do it over and over again. After all, once you have figured out the best, or most efficient, way to do something, WHY change it? Also Deltas. WHY? Because they are realistic and risk averse, so they can be considered "boring."

Fear of loss

If you have a strong need for Certainty, then you may develop a strong fear of loss. Certainty may mean routines, habits, traditions, and small social circles. Losing someone or something, having something damaged, or having something taken away from you can trigger Uncertainty and pain, for you more than others. If you have your car stolen (or wrecked) this will be more impactful for you because now you have to go get another car. These things can take you out of your comfort zone, which will affect you more than others. People with a fear of loss may develop overprotective, security conscious, controlling, or jealous behaviors in an effort to minimize loss. A fear of loss may also trigger anxiety.

What kind of job do you think someone may have if they have a strong Need for Certainty in their life?

1. Salaried position with vacation time (hello Deltas)

2. May work for a large company thinking the job is more stable (won't catch a Sigma nor Gamma doing this for very long, if at all)

3. May work in the same place for a long time (again hello Deltas)

4. Wants to know exactly what the company policy is to get promoted (hello Analyticals)

4. THE NEED FOR UNCERTAINTY

AGAIN PRO TIP: The Need for Certainty and the Need for Uncertainty may constantly struggle to balance within you.

Uncertainty is (for some) exciting! For others, it's torture. Uncertainty provides short term dopamine hits, which can be fun. "Where am I going next?," "Who will I meet next?," and "What will happen next?," can all be exciting. The problem with a strong Need for Uncertainty is sustainability. One has to keep increasing the adventure, the risk, or the danger, aka trying to one-up the last Uncertainty, to equal that last dopamine hit. This can lead to unhealthy behaviors.

Example: If you are in a restaurant and spot a celebrity you may be fascinated by this novelty, and it may be the topic of discussion when you get home. You may even message your friends "You'll never guess who I just saw!" Let's change this scenario to say you work in this restaurant and this person comes in all the time. The 20th time you see this person the fascination and novelty probably wear off.

Someone may have a strong need for Certainty in their financial life but every weekend they get in the car and drive to a new town without making hotel reservations. They balance the Certainty of having a strong financial foundation with the Uncertainty of what is going to happen next when I am on vacation. They may have a map of the world on the wall, blindfold themselves and throw a dart at the map. Wherever it lands is their next place to visit! One may be a "10" in Certainty in some parts of life and a "8" in Uncertainty, in others.

By the way: the two don't have to equal "10" in order to balance. If you have a "7" Need for Certainty and a "4" Need for Uncertainty and that balance that works for you, great! Whatever makes you feel balanced is your WHY.

One thing to discuss before entering into a relationship is what are each of your Need levels for Certainty and Uncertainty. You don't want to get years down the road to find out one of you is now out of balance and wants to quit their job to start a new business, and the other one does not have that tolerance for risk. Hello Sigmas and Deltas.

There are other traits that follow along with having that strong Need for Uncertainty. These people may try a new restaurant every time they go out. If they go to the same restaurant, they will order something different every time they go. They may not have a solid relationship. Because the "next good thing around the corner" mentality may apply to romance as well.

Entrepreneurs (Alphas, Sigmas, Gammas and Omegas are typical) are looking for the next thing that will make them rich. They probably do not do well in the corporate environment (hello Sigmas.) The Uncertainty of what may be around the corner is thrilling to them. The next big invention or the next company that comes up for sale is unknown, and very exciting. What do you think an entrepreneur's need level for Uncertainty is? Probably pretty high.

Self Employed people are probably one notch down in Uncertainty. They are usually self-employed in a field they are good in. If I am a plumber and know that I am one of the best plumbers in town, then I may feel Certain that I can drum up business by referrals. The Certainty in their skills makes the Uncertainty of starting a business less daunting.

Straight commissioned people have a need for Uncertainty on some level but not as much as an entrepreneur nor a self-employed person. The reason I say that is because they do have the safety net of working for an organization. A straight commissioned person (like a salesperson) may be Certain in their abilities to sell, which means they know they will get paid. For them, the thought of being in a "dead end job" or being on a salary would mean capping their income potential. The Uncertainty of "how much can I make?" is exciting. If this person works for a large company, then the Certainty of job security may be there. If they work for a small company, then they probably have stronger Need levels for Uncertainty since a small business is more likely to go out of business.

My mother (she is a Delta) once asked me if I have a salary. I replied "no, I work straight commission." She asked me how I can sleep at night with a job where you don't have a minimum you can make. I replied, "I am so Certain in my abilities, I can operate in an Uncertain world." That's balance.

If you are one of the people who can't imagine the Uncertainty of being an entrepreneur, starting a business, or working straight commission, then you have a stronger Need for Certainty, than Uncertainty.

Other Uncertainty traits:

- Being a "free spirit"
- Travel without a destination in mind
- Travel without making reservations
- Go to different restaurants
- Loves to try something new
- May not "settle down" or commit in their relationships
- May move to a new house every few years
- May move to a new town every few years (military families come to mind here. The security (Certainty) of being in the military and having my rank, job, or position is comforting; however, the Uncertainty of not knowing where I am going to be stationed, is exciting. Feeling stable in the military while moving around a lot, may fill both needs perfectly)

- Have a job where they travel (again good balance between the Certainty of being employed and the Uncertainty of what tomorrow will bring)

- Have a job where "no two days are the same" (again good balance)

- May lease their cars for 2 or 3 years (instead of buying them) so they can get a new one every few years

- No fear of the unknown

- Only watches a movie once

- Redecorates their home frequently

- Changes their hairstyle or hair color frequently

So, based on this list of possible behavioral patterns, is everyone that has a strong Need for Uncertainty an entrepreneur, self-employed, or a straight-commissioned salesperson? Absolutely not. I am sure you know people who do some, or all, of the things on this list but they have a job or a relationship filled with Certainty. Do you know a couple that has been together for a long time but frequently loves to do new and spontaneous things together? They balance the Certainty of having a relationship with the Uncertainty of doing new things together. Some people are even in open relationships. What do think may happen to a relationship if one person's Need levels change? What if one person, through the natural course of getting older, begins to feel a stronger Need for Certainty? If the other person does not change with them, the relationship may start having problems. They may start fighting about the way they "used to be" but what they are really saying is "we used to have fun through Uncertainty and now that has changed." This is the language we should use to articulate ourselves.

Want to know your balance of Certainty/Uncertainty? Sit in a room and play a song that you like a lot. Play the song on repeat.

The first time you hear the song you may be smiling, moving around, dancing, and enjoying yourself. What about the 10th time it played? 50th? 80th? At what point did you want to turn the song off? More importantly, WHY did you want to turn the song off? After all, it is a song you like a lot, or should I say used to like until you played it 80 times. So WHY did you turn it off? The song didn't change, you did. You were Certain you were going to like it the first time you played it but eventually you got out of balance and needed Uncertainty. The less you played the song, the greater the Need for Uncertainty. If you could enjoy the song on the 80th time you played it just like you did the first time you played it, the greater the Need for Certainty.

5. THE NEED FOR LOVE

"What is real love? Real love is when you love someone so much you put their Needs above your own. Once you measure what they have done for you in return, the relationship becomes a transaction and is not a relationship."

~Tony Robbins

Amiables this doesn't apply to you until you have established, and can enforce, your boundaries. WHY? Because until you have the ability to do that, you won't know what a healthy relationship is.

Hopefully the Need for Love is self-explanatory. Everyone has the Need for Love on some level. Some people live their life to Love and to be Loved. People that have a strong Need for Love may use this as fuel for a strong Need for Connection. There is also a certain level of Certainty in loving and being Loved. Love can be towards people, animals, or even inanimate objects. What if a father and son built a car together? I am sure they both Love that car and it is a symbol of the Connection between the two of them. How much is a car like that worth? I am sure there is a market price for it but how much would that particular car be worth to the son after the father passes away? How much would that car be worth to the father if the son passed away? Hopefully priceless. The car would literally not be for sale. However, it is also possible the car may immediately go up for sale by the surviving person for half of its market value just to get rid of it. You may be asking "How could someone possibly do that?" Remember not everyone is like you. The survivor probably has a strong association toward that car and every time they see the car they may remember their Love for the deceased. They may have to get rid of the car just to try and deal with their loss.

Some people fulfill their need for Love through animals. How many people have pets? How many people work in animal shelters? How many people are part of an organization whose sole purpose is to save a species (like Manatees.) They are fulfilling their need for Love and their Need for Growth and Contribution through participating in the organization. They are literally Contributing to something they Love.

Some people just Love people. Some people do not love animals and think inanimate objects are completely replaceable. If you can fulfill your Need for Love through one category, then that works for you. Some people need more than that. I may be a 10 in my Need for Love and may fulfill this Need by having a spouse, a kid, a foster kid, 2 good friends, 6 dogs, 4 cats, a horse, a car collection, and contributing to the local animal shelter. Everyone is different. I may be a 2 in my Need for Love and may like to live alone. I may have friends that I Love like siblings, and I see from time to time when I feel out of balance. I may have a bird feeder and feel like the birds that come and go are my pets and I Love them. Again, the important thing to understand is how Need levels affect actions and behavior.

5. THE NEED FOR GROWTH AND CONTRIBUTION (GC)

This category encompasses many actions. Need levels for Growth can be fulfilled in many different ways. The focus can be placed on the Need to Grow as a person either in your personal life, professional life, or both. Focus can also be placed on the Need to Grow a business or Grow as a family. The Need to Contribute can be achieved through personal Contribution or through joining and supporting organizational groups that help people, animals, or causes.

Keep in mind the difference in actions that can occur when a person has a strong Need for GC in one category and not another. Let's say someone has a really strong Need for Certainty in their finances and also a strong Need for GC. They may have a salaried position that pays well enough to support their lifestyle yet may have no interest in having more responsibility or growing professionally (hello Deltas.) So what does this person do to fill their Need for GC, since they don't want more responsibility at work? In their personal life they may take piano lessons, foreign language lessons, golf lessons, and volunteer their time at the local animal shelter on weekends. Do you think they could fulfill their Need for GC in this manner? I would say yes. Even if their Need for GC was a "9" this may fulfill their Needs.

Now let's reverse that situation. Let's say I have a strong Need to Grow in my professional life but not my personal life. I may study my craft constantly even at the expense of my relationships, my health and balance in my life. Have you ever met a workaholic? It may be because they have a strong Need for Growth or to Contribute to their industry (like an Omega who is a scientist.) On the other hand, it may also be because of their strong Need for Certainty (trying to build a nest egg.) What if a scientist was a workaholic? We might mistake that person for having a strong Need for GC. After all, they are obsessed with making progress in their field. That may be the case but are there other possibilities? What if that person has a "10" Need for Significance and is a workaholic because they want that "huge discovery" which puts their name in the history books? Remember, everyone is different. We can't generalize behavior. Each behavior has different reasons for people. The easiest way to figure it out is to have a conversation with that person and ask questions.

People that have a strong Need for GC should have a high tolerance for failure since you may not succeed every time you try to Grow or Contribute. They should actually learn to treat failure as good news. Now you may be saying "Ok, hold on Rob. How can failure be good news?" Whether you succeed or fail, you have knowledge that you didn't have before. You have Grown and have a greater ability to Grow in the future with that knowledge. To people with a strong Need for GC succeeding or failing is always good news because they Grew (through learning) and Contributed to the outcome, because we know what does or doesn't work.

People who do not have a strong Need for Growth lack the desire for self-improvement. MA personalities do not have a strong Need for GC. This lack of desire for self-improvement, makes them closed off to suggestion and makes them unwilling to accept criticism. They spend a lot of time defending their position out of pride rather than listening to what someone may have to say.

By the way, you have at least a medium "5" Need for Growth, maybe higher. WHY do I know this? Because you are reading this book! We are Growing!

Let's reiterate the goals of the chapter and see how we did

Goals of this chapter

1. Understand your current need levels (let's use a 1-10 scale with 10 being the strongest)

2. Decide if this level makes you happy and fulfilled

3. Figure out what actions you have created to fulfill or maintain your current Need levels

4. Make a conscious decision if changes in your levels and actions will improve your happiness and quality of life.

    Remember your Need levels right now are just that: your Need levels right now. Now can be different than yesterday and tomorrow has endless possibilities. Don't limit yourself. Several things may change your levels throughout your life. When you get older, have different experiences, different goals in life, or just decide the actions you have created to maintain your current levels do not make you happy. At this point you may decide to change. It may not be a conscious decision. It may happen naturally. For example: what is your Need level for Certainty when you are in your school years compared to when you have a house, a spouse, and children? I would guess they changed a lot whether by active decision or natural change. You may have very different Need levels at the end of this chapter than you did at the beginning.

    Besides understanding ourselves what else can we do with all this information? I will elaborate more in the upcoming chapter "Bringing you all together."

CHAPTER 105:
Capacity

Capacity defined (per Google):
ca·pac·i·ty
/kəˈpasədē/
noun

    1. the maximum amount that something can contain.
"the capacity of the refrigerator is 25.1 cubic feet"

    2. the amount that something can produce.
"the company aimed to double its product generating capacity"

    3. The maximum amount one can handle
"within people it's the maximum of life that one can handle without assistance"

WHY definitions of Capacity within people: are you a 1, 2 or 3?

1. 1's don't have enough Capacity to handle their life. 1's need help because life runs them over. 1's seek help. In many circumstances, relationships with 1's are one sided because they don't have the Capacity to even be a good friend, family member, nor partner. They want to be, they just can't. 1's are Capacity suckers. They latch onto people and draw from their Capacity. Amiables watch out! They are coming for you. Capacity 1's, who themselves are Amiables, will give from their empty cup and rarely get anything in return, not even gratitude.

2. 2's have just enough Capacity to handle their life. They typically do not need help; however, they do not have enough Capacity to handle their own lives and to help others.

3. 3's have a lot of Capacity. They handle their life with ease. They have things figured out. 3's may have resources, they may be resourceful, or both. Their cup is full and they can give from that full cup. They live by the motto "make sure to put your oxygen mask on before helping others." We hear this statement each and every time our plane prepares for takeoff. 3's apply this to their daily lives.

So, which one are you? Are you a 1, 2, or a 3? If you like to rescue people, like to feel needed, or just like to help people, we must understand that we cannot give from an empty cup. I can hear some of the Analyticals asking "what is this empty cup thing?" It is a metaphor for how much you take care of yourself. You take the time to handle your business, manage your appointments, recharge (metaphorically) your batteries, and prioritize things in your life appropriately. You also get very good at it. Once your life is handled and your work is done (full cup) you can help others if you have time. Capacity 3 people are Evolved and have a wholeness about them (more on this in the chapters to follow.)

I don't know the statistics as I am writing this but if I had to guess I would think Analyticals, Drivers and MT's have an advantage here. An Analytical will figure out the best way to accomplish their tasks and increase their ability to do them. A Driver develops the skills needed to better accomplish their tasks, so both of these personality types should naturally develop more Capacity. An MT is motivated to get things done, which builds Capacity.

If one tries to give from an empty cup, they feel themselves being drained. They may also feel used, unappreciated or like they are being taken advantage of. A giver should not be with a taker because a taker has no limits, and a giver has no boundaries. Just ask any Aimable to explain what I mean and they will be happy to unload on you. That is until the Aimable thinks listening to them is making you unhappy, then they will stop. People giving from an empty cup are helping others before they have their life in order. Yes, sometimes this is noble; however, this should be an exception and not your normal.

What is Capacity within people?

The maximum amount someone can handle within their life. Sometimes you may have enough Capacity to handle your life and other times you don't. This even applies to 3's. Capacity 3's have learned to set boundaries when they feel their Capacity levels dropping. If a 3 gets too much on their plate at one time they will stop helping others, tell people to leave them alone (with or without explanation) and focus on the extra effort it takes to get everything handled. Once the fire storm has been handled, they can focus on what others are asking of them. Setting boundaries is key. Note: having a lot of Capacity and being a Capacity 3 is a way to serve the Need for Significance and Connection. Significance: people may brag about you and say things like "Sally always has her act together. Not only does she handle her own stuff, but she handles the ancillary needs of the family (or team/group) and still has time to help other people. She is a rock star!" Connection: people may say "Sally is so nice and helpful. Whenever I need something, Sally just seems to be ready to help. She is so nice and I really appreciate her!" If Sally is special to you then you may want to watch her because Sally may never ask for help. Sally thinks that if she does, she is no longer the rock star or no longer the one who always has her act together. Remember filling the need for Significance and/or Connection is a NEED. Sally has a fear that if she asks for help, she will not be revered in the same way. So one of the behaviors Sally has designed for herself is she will not ask for help.

Uncertainty requires more Capacity

The highest level of Capacity is an Evolved Capacity 3. Evolved 3's do all of the things I just described except they know when it is time to ask for help. What Sally has to understand is if Sally never asks for help, she is robbing her friends and loved ones of their opportunity to give back to her. This is unfair and unbalanced. Give people the opportunity to help you and it will strengthen the relationship. Don't be a martyr.

Analyticals are asking, who is Sally? I just made Sally up. Don't focus on the tree, focus on the forest.

Varying and situational Capacity levels

Example of situational Capacity levels: let's say you share custody of your children 50/50 with their co-parent. When you don't have your kids, life is easy and you have a lot of Capacity. The house stays clean, your animals are cared for, and you have extra time to focus on your work or your social life. You feel like a (C3) Capacity 3.

However! When you do have the kids…O…M…G. The house looks like a bomb went off. I can't find the cat, let alone know if he ate today. There is a smell coming from upstairs that might be lethal and everyone is asking me what is for dinner! These miniature adults have outnumbered me, they don't follow the rules, and I think one of them is hiding the cat. I hope that smell is not the cat but hey, at this point it's every man for himself! [Insert swear word here.] You feel like a Capacity 1, and can't handle your life.

First of all, this is perfectly normal. We need to identify if there are times in our lives when our Capacity changes. Another great example is an accountant. In the months before the income tax deadline, they are busy, busy, and more busy. They have so much work that they cannot handle one more thing in their lives and may be asking family and friends for Capacity. The day after the tax deadline, they are on vacation to decompress and then their normal Capacity returns. When this extra draw on our capacity happens you better have resources, or be resourceful, or you are going to have Capacity issues. In the coming chapters we are going to talk about Maslow's Hierarchy of Needs to further explain varying Capacity levels based on situations and circumstances.

Example of resources:

You have the money to hire a nanny, housekeeper or some form of help.

Example of resourceful:

My next-door neighbor doesn't have anything to do on Wednesday evenings so they come to my house and act as a second parent. In exchange, while I am on my lunch break at work, I do the bookkeeping for their business. Your neighbor is using their Capacity when they have more of it and you are using your Capacity when you have more of it.

Several years ago, my son texted me at 4pm on Halloween. He was trick-or-treating elsewhere and he told me he forgot part of his costume at my house. Before this text arrived, I had everything figured out. Capacity was no problem. I had plans to make my home ready for Halloween including last minute decorations and getting my own costume on. This was going to take me about an hour and I wanted to be ready by 6pm to receive the neighborhood trick-or-treaters. I had plenty of time. All of a sudden, my Capacity was being challenged. Rush hour traffic was coming up so driving to him could take me well over an hour and possibly two hours. I don't have time to do this on my own and do what I wanted to do before 6pm. What do I do? Do I disappoint my son? Do I disappoint myself? I called an Uber. When the Uber driver arrived, I put my son's missing costume piece in the front seat and said to the driver "here is your passenger. You are going to make a young boy very happy!" I paid a $50 fee for the ride and texted my son that his costume piece would be there well before 6pm. Morals to the story are Capacity levels can get reduced very quickly (they can also be raised very quickly) when a situation changes and resources (also resourcefulness) can increase Capacity levels.

Let's revisit that Halloween situation. I was able to increase my Capacity in that situation because I had the (money) resources. What if I didn't have the resources? I would have to check my resourcefulness. I may have gone to the community social media page and asked if anyone was headed to the town where my son was. If someone said yes, then his costume may have been able to be brought to him by a nice neighbor. This is an example of resourcefulness as opposed to resources. Resourceful and resources may have combined as I could have called a neighbor with a teenager who recently got their license (and loves to drive) and offered for them to take my car for a long drive. Maybe I had to pay the teen a few bucks (and it cost me money in gas) but it may have been cheaper than the Uber. So my resourcefulness found a less expensive option and it was within my resources to make it happen.

WHY is capacity so important?

When we don't have Capacity, our lives may be in disarray or even in shambles. Things, people and relationships may get neglected. We don't have good time management. We look at the clock to discover it's the end of the day and our work isn't finished. We also realize we forgot to eat. We look at the calendar and realize tomorrow is our anniversary and we are not prepared. Perhaps even worse, we look at the calendar and we missed someone's birthday. We are overweight or underweight, haven't been to the dentist in years and our credit report isn't what it should be because we forgot to make the monthly payments we promised to pay. Even worse, people with low Capacity get annoyed easily. Especially when trying to accomplish tasks. They may even blame others for making their circumstances harder. You might hear them say "OMG who put this in my way! People are so inconsiderate!" Bashing others gives them temporary relief from their painful life. Does this sound like a life you want to live? Hopefully you said no. If this the life you are living, then you may be asking "what can be done to increase capacity?"

What makes Capacity?

It's a combination of things. Any one of these will increase Capacity but all of them will increase Capacity immensely! Let's dive in...

1. Boundaries! Withdrawing when you need time to handle your life. Telling people you cannot help them right now. Perhaps reassure them that you really want to, but it is not within your Capacity to do so right now. Reschedule appointments or events when needed. Cutting Capacity suckers out of our lives. This includes family.

2. Make good choices the first time! Hire a good employee, get the right job for yourself, buy the right car that suits your lifestyle, and find the right romantic partner rather than settling for someone that is not good for your personality type. These are all just examples of do it right the first time, but there are hundreds more. Those who do not take the time to make good choices the first time, definitely do not have the time to do it over!

3. Become good at doing the things you do over and over again! I used to say that I could do my job with a head injury. I have scripted what I am going to say (but it doesn't sound scripted), I know my guidelines/product knowledge and I have learned from each situation to the point that I could "do it in my sleep." Well one day I got in a car accident and walked away with a concussion. I was correct and I literally

did my job, for the next couple weeks, with a head injury! I don't suggest testing this theory.

4. Do things right the first time. Don't do things half assed and then promise yourself that you will come back to it. Do it right the first time even if it takes an extra bit of time. This sounds like #2, but it is different.

5. Minimize your losses! When something happens, which seems to be a setback, don't make it worse by letting something else make another setback. If you are driving home from an appointment that didn't go well, don't lackadaisically drive home, veer off the road and get a flat tire nor cause damage to your car. Because now you have the bad news from the appointment, and you have to pay for a tire. If you caused damage to your car you just devalued it, and that lesser value may be the difference between you being able to trade it in at a later date for the car you really want. Setbacks add up and decrease Capacity.

6. Budget resources for your mistakes.

7. Increase your resourcefulness! Ask friends, family, co-workers, and neighbors what they do for a living, what their interests are, and if they needed help in their lives in which area would it be? Create a network of people you can refer business to and teach them how to look for business for you. Perhaps barter for assistance by helping people find clients. Hey teenage babysitter, if I help you find clients on weekends will you watch my kids on Thursday evenings for half price? Hey high school student, if I find you a math tutor will you cut my lawn? Yes? Great! Hey math tutor, is that your side job? It is?! What do you do for a living? CPA? Great! If I pay you to do my taxes, will you help this high school student with his math? Yes?! Fantastic. Networks of people helping people create resourcefulness.

8. Keep your life in Balance (more on that in a later chapter.) Being out of Balance causes stress and anxiety which lower Capacity.

9. Focus on things you can control, rather than things you cannot control. Reinhold Neibuhr wrote: "God grant me the serenity to accept the things I cannot change, the courage to change the things I can, and the wisdom to know the difference." Learn it, live it, love it.

10. Time management. The 2 most important parts of this are: 1. Do what you need to do before you do what you want to do. Self-explanatory. 2. Back into your important timelines. Example: My flight takes off at 4pm (hard deadline.) So I need to be at the airport at 3pm. It takes me 30 minutes to get to the airport, so I need to leave at 2:30pm. It will take about an hour to finish packing, so I need to start packing at 1:30pm. I need to shower before I go which takes about 30 minutes, so I need to get into the shower by 1pm. I need to run errands before I do all of this which is going to take me about 2 hours, so I need to leave to run errands at 11am. Oh no, it's 10:45am and I am not even dressed yet, I need to get off the couch and get moving! I thought I had a lot of time to spare when I actually don't! Backing into timelines is huge tool for time management.

11. Versatility. Try new things and consider other options. We don't have to be so rigid. We can appreciate other perspectives. Our ability to be versatile increases Capacity.

When someone tells you that you have been grumpy lately, this is a time to reflect on what has tested your Capacity and has taxed your ability to handle life. What is the #1 Capacity drainer? Want to guess? Drumroll please......CHILDREN! After all, what are children but full-time Capacity suckers! Money problems, medical issues, and moving to a new home round out the top 4. Any of these can instantly drain Capacity.

How much Capacity you have, and what you decide to do with that Capacity, is a big determining factor of the quality of your life. Specifically, your emotional well-being. Oh, and by the way, for everyone with a strong need for certainty (and is bored with life), this means you should have a lot of extra Capacity that you can give away. Boredom = Capacity. If you are bored with your life, and have extra Capacity, volunteer your time somewhere or do something to make someone else's life better. Raising your need for contribution and giving back to people is a great cure for boredom and it's very fulfilling! Deltas have a lot of Capacity because they typically have a good work/life balance.

CHAPTER 106:
The 5 Love Languages

I would like to thank Gary Chapman for his work and give him credit for the creation of this list. The 5 Love Languages are the way we give and receive love. There are three reasons WHY I am including this in my book.

1. many actions and reactions can be traced back here.

2. to bring awareness to this list because Mr. Chapman wrote his book in the early 90's; however, I did not learn about this concept until 25 + years after he wrote it (and I wish I had learned it earlier in life.)

3. to expand the understanding of this list because, in my unhumble opinion, it not only applies to romantic relationships, it also applies to other aspects of life and intertwines with our other personality traits. In short, it is part of our WHY!

Just like the other personality types, this is in no certain order, this is not a hierarchy nor is it a tier system and one is not better than the other.

THE 5 LOVE LANGUAGES

1. Acts of Service
2. Gifts
3. Physical Touch
4. Quality time
5. Words of Affirmation

Some people read that list and say to themselves "I want all of them!" Yes, of course you do; however, this is not a Christmas list. One of these is the primary way you give and receive love. We have to take a step back and really think, which one makes you feel loved. Everyone may appreciate a gift on their birthday, anniversary, or holiday, and it may make you feel remembered or special, but it may not make you feel loved. Which one of these makes you feel (key word) "loved?" Again, this is not a hierarchy, and one is not better than the other. I literally listed them that way because that is alphabetical order.

I'll do some brief explanations as I understand them.

1. ACTS OF SERVICE (AOS)

AOS is when you help someone with their life by doing something to make their life better or easier. This Love Language is dominated by females so I will use that as an example. Guys pay attention! If this is the primary Love Language of your romantic partner then it's time to start knocking out the "honey-do" list. If you cut the grass, emptied the dishwasher, or cooked dinner, you got your romantic partner's attention. If you did it without her asking you to…boy!…let me tell you what!…you may be in for some extra hugs and kisses tonight. Ladies, when he does these things for you, it's a really good idea to recognize it. How do you recognize it? Well this book isn't called HOW, but I'll give you another freebie. You recognize it by responding with his primary Love Language! If it's Physical Touch, do that. If it's Words of Affirmation, do that. If it's Quality Time, do that. When he gives you your Love Language and you reciprocate, you are on your way to a healthier and happier relationship.

What else is AOS? If she says "my head hurts," get up off the couch and go get her pain reliever and a glass of water. If she has a trip coming up. Go to the garage, or storage shed, and get the suitcase(s.) If she is working late one night, have dinner ready for her when she gets home (even if you just order take-out.) Doing it when she asks is level one. Doing it without her asking you is level two. Anticipating her needs and surprising her with it is level three, off the charts! Give that guy the gold medal! If your wife's Love Language is AOS and you consistently operate in level three, your chances of divorce just went down to less than 1%.

2. GIFTS

This one sounds easy; however, it may be the most misunderstood. Again, mostly female dominated so I will focus on that. When I first heard of this list and found out there are women out there who have the primary Love Language of Gifts, I rolled my eyes. I was thinking, you mean to tell me I have to come home with a diamond necklace every night or she isn't going to feel loved? No! That isn't the case at all. This was my complete ignorance because once I understood these people, it made a lot of sense.

Gifts are exactly what they sound like, but they don't always have to be extravagant. Gifts is something you bought her, which may have just been something thoughtful. Let's say she really loves strawberries and on the way home you stopped at the farmer's market and bought her some fresh strawberries. Base hit, good job!

Let's say you took her car in to be serviced (yes this sounds like an AOS but stay with me) and you noticed that her tires are starting to hit the wear sensor. So you ask the service center to put new tires on her car. When you come home you tell her you bought her a present. When she asks what it is, you can bring her outside and say "I inspected your tires for you and was concerned they wouldn't keep you safe, so I bought you new tires." Doesn't sound like much because you and I know that one thousand miles from now she would have heard a noise in her car and asked you to take care of it. Then you would have bought her new tires anyway; however, in my scenario you are the hero who bought her a Gift to ensure her safety. That's a standing double right there.

Let's say this anniversary you went to the jewelry store and got her earrings to match the necklace you bought her for your last anniversary. If you did this, without her hinting that it might be something she wanted, and you surprised her with it, even better! That is a nice Gift. It doesn't have to be expensive because it was thoughtful. It is something she may not know she wants and something she might not buy for herself. That might have been a bang bang play at third but you were called safe so stand up, pound your chest, and ask the umpire for time!

Let's say you planned a trip to go out of town, got a hotel room right by the art district (in this scenario your romantic partner likes art) and when you arrived at the hotel you arranged for fresh strawberries and champagne in the room. Home run baby! Over the fence, that one is outta here!

PRO TIP: When you present it to her you say "I bought us a present! I bought us plane tickets (tangible item), a hotel room for the weekend (tangible item) and a few other surprises (teasing her with anticipation of tangible gifts/surprises to come.) WHY do you present it this way? Because this could also be an Act of Service, so you want to drive the point home that these tangible items are Gifts…you're welcome.

By the way ladies, I am not trying to be manipulative here. I am trying to help some of the guys who may find this Love Language a bit daunting…you're welcome. Some guys may be saying "I am typically not this thoughtful and this seems to take a lot of time to have to think of these things." To that I say "you are right, but you are not cutting the grass, emptying the dishwasher, nor cooking dinner (like the guy above) so it seems as if you have some extra free time on your hands to start thinking about Gifts! After all, you chose her as your SO. If you want to keep her and have her feel loved, become a good Gift giver.

One more thing: if your Love Language is Gifts and you choose to move forward with a relationship with someone, you both need to understand the financial ability the Gift giver has. More importantly, both of you need to accept the Gift giver's ability. Meaning, if your last Gift giver had the financial ability to buy you diamond necklaces and expensive cars (and that is now your standard level of Gifts for feeling loved) then this should be discussed. A Gift giver's ability should be understood and agreed upon, meaning you might be driving to your vacation spot or flying coach. If Gift recipient is expecting private planes, limousines, and Ritz Carlton suites, the relationship has a bomb in the building.

On the other hand: a Gifts Love Language person may the ideal mate for a man who is a workaholic and doesn't have a lot of time to spend with his romantic partner. He might even have his secretary buy the Gifts for his romantic partner (hopefully he presents them but maybe not.) The more he has been out of town + the greater the occasion = the more expensive the Gift! The Gift receiver may be supportive of the business' demands on his time and may feel loved because he is willing to spend a lot of money on her. Hey, don't judge, this relationship may work for both of them. It certainly wouldn't work for a person whose Love Language is Quality Time.

3. PHYSICAL TOUCH (PT)

PT is just as it sounds, but I need to clarify a few things. Since this is a male dominated Love Language, I will focus my thoughts that way. Ladies might be thinking "he just wants sex" or "every time he touches me, it's just for sex." Well you may be right but I am here to tell you that PT is probably not that man's primary Love Language. A man who has PT as his primary Love Language wants to touch you all the time and wants to be touched all the time. This could be sitting next to one another on the couch, holding hands, hugging, just touching hips when sitting on the couch together and yes of course, sex. Sex is very, very important to men but a man who only touches you when he wants sex, may have a different primary Love Language. It is possible that you are just a trophy and he doesn't really love you, but if that is the case you have bigger decisions to make. Anyway! Assuming his intentions are pure and he is in this relationship for the right reasons, he wants to touch and be touched. If you are with a romantic partner where their primary Love Language is PT and you don't like to be touched that much, you two are not compatible. You probably should not have gotten into a relationship with this person because it is going to be a struggle. In contrast, if you have ever seen a couple who are always stuck together like Velcro, it is very possible both have PT as their primary Love Language.

WHY do you think men have a problem with other people touching their significant other? Because for many men, their primary love language is Physical Touch! Pro tip ladies: if a man is romantically interested in you, they will slowly initiate Physical Touch. They may do it consciously or unconsciously. They may start with a "high five." A man might Touch your shoulder, playfully push you, shake your hand, or put his hand on the small of your back as he walks by while saying "excuse me." These are all done to initiate contact, get you used to being touched by them, and check your tolerance for being touched. If you receive those he will upgrade to a hug, standing close in an elevator, or sitting too close to get you used to him being in your space.

Other males know these techniques and are on the lookout for them. If another male initiates contact, which sends up a red flag for your romantic partner, you partner will have a problem with that. Sigmas may be the first to take issue with this because of their highly intuitive nature. So if a man is touching you too much and your man takes exception to it, realize this is a real thing. Your significant other's reaction is a positive thing (he should handle it by speaking calmly to you.) Do not dismiss the way he feels! WHY? Because if he didn't care, he wouldn't care! Men, if she dismisses the way you feel, she is not ready for a quality relationship. I can also assure you she has other behaviors you are not going to be happy with.

4. QUALITY TIME (QT)

QT is exactly as it sounds and is a Love Language that is shared by all genders. People like to spend QT with one another. I actually changed this one for myself. Mr. Chapman wrote that it is Quality Time; however, for me it is "Quantity Time." What do I mean by that? I want to spend a lot of time with my wife. I enjoy her company and I feel "at home" when she is near me. When both of us work from home, she goes into her office and takes work calls. The house feels different when she is home, I know she is there, I can hear her voice, and every once in a while she pops out of her office to get something from the kitchen. To which I take that opportunity to hug or kiss her. That is Quantity Time. Once work is over, we may snuggle on the couch, or go out on a date, and have Quality Time. So for me, we will have Quality Time within our Quantity Time, but I want to feel her presence in one way or another.

Some people have to go to the office, or to the jobsite, and may not have the option to have as much Quantity Time as they would like. If their primary Love Language is Quality Time, then it is important to them to focus on one another when you have the chance to.

If your relationship is struggling and one or both of you work a lot, take a look to see if one or both of you have QT as your Love Language.

5. WORDS OF AFFIRMATION (WOA)

Another one that is shared by all genders. I didn't know my Love Language was WOA until my wife pointed it out to me. This is how it happened:

One year, my wife bought me an expensive gift for Christmas. She really liked how much it made me smile. Then one random day, she commented she thinks I am handsome, smart, and she loves how much I take care of her. She was shocked to see my response was an even bigger smile than the expensive Christmas gift. Her light bulb went on! She said to herself "wait a minute, you mean to tell me all I have to do is tell this man how much he means to me and he will smile bigger than any gift I can give him?" Yes! That is exactly correct because my Love Language is, unbeknownst to me, WOA. I enjoyed the gift and appreciated her thoughtfulness; however, the biggest impact she can make on me is WOA. Until she discovered this, I misdiagnosed myself because I had never had Words of Affirmation before.

This is how easy it can be to misinterpret who we are. Once we misinterpret who we are it is easy to not feel loved, not feel fulfilled in our relationship, and inadvertently give mixed signals to our partner.

Back to WOA. WOA is simply telling your partner how much they mean to you, acknowledging they did something smart or thoughtful, or simply telling them they look attractive today. It can be heartfelt and loving Words or it can be a simple compliment. If you struggle with giving this Love Language to your partner, here is your Pro Tip:

PRO TIP: If you see something, say something. If you are thinking to yourself *Wow, they look really good in that outfit today,* **then say it. If you think they did something smart, say it. If you are thinking about how much they mean to you, tell them. If you are missing them, send them a simple text telling them exactly that. You will be surprised how impactful those simple things are to a person who has WOA as their primary Love Language.**

I heard a woman (from a different culture than me) say "a real man does not need this!" To this I say "I hope you evolve one day." There are plenty of "real men," from all personality types, who have WOA as their primary Love Language." Not only is that OK, it's beautiful. The problem is men usually don't receive compliments, so men who have this as their primary Love Language have had it beaten out of them. If you find a man like this, he may just be a diamond in the rough. Give him the WOA he has never gotten, reassure him it is ok to accept your WOA, and he will bond to you more than he has with anyone else. Happy hunting! I have heard the most attractive men don't always end up with the most attractive women. WHY? Because they prefer how they are treated over appearance and the most attractive women may not feel as if they have to try that hard.

PRO TIP: If your partner's Love Language is WOA then negative Words will impact them more than others. If someone is verbally disrespectful or rude to them, it will be more impactful on their emotions and they may have a stronger reaction than others. If the person they love (you for example) says something to them that is negative, rude, or disrespectful then fasten your seat belt because their reaction will be more severe than others.

One of the things you probably noticed about my explanations is they were geared towards couples. That is because the original list was meant to help couples have lasting love through understanding. I love that!

I suggest we make a descending list for ourselves. Which one is our primary? Which one is secondary? Third? Maybe the other 2 are impactful for you, or maybe they aren't. For me, I have a top 3. The other 2 really don't mean that much to me. Everyone is different. Maybe 4 of them make you feel loved, and one doesn't. Remember: even if 4 are impactful for you, there is one that is the strongest, another that is second strongest etc. Share this list with your partner. If they struggle with giving Love that way, give them techniques that both of you enjoy. Remember relationships take work so be willing to put in the work.

Also! We should make our list and share it with our loved ones. Not just your romantic partner, but your family as well.

Story time!

About ten years ago, I was having lunch with a friend of mine and he was telling me that he and his wife are not getting along. Of course, I asked WHY!? He went on to tell me that he has been trying "everything he can think of to make her happy." He told me they went on a date a couple of nights ago and they really didn't connect, so I asked him to describe the date to me.

He said he planned the date and made a reservation at a nice restaurant. They got ready together, left the house together wearing nice clothes, he drove to the restaurant, parked, opened her door for her, they went into the restaurant, and had a nice dinner. Most people are thinking "what is wrong with that!?" Let's dive deeper…

I asked him the following questions:

Me: When she was getting dressed did you tell her how sexy she is to you?

Him: I don't remember

Me: After she was dressed, did you tell her how pretty she is to you or compliment her outfit?

Him: Maybe, I think I did

Me: After you opened her car door for her, did you hold her hand while walking into the restaurant?

Him: No

Me: Did you open the restaurant door for her?

Him: Yes

Me: Did you sit on the same side of the booth or opposite sides?

Him: Opposite

Me: Did you hold her hand from across the table?

Him: No

Me: Did you ask her about her day and find something she said to tell her good job and compliment her?

Him: No

Me: I may have found your issue. I am going to go out on a limb (not really) and saying Acts of Service is not her Love Language. You give Love by doing Acts of Service (planning a date, opening her car door and opening the restaurant door) for your wife; however, she does not receive Love that way. Her Love Language may be Physical Touch. You didn't hold her hand walking into the restaurant. You didn't sit on the same side of the booth as her. You didn't hold her hand from across the booth. I didn't hear anything about hugging when you were describing your date. I didn't ask them if they had sex but if they did, she may have been thinking "oh yeah, now you want to touch me!" See the disconnect here?

What if her Love Language is Words of Affirmation? You didn't tell her she looks sexy to you when she was getting dressed. You may not have told her she looks pretty after she spent a lot more time getting ready than you did. Pro tip guys: she probably spends more time getting ready for your date than you do, appreciate the effort. You didn't ask her about her day and find something she did well to compliment her. If WOA is her Love Language, she didn't feel loved. Yes, she appreciated the effort you put into the evening, but you missed the mark! A few simple changes could have turned that evening from feeling appreciated to feeling loved! See the difference?

Him: so how do I know what her primary Love Language is?

DRUMROLL please…..

ASK! It's that simple. If your romantic partner has never heard of this list, introduce them to it, and ask them to tell you which one resonates with them the most. Once they tell you, do it! It's that simple.

If you are the blunt instrument who is saying to yourself "that guy didn't do anything wrong and if I put that much effort into a date and she still isn't happy, then I'm out of that relationship!" These responses are one of the reasons WHY the divorce rate is 50% for first time marriages and 75% for second time marriages. How about we learn our partner's Love Language, make them feel loved, and not get divorced? Maybe your kids will thank you. Maybe your bank account will thank you.

The biggest mistake we make is we give love a certain way, like my friend in the story above. He gave Love by doing AOS and didn't know his wife doesn't receive love that way. AOS is not his wife's Love Language. That is WHY they had a disconnect. In fact, you only have a 1 in 5 chance of getting it right if you guess! The other big mistake we make is not knowing our own Love Language so we can effectively communicate who we are with our partner. So if your current relationship is working out because "he just knows what I like" and your last relationship didn't work out and you don't know WHY, I am here to tell you it was blind luck because you didn't know your Love Language. Have a relationship by design, not by chance, and you will have much better results.

Oh and what happened to my friend and his wife? They learned about Love Languages and since then they have reconnected, decided to have a 2nd baby, and are currently living happily ever after. Another successful WHY story!

How does this apply outside of romantic relationships?

If you are the boss and you want to show your employees how valued they are, you have to make sure you are doing it the right way. If you keep telling them how great they are but their primary Love Language is not WOA, then it is not as impactful for them. If their primary Love Language is Gifts and you get them a gift to show your appreciation for them, they will feel loved and valued by the company.

If your employee has WOA as their primary Love Language and you tell them privately, publicly, in an email etc how great they are doing, how valuable they are to the company, highlight their tenure with the company etc, it will be more impactful for them.

If the employee's Love Language is Quality Time and you give them an extra day off to spend time with their family, it will be more impactful for them.

If the employee's primary Love Language is AOS and you give them tools to make their life better, like an ergonomic desk or an upgraded desk chair (these may seem like Gifts but these items are geared more towards making their life easier / better so it falls into the AOS category) they will appreciate those Acts of Service more than others.

If their primary Love Language is Physical Touch, then you might want to be careful with this one because physical touch is more impactful for them positively and negatively. Let's say you called them up to the front of the room to tell everyone how great of a job they are doing and (if appropriate) put your hand on their shoulder while telling everyone what a great job they did. Maybe you grabbed their wrist and raised their hand in the air because they got first place in the company work contest and you literally raised their hand like a prize fighter. Maybe after your speech you turned to them to shake their hand and maybe (big judgment call here) gave them a hug at the end of your speech to show how valued they are, it will be more impactful for them. OR maybe you get a call from HR. LOL. Hey, I told you it was impactful for them!

If you correctly make employees feel appreciated and loved by the company there will be less turnover, less time spent on training, a healthier work environment, less shrink (employee theft,) and more productivity! You're welcome.

Other aspects of life

If Primary love language is Acts of Service and some random person does an Acts of Service for you, it will be more impactful including feeling more attracted to that person.

If primary love language is Words of Affirmation and someone gives you a compliment, it will be more impactful to you. On the other hand, if someone says something less than pleasant to you, it will have a harder negative impact on you than someone who doesn't have this as their primary. So when someone says, "WHY did you take what I said so seriously? I was just joking." The answer is because Words mean more to you than others.

If your Love Language is Quality Time and you end up spending a lot of time with a co-worker (that you are attracted to) then you may inadvertently be putting yourself at higher risk of infidelity.

All of these statements apply double if you are out of balance. That chapter coming up…

CHAPTER 107:
The 5 WHYs

I have invented so many things in my lifetime. After I invent something, I do research to see if what I invented already exists. Almost always, it had already been invented. I was just not aware of it, when I came up with it. This one is no different. I invented this idea; however, Mr. Toyoda (founder of Toyota Motor Company) also came up with it years before I was born. So to give credit where credit is due…

I have never worked for Toyota but through research I discovered Toyota has a training program they call "The 5 WHYs." A problem solving technique that helps get to the root of the problem. It typically takes asking WHY 5 times in order to get to the root of the problem. For our purposes, it takes asking WHY up to 5 times in order to get to the root of the behavior, desire, or reason. Aka your reason WHY. Basically I ask WHY until the onion has been peeled all the way and the root/core of the problem, issue or behavior has been discovered.

Examples:

Person 1

    I want to be a doctor

    WHY?

    I want to help people

THE 5 WHYS

WHY?

Because when I help people, they will be happy and grateful that I helped them

WHY is that important to you?

Because when people are happy and grateful, I will feel needed and fulfilled

WHY is feeling needed and fulfilled important to you?

Because I have a strong need for connection and I think I can fill it this way (the root of the real reason)

Person 2

I want to be a doctor

WHY?

So I can help people

WHY is that important to you?

Because then everyone will look up to me

WHY is that important to you?

Because when I was a child, I saw a person in need of medical attention and when one person in the room said "I am a doctor," the whole room stepped aside and watched as they saved this person's life

WHY was that impactful for you?

Because that person was significant and I want the same significance

WHY you do want that same significance?

Because I have a strong need for significance

Person 3

I want to be a doctor

WHY?

Because my Mom died in a car accident

WHY? What will that do for you?

I loved my Mom very much and I feel it would honor her

WHY?

Because I feel that I can, in some way, keep my connection with my Mom by doing this

WHY is that important to you?

Because I have a strong need for connection and there is a void now that she is gone

WHY?

Because I have not found anything nor anyone else who can fill that void

Person 4

I want to be a doctor

WHY?

Because I want to make a lot of money!

WHY?

Because I want a nice house and flashy cars

WHY?

Because I want everyone to know I am rich and successful!

WHY?

Because I have a strong need for significance

Person 5

I want to be a doctor

WHY?

Because doctors are so smart and educated

WHY is that important to you?

Because I crave information. I can't get enough of it.

WHY?

Because I am an Analytical who just craves more and more information

WHY is that important to you since not all Analyticals have such a high drive for so much information?

I have a strong need for Growth and Contribution

See how we uncovered multiple reasons here? We found out this person is an Analytical with a strong need for Growth and Contribution. This is what is really motivating/driving them.

These examples are five completely different people, who all have the same goal, for completely different reasons. Now we know their WHY. So WHY is this important?

Epiphany time!: Once you realize what is the real driving force, you can make conscious decisions and changes in your life accordingly. Maybe the people in these examples don't have to become a doctor to fill their needs.

Person 1 is just trying to fill their need for Connection and thinks they can do it this way. Once they realize this they may say to themselves, if I simply stop being such an introvert and make more friends, I can achieve my need for connection.

Person 2 and Person 4 are just trying to fill their need for Significance. They may not even want to be a doctor. They may just want the Significance it brings. Once this person realizes the Need for Significance is not fulfilled externally. You don't need other people to recognize you and tell you that you are fantastic. All you need to know is that you are significant to your family, your community, or your friends. Maybe you are significant to just one person and maybe that one person is you, that's ok! Your Need for Significance should be filled internally, not externally.

Person 3 is just trying to fill a void. They felt a strong connection with their mother and now that hole is still there. WHY? Because they haven't filled it by furthering their current relationships, making new relationships, or replacing the confidant that their mother was. So rather than doing these things they are going to go to school for years, and rack up tons of school debt, in an effort to fill their Need for Connection.

Person 5 may be right where they need to be. Remember how I said earlier that you did not choose your job, your job chose you? This is the perfect example. This person has the right job, for the right reasons, and is serving their personality type while fulfilling their strongest of the six basic human needs. They will love and thrive in this position. They will also not work a day in their life because it won't feel like work to them. It will feel "right" because they are right where they are supposed to be.

Do you see how the 5 WHY's derive the real reasons WHY and how it impacts our decisions and behavior? I am not trying to get a lot of people to quit medical school here! I am just trying to accentuate that even the grandest of behaviors may have the simplest of reasons, once we understand WHY. Understanding the root of the behavior can change the trajectory of our life!

CHAPTER 108:
Bringing YOUR WHY NATURE All Together

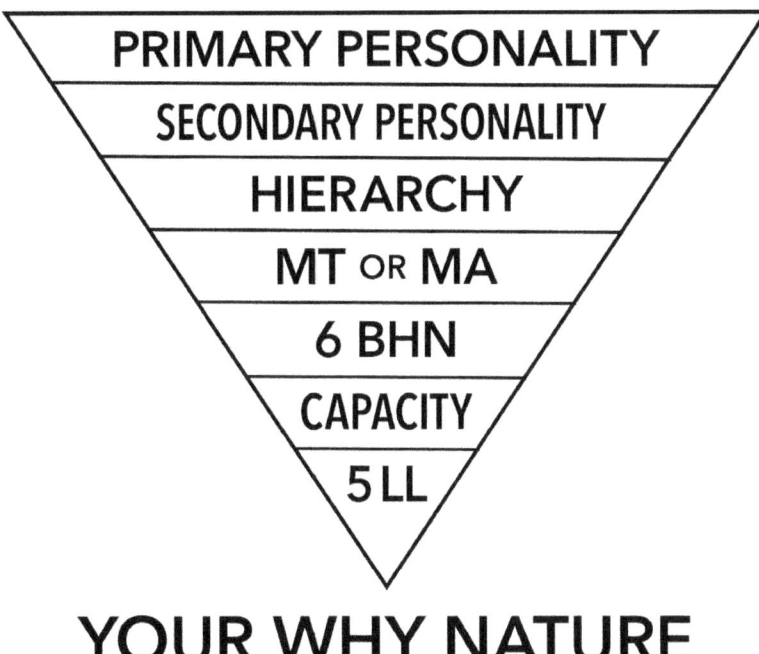

Do you know how rare you are? You are:

- One of 8 Primary Personality Types
- One of 8 Secondary Personality Types

- One of 6 Social Hierarchies
- One of 2 MT or MA personalities
- Have 18 different variables of your Basic Human Needs*
- One of 3 Capacity levels
- One of 120 combinations of Love Language order

There is literally a 1 in 5 million chance (4,976,640 if you actually did the math…I rounded up) chance that YOUR WHY NATURE is what it is. Learn and embrace what is special about you!

* WHY 18? Because if we have a low, medium, or high Need, then that is 3 different options times the Six Needs = 18. I still want you to rate your Need level from 1-10, but a 2 and a 3 behave very similarly. Once we go from a 2 (low Need) to a 6 (Medium Need) or a 9 (High Need) then behavior is noticeably different.

In the beginning of the book, I thanked you for taking the first step towards improving your life. If you have made it this far, you are well on your way. Great job!

In the introduction I told you we would learn WHY you do what you do and through that understanding, who you are as a person. I promised we would learn a language so you can talk to yourself about your WHY, and articulate who you are with yourself and others. Others can also use this language to share who they are, so we can easily understand. The first section of this book is all about what is inside you, YOUR WHY NATURE, which is who you are in your core. This is the root of your nature based behavior and WHY you handled your experiences the way you did. I made you a lot of promises and if I haven't fulfilled them yet, I will by the end of the book.

I only want one thing in return! I want you to be a good human. Which means sweep your own front doorstep. Learn who you are and who others are. Through that new understanding have tolerance for your fellow man and help others to have tolerance. It means growing your tolerance into acceptance and through acceptance, do your part so the world can have peace and live in unity. Live and let live. That's what I ask of you.

Are you a good human? Do your part!

> *"I'm starting with the man in the mirror. I'm asking him to change his ways. No message could have been any clearer. If you want to make the world a better place, take a look at yourself and make that change."*
> ~Michael Jackson

> *"Focus on what you are doing and get better at what you are doing. Everything else is a complete waste of time."*
> ~Roman Emperor Marcus Aurelius 121 AD—180 AD

When you master the first few chapters, you will be well on your way to knowing YOUR WHY. You will also understand other people on a higher level. Basic understanding is through people telling you who they are. The next level is by asking people questions and figuring out who they are based on their answers. The highest and most fluent level of understanding is through observing people. When you can observe people, establish patterns of behavior, and know their WHY through observation, your life will change dramatically. Especially when you can predict behavior.

So, what's next?

Have you ever seen the movie *The Karate Kid* from 1984? In that movie the teacher has the student wash the car, paint the fence, and sand the floor using the same motions over and over again.

The student became frustrated from doing the chores and using the same movements over and over. The student was not aware he was actually practicing the techniques he needed to accomplish the larger goal, to learn Karate.

In the previous chapters we discussed the pieces of YOUR WHY NATURE. We did it in pieces, just like "The Karate Kid," and now we are going to bring all the pieces together just like Mr. Miyagi did in the movie.

WHY ARE WE SO DIFFERENT?

Your parents got together and made you

- They were the product of 4 people
- Who were the product of 8 people
- Who were the product of 16 people
- Who were the product of 32 people
- Who were the product of 64 people
- Who were the product of 128 people
- Who were the product of 256 people
- Who were the product of 512 people
- Who were the product of 1024 people
- Who were the product of 2048 people
- Who were the product of 4096 people

You are the unique and special combination of those 4096 people. Recessive traits from an ancestor from hundreds of years ago may have surfaced within you. Each generation (including your ancestors from 12 generations ago) had different ideals, struggles, knowledge, education, outlook, intelligence and each had their own unique DNA. These people passed down active traits, latent traits, and instincts that make up you.

If you have a sibling, from the exact same parents, they may have different traits that are dominant or recessive within them. This is the reason your brothers and sisters don't look exactly like you. You both will also become different from being treated differently by your parents, by birth order (Birth Order is the next chapter and it is so enlightening!), and opportunities given or withheld.

If your full sibling can be that different, just imagine how different half siblings can be. If a half sibling has one parent in common, they are the product of 2048 of the same ancestors as you, and 2048 different ancestors from the different mother/ father.

If siblings can be so different, and half siblings can be so different, then what makes you think you are remotely the same as a non-relative? You are the product of those 4096 people (nature) but also the product of your environment (nurture.) Your DNA and psychological make up reacted to how you were raised, how you were treated by your family, the environment you grew up in, who you associated with etc. What I am trying to say is, you are unique and special! You should understand and discover what is special about you, rather than comparing yourself with others.

We gravitate toward people who are like us. We call them friends. WHY? Because we actually like ourselves and we like people who are like us! It's part of our need for connection and need for love.

OK KARATE KID, LET'S HAVE SOME FUN

What is the behavior of an Alpha with a strong Need for Significance?

Authoritative, demanding, strong tone of voice maybe even yells at people, physically intimidating

What is the behavior of a Beta or Gamma with a strong Need for Significance?

Undermining, outspoken, demanding, possibly rude, unapologetic

What is the behavior of an Amiable with a strong Need for Connection?

Caring, nurturing, always available, reassuring, Friendly

What is the behavior of a Gamma with a strong Need for Connection?

Relationships may be a constant struggle for them. Being insecure, jealous, avoiding conflict, and their inability to compromise might make for a turbulent relationship. They may be committed to making it happen if they understand their traits are hard on a relationship. If they don't want to grow then "knowing their worth" they may just move on.

What is the behavior of an Analytical with a Moving Away from personality?

They are going to be very difficult people. They are unmotivated and calculating so they will do the absolute minimum they have to do, in order to get by. They are trying to figure out ways to cheat the system, get something for nothing or maybe get rich quick. If they have a low Need for Connection they may use people or make people close to them think everything is your fault. If this person is a Gamma, then they may resort to gaslighting.

What is the behavior of an Amiable, with a strong Need for Connection and a primary Love Language of Words of Affirmation?

They are very sensitive and caring people. When you tell them something, positive or negative, it gets taken to heart. They may strive for your approval, apologize a lot (even when they don't need to), and will ask you for verbal conformation if they are making you happy (or what would make you happy.)

How do you think a Driver with a "10" Need for Significance is going to answer your question?

Direct, curt, maybe with destain, and a glare that says "how dare you question me" to go along with the answer. Do you see how the behavior changes? Also, do you see how the need for significance can be at odds with the need for connection? This Driver with a 10 Significance is rarely connecting with anyone when they behave like this. When they accomplish their goal, damage control is needed because all of the people they upset.

What is the behavior of an Expressive, who is an Alpha, with a strong Need for Significance, a Moving Towards personality, and a primary Love Language of Acts of Service?

Think Diva who wants to be on stage. Annoying, difficult, driven, and will run you over to get what they want. They know a huge web but with very few deep relationships. Threatening if they don't get what they want, will demand satisfaction and will be forceful in their behavior.

Another example

Personality type: Sigma, Driver, with an "8" Need for Significance, whose primary love language is Words of Affirmation. Situation: you say something to them that is not nice (violates their boundaries), what do you think their response might be? If you said their response might be harsher than someone who does not have all of those traits, you are correct! They may retaliate verbally but the Sigma portion of their personality will probably prevail. They will turn ice cold and will cut you out of their life. On the drive home they told their significant other, "we don't ever need to speak to that jerk again." Their significant other, if they don't understand

WHY, may reply with "WHY do you have such a harsh reaction?" The Sigma now tries to explain themselves and a debate may ensue. Not understanding the Sigma behavior may cause strain on their romantic relationship.

Another example:

When figuring out who you are, or who anyone is, you need to figure out the level of their needs. Then you can begin to establish a pattern. Look at this person's need levels. What do you think a person with these need levels does for a living?

Significance = 2

Connection = 10

Certainty = 9

Uncertainty = 0

(Remember: certainty and uncertainty do not have to add up to 10. They are independent of one another even though they are opposites.)

Love = 5

Growth and Contribution = 4

Answer: This guy is a trash truck driver in a small town. Go back over his need levels and see if you can figure out WHY he is a trash truck driver in a small town.

* Explanation at the end of the chapter

Another example:

I was astonished the other day. I was talking with a woman who has very little need for GC. So, I decided to ask her WHY she never chose to better herself? WHY she never tried anything new in relation to improving herself or learning. When I say never trying anything new I mean she wouldn't even try new techniques related to the things she knew she was good at. I mean if she was an avid skier she wouldn't try shorter skis because she was fine just the way she was. Her answer opened my eyes as to the strength of her needs. She said the reason is because she doesn't want to look stupid. If she tries something new, she probably won't be good at it right away. During the initial learning period she would look stupid and can't have that. So, what did I learn from this? Starting something new and looking stupid while learning would be what for her? Uncertainty. If she always does the things she knows she is good at, what is that? The need for Certainty, right? There is more. If you always want to be certain and don't want to look stupid, what is that a recipe for? Significance! She didn't tell me initially that she doesn't want to learn anything new. She said she doesn't want to look stupid while doing it. Notice the word choice there. Interesting what we can learn from that simple answer when we listen, right? I have to try to establish more of a pattern but right now my theory about her is these are her need levels:

1. Significance: 7 or higher

2. Connection: 5 or lower

3. Love: unknown

4. Growth and Contribution: unknown
   but I am guessing a 3 or a 4

5. Certainty: 9 or higher

6. Uncertainty: 3 or lower

In thinking about this more I understand that she wants to learn new things, but she will only do it if she can be certain she does not look stupid. This is the astonishing thing I learned. The strength of some of her needs made some of her other need levels weaker! Wow!

She is so strong in her need for certainty and significance that she will sacrifice GC and probably connection in order to achieve the stronger needs.

Here is an example of how she may sacrifice connection. Let's say a bunch of her friends want to get together to go horseback riding but she doesn't know how to do it. She probably won't go because her desire not to look stupid (need for certainty and significance) will outweigh her need to connect with everyone. Thus sacrificing connection for certainty and significance. Alternatively, she may try to sway the group's decision to do a different activity, but ultimately she won't go horseback riding. If she did go with the group to achieve the connection, she wouldn't get on a horse. Are you seeing how need levels directly affect behavior? If you didn't know this about her and were one of the people in the horseback riding group, you would have no idea the reason this person wasn't riding was because of all that. One may misinterpret her actions thinking she is injured, scared, or is being rude.

The key to all of this is to understand that your need levels will dictate many of your actions.

What about these questions: "So Rob do you mean to tell me that if I go to a football game that action has some sort of meaning? Am I really trying to fulfill one (or more) of the six basic human needs?" Are you saying a Driver wants to go to a football game more, or less, than an Expressive? No, but the way you go to the football game does. WHY? Because going to a football game is not the entire action, is it? What about: whom you go with, who drives, how much conversation and the depth of conversation you have with the person you go with, what you drink (and how much), whether or not you tailgate, if you talk with strangers sitting near you, where in the stadium you sit, and how much of the game you watch compared to how much you socialize? Did you wear your game used, hand signed jersey that you paid a lot of money for (need for significance), or a t-shirt to blend in? The person who wore a t-shirt to blend in may be an Amiable or a person with a strong need for connection. Have you seen the people with face paint, pink wigs, and a chain link necklace thick enough to restrain a horse? If you think those people are Expressives, you guessed right! All of these actions encompass going to a football game. How you accomplish all of these actions are directly related to YOUR WHY.

Another example:

What about a Driver who is low on Capacity, how do you think this person will behave?

Answer: their Unevolved Driver is going to come out. They are probably going to slam things into place, use force to make things happen, speak using very few words, it may not be the best time to engage them in conversation, have little patience and have zero tolerance for other people not doing their part/carrying their weight. Once they recharge their batteries they may apologize for their behavior. An evolved driver with a strong need for GC will use this opportunity to reflect on what they need to work on to grow as a person. If they have a strong need for connection, they will include you in their reflection. If they have a strong need for significance, they won't include you in their reflection because they don't want to appear weak (aka less significant.)

Another example:

What about an Analytical who is a Moving Away (MA) personality, who has a strong Need for Certainty and Connection, is a Capacity 3, and their love language is Words of Affirmation?

Answer: when they are faced with a problem, they are going to come to you (Certainty), their friend, for guidance. Helpful hint: the request will be disguised as a request for guidance; however, is not really guidance they seek. They want reassurance (WOA) and conformation from you (Connection) about which options they are considering (Analytical can't make up their mind due to overthinking) because they don't know what else to do (Capacity 3.) Amiables watch out! The capacity suckers are knocking at your door!

Tony Robbins says, "When three or more of the Six Basic Human Needs are met with one action, that action will become a habit"

With this in mind, let's revisit the last person we just discussed. That Analytical coming to you is filling their Need for Certainty, Connection, and Love all in one action. Meanwhile you are telling them it is ok to Move Away from pain and validating their behavior. Think their behavior will become a habit? Absolutely!

Another example:

You are at the office, speaking with co-worker Tracy. The conversation goes like this:

Tracy: Hey you! I haven't seen you in a while.

You: Hey, I just got back from vacation. We went to XYZ beach.

Tracy: Oh that's great! My husband and I have a house down there. We go all the time. The kids love it.

You: It was our first time there. We liked it a lot. Do you always vacation there?

Tracy: Yes! It's such an easy drive to get there, the whole family loves it, and we always have a great time. Traveling to other places sometimes sounds like a good idea but we always end up at the beach.

You: That's great that you love it so much. I don't think I ever asked you how long you have been working here.

Tracy: Oh I have been here for 18 years. About 10 years ago Mrs. Jones asked me to be her Executive Assistant and I just love it. I mean, it's not as glamorous as some of the other jobs this company offers but I enjoy it.

From this simple and typical exchange, what might we start to determine about Tracy's personality type?

Tracy has a strong Need for Certainty. WHY do we know this? 18 years with the same company and 10 years in the same position. Tracy also vacations at the same destination. Tracy wants to be so certain her family can go to the beach whenever they want, they bought a house there. The house purchase is also a tell tale sign that they don't like change. Tracy made the comment that they consider going other places, which may mean she gets bored of the monotony and may get out of balance once in a while (chapter "Balance" is coming up); however, they always do the Certain and easy thing.

Tracy may be a Delta personality. Go back and check the characteristics of the Delta personality and you will see Tracy exhibited a lot of those characteristics in her statements. However! Tracy also made the comment her job is "not as glamorous as some of the other jobs" which has a hint of envy and jealousy due to working in the background, which are Beta traits.

If you want to know if Tracy is a Delta or a Beta, ask one simple question: "Would you prefer one of those glamorous and more stressful jobs or would you prefer to just put your head down, knock out your work in exchange for a solid buck while having a good work/life balance?" Her answer will tell you because the Beta would prefer the more glamorous job and the Delta wants solid work for solid pay and work/life balance.

Do you see how easy this is now? If you listen to people, not just hear them speaking, they will tell you a lot about themselves. WHY gives us the language to understand.

PRO TIP: If you find yourself asking people "WHY are you so difficult to speak to sometimes?" One reason is because each of you toggle back and forth into your primary and secondary personalities.

I am a primary Driver with a secondary Analytical.

My wife is an Amiable with a secondary Driver.

An Amiable speaking to an Analytical is a very different conversation than a Driver speaking to another Driver!

So what are the things we can change vs what we cannot change?

THINGS WE CAN CHANGE

Your Six Basic Human Needs—this simple choice and lifestyle change can make a huge impact on your life.

Examples:

Significance:

1. If you have a low Need for Significance and have realized it is making you unhappy, then it is time for a change. Start taking credit for your work, ask/demand to be recognized and set more boundaries in your life. You don't have to shock everyone, you can be upfront about your new boundaries. Tell people you feel you are too readily available for them and you feel taken for granted. Tell people your relationship with them is out of balance because they take too much. Note: relationships should not be a tit for tat transaction, but at the same time they should not be perpetually imbalanced. Tell people you need more "you time" and they will have to wait. Buy yourself a present. Take yourself on a trip. Tell people you are going to focus on you, your well being, your personal growth, and you need time to read this book a couple more times which means other people will have to take care of themselves for a while! Insert a "you go girl" or "ata boy" here. Here is the good news: if this change makes people not want to be your

friend anymore, they weren't your friend to begin with. True friends will support and congratulate you. Great friends will ask how they can help you. Weeding out your non-friends will be very cleansing.

2. If you have a strong Need for Significance, this will be a struggle. No one will actually think you are Significant because you feel this way. When you truly are Significant, like a famous actor or athlete (the most followed person on the planet right now is Cristiano Ronaldo with over 1 billion followers), people will tell you. The more you have to tell people you are Significant (it doesn't work by the way) the more you will push people away. In fact, when you are not in the room people will say "he thinks a lot of himself and for no good reason." One day you will realize your strong Need for Significance inhibited your Need for Connection, while no one really thinks you are Significant. When you are truly Significant, humility will add to your Significance (because people will be impressed.) By the way, every time I have heard Cristiano Ronaldo speak, he was classy and humble which validates my point.

Connection:

I know a lot of rich people and the one thing they all have in common is they say "their family is the most important thing to them." Ironically poor people typically feel the same way. It's the people in the middle who lose sight of this. If you have a strong Need for Connection, keep it. If you have a low Need for Connection and don't really like people, just be careful this doesn't come around to bite you one day. The good news is, as long as you still have air in your lungs, it's not too late to make any change. Oh and...

PRO TIP: When you Connect with people, this will make you feel Significant and Loved.

Certainty:

Remember, Certainty is boring. If you are bored of your life, reduce your Need for Certainty. Work on your versatility. Versatility is also one of the tools of Connection. WHY? Because the more people you can relate to, the more Connection you will have. The more people you know and can relate to, the more positive Uncertainty you bring into your life. Remember, balance is key. Try something new. Travel somewhere you haven't been before. Do something that positively (key word) takes you out of your comfort zone. You will be surprised how much being versatile has a positive effect on you.

Uncertainty:

Uncertainty is fun and exciting. If your life is boring to you, consider making the conscious decision to add more Uncertainty into your life. Aka raise your need for Uncertainty. Be careful about what type of Uncertainty you add though. Positive Uncertainty is healthy and safe. Negative Uncertainty (taking risks, gambling, and doing things that are not good for you nor others) may be exciting, but they are not sustainable and are detrimental in the long run.

On the other hand, if you already do too much to fill your Need for Uncertainty and it is extreme, not safe, not healthy or not sustainable, then consider dialing down your Need for Uncertainty.

Repetitious boredom:

My definition: "the mundane but necessary actions and activities necessary to sustain life"

Elaborated:

- Having to be at work every day at 9am
- You take the same 8:30 train to work
- You drive the same car

- You wear the same thing (scrubs, lab coat, uniform, clothing line or even similar suit and tie every day)
- You repeat the same script every day, or multiple times per day. This applies to everyone from people who work in a call center and say the same thing on the phone, to a doctor who asks people the same health questions, to a dentist who has to explain proper dental care, to a teacher who has been teaching the same subject for years, to a lawyer who has to discuss the same laws they specialize in, to a coach who has to remind his student of their fundamentals.

Before you make big decisions about your Need for Certainty or Uncertainty, make sure you have mastered Repetitious Boredom. If Repetitious Boredom is creating too much Certainty in your life, you have to get over it. We all have it. Everyone. Think a movie producer doesn't have it? They have to deal with extras having issues, stars of the show being a pain in the butt, people forgetting their lines, etc. They may say "same crap, different location!" What about the President of your country? They wake in the morning and the briefing of what happened yesterday is sitting next to their coffee. They have to read it. 7am their advisor walks in to touch base on the day's events. 8am they meet with their military advisor to understand the state of the union. 9am they jump in the shower to get ready for their 10am meetings, and so on! It's the same thing every day! We cannot escape Repetitious Boredom so we should reframe it, master it, and make friends with it.

Love:

If you do not have a strong Need for Love, that's ok. Just watch that this doesn't impact your Need for Connection because Connection is important.

If you do have a strong Need for Love, watch the way you fill your need. Sleeping around, giving your Love and Capacity to those who do not reciprocate, and falling in Love too quickly can be detrimental. WHY? Because it can lead to an emotional roller coaster. Being a student of WHY will help you understand which personality types are a good match for YOUR WHY NATURE.

Growth/Contribution:

We have been talking about versatility and how it can have a positive impact on your life. Becoming versatile is personal Growth! Learning your WHY is Growth! Raising your Need for Growth also feeds the need for positive Uncertainty. These are recipes which fuel happiness. Raising your Need for Growth is a positive thing. Growing your career or business are certainly beneficial to your finances; however, personal Growth is irreplaceable.

Raising your Need for Contribution can lead to feelings of being personally fulfilled. If you give back, help people, and Contribute towards positive things, you are the one who actually benefits. You can Contribute financially towards groups, societies or causes or Contribute your time by teaching, coaching or mentoring. One of the greatest times of my life was coaching Little League baseball. Contribute towards your community and you may just fill other needs, like Love, Certainty, Uncertainty, Connection, and Significance (hmmm, isn't that all of your needs filled with one action?)

Moving towards: if this is your personality type, you don't want to change. You might severely dial back the drive when you get rich, get fat, or achieve the goal (or a combination of all three) but once you see something you want again, the MT will kick right in.

Moving Away: you have to make conscious decisions and create motivation to emulate an MT. It's a struggle, sometimes a major struggle, but you can do it.

PRO TIP: An unmotivated MT may easily be mistaken for an MA. Remember I said an MT has to want the prize, award, or goal. A perfect example may be a young person, with an MT personality, in school. They may not see the value in getting their schoolwork

done and may be more interested in hanging out with their friends. Once they join the workforce and start making money, the MT personality will emerge because they will be motivated to make more money.

Capacity: some people are just good at it. They are natural Capacity 3. If that is not you and you are a natural Capacity 1 or 2, then mastering the Capacity raising techniques I mentioned will go a long way.

5 Love Languages: These may change naturally with age or with a different romantic partner, but your list probably won't move around too much. Meaning: your primary and secondary Love Languages may switch places, but they will most likely always be at the top.

THINGS YOU CANNOT CHANGE

PRO TIP: You can evolve and fine tune these, but they won't change from one to the other.

Your main personality: Once a Driver, always a Driver, Once an Amiable always an Amiable etc

Your Secondary personality: same as primary personality. Whatever you were born with, won't change.

Your Third personality: it's rare but some people have a pronounced Third personality. If they do, there is a super high chance this personality type is Unevolved (more in that chapter) because they rarely toggle into it.

Social Hierarchy:
Dominant personalities might dial down their dominance with age, but it will always be there.

Submissive personalities: if you think this has a negative commutation or don't accept it's ok to be you, then you have an Association or Trigger you have to clear. There are a lot of positive traits about each personality type. Again, your focus determines your reality. You may not change hierarchies, but you can evolve. Example: if you are not a natural leader, but want to be, you can take classes and learn how. Don't emulate other hierarchies and sell yourself as something you are not, it won't end well.

NOW THIS GETS REALLY FUN

Remember our definitions:

- YOUR WHY NATURE (Section 100) is who you are as a person, at your core
- YOUR WHY NURTURE (Other Sections) are the experiences you had during your life and how they shaped you

Examples of YOUR WHY NURTURE:

- The family you were born into
- Your parents had different qualities
- Learned behavior from your family
- Grew up with certain expectations placed on you
- Being placed in different circumstances
- Had different experiences
- Growing up in different regions with different customs
- Had unique influences
- Taught different belief systems

How you, with YOUR WHY NATURE, handled your unique experiences and how your unique experiences shaped you, is the overall final product you see in the mirror today.

Said another way, YOUR WHY NATURE x YOUR WHY NURTURE shaped you into the unique person who is YOU.

Now let's learn YOUR WHY NURTURE!

But first: WHY is that guy a trash truck driver in a small town? He has a low need for significance, so the job doesn't define him. He has a very strong need for connection, so he lives in a small town where everyone knows one another for a long time. A strong need for certainty made him gravitate toward a recession proof job. After all, there will always be trash, right?! Need for uncertainty is very low, so running his daily route in a small town means nothing changes and no surprises, just the way he likes it. Need for love is right down the middle and is filled through the love in his community and possibly a romantic partner. Lower need for GC, which means he doesn't need to be in a job with a lot of room for growth potential. He is contributing to his community by keeping it clean. Whether everyone appreciates his efforts or not, he knows he makes his community a better place for his loved ones. Oh and bonus answer: he is a Delta.

Now get ready for a VERY fun chapter we can all relate to…
BIRTH ORDER.

SECTION 200:
YOUR WHY NURTURE

This is what happened to you

CHAPTER 201:
Birth Order

I struggled with whether to put this chapter in the Nature section or the Nurture section. Because the Nature part is: you were born first, second, third, only child etc. The Nurture part is: your parents, your siblings and your family treated you a certain way due to that Birth Order. After much deliberation, I decided to move it down and kick off the Nurture sections with Birth Order. This is where the rubber meets the road, as they say. WHY? Birth Order is the first experience that unique person (you) experienced.

Think of it like a brand new car that was just taken off the showroom floor and driven to your house. That brand new car is unique, including having a unique VIN number. The life that car experiences (driving habits, climate, and level of care) will change the car. A different car may have held up better (or worse) in the same environment; however, the same car may have may have had a better (or worse) outcome in a different environment.

So to continue the metaphor: Fasten your seat belt, here we go...

Alfred Adler developed Birth Order theory in the 20th century. I find this interesting and relevant to behavior, EBR (Expectations, Beliefs, and Rules chapter coming up soon), and the way we think. After all, behavior is nature and nurture. Birth Order is a contributing factor to nurture.

Adler's theory is a person's Birth Order can impact their personality and development. Adler's theory suggests that the order in which a child is born can lead to both positive and negative life outcomes. Adler said: "*It is a common fallacy to imagine that children of the same family are formed in the same environment.*" This means even though siblings were born from the same parents and grew up in the same household, they were treated differently by their parents and family members and did not have the same experience? How fascinating!

Before I go farther let me tell the parents something they should never forget. If you want to raise an overachiever and hyper successful child, then listen up. The number one reason a child grows up to be a hyper successful adult…the number one reason…is this:

Hyper achieving adults, from world leaders to rockstars, have one thing in common. Just one and it's this: when they were children, their parents (usually the parent of the opposite sex is most influential here) had an unconditional belief in the child's ability. That's it. The way you speak to your child when they try to do something, or ask if they have the ability to do something, is key. I will elaborate in the upcoming chapter "Communication."

Rob's Birth Order definitions for WHY:

- Only Child—has no siblings in the household
- First Born Child—is the oldest of the siblings in the household
- Middle Child—has older and younger siblings in the household
- Youngest Child—has only older siblings in the household

Important to note these definitions are predicated on which children are in the household because this affects the way a child is treated by their parents, siblings, and other family members.

Clarifications: here is where we go fast. Make sure you digest these clarifications.

The first born child is born an "Only Child." They become a "Frist Born Child," by definition, only if siblings are born. Note the difference between "the" first born child (by order to appearance) and "a" First Born Child (by definition).

The second born child is the "Youngest Child" when they are born.

If a third child is born, they are a "Youngest Child" and the 2nd born child becomes a "Middle Child."

If a fourth child is born, they are a "Youngest Child" and the 3rd born child changes from a "Youngest Child" to a "Middle Child." The second born child remains a "Middle Child" and the oldest remains a "First Born Child."

If a child or children emancipate from the household (move out of the house or go off to college) and then another child is born, then the last child is an "Only Child" because they are the only one in the household.

Birth Order may also change if siblings pass away, if siblings get separated into different households, or blending of families through divorce/remarriage.

What about twins? By Birth Order they go to the same definitions as above.

Don't proceed until you have these definitions down. Go back and read again if needed.

Now that we understand my definitions and when/if a child changes definitions, let's dive deeper…

ONLY CHILD

- Likely characteristics:
- spoiled
- difficulty sharing
- difficulty compromising
- selfish / self-centered
- independent
- may be headstrong
- bossy

- self-reliant
- resourceful
- more mature than classmates (since they spend more time around adults without other kids)
- high achieving
- leadership skills
- poor social skills
- maladjusted
- lonely or likes being a loner

An Only Child with a strong sense of self-worth may have a "naive sense of entitlement" that will take them far in life. WHY? Because there is no doubt in their mind they don't deserve it. With this attitude they may not attract many friends, but they will "go far." If you teach this child to ask themselves "WHY not me?" while giving them unconditional belief in their ability, they will go even farther in life.

What happens if your Only Child is a Sigma personality? A Sigma is described as a "lone wolf." This person may really like to be alone, even as an adult.

What happens if your Only Child is a primary Expressive? Their personality type may exacerbate many of the Only Child traits. This child may be difficult to raise and will be a drain on capacity levels. The parent also becomes the toy they want to play with and get attention from.

Parents may have high expectations of an Only Child or the child may receive more coddling than if they had siblings. If the Only Child is the result of the death of a sibling, or even a miscarriage, then being coddled and overly protected by a "helicopter parent" may result. These kids are less likely to have developed skills, since their parents did everything for them. This smothering will likely backfire on the parent/child relationship later in life, or you will raise a completely dependent person who won't grow up and will constantly come to you for their needs.

FIRST BORN CHILD

May be more likely to develop a strong sense of responsibility and be a leader. They may also be expected to set an example for their younger siblings. However, they may also feel like they didn't have a "proper childhood" and may develop anxiety or depression. Some say a First Born Child has an increased susceptibility to both drug use as well as positive educational outcomes. In other words, they seem to focus, and have great success, or fold (emotionally) and fall by the way side.

WHY? Because of extra pressure being put on them to be more grown up or to be "the example" for the younger kids. This is a lot of pressure. This is also WHY they may feel like they didn't have a proper childhood as they were pushed to grow up faster.

What a First Born Child is likely to have to deal with from parents, family, teachers, friends and even other kids:

"Hey, you are older than everyone else and I expect more from you!"

"You need to set a good example for the other kids."

"Other kids look up to you so they can see how to behave. What are you teaching them by acting like that?"

How do you think this pressure and these expectations affect this child? When did this child sign up to be someone's teacher? This volentold position and expectations make some kids step up to the challenge. The kids who step up may be using this to fuel their need for significance. If you know an adult (maybe I am describing you) who feels like they have to take care of everyone, or everything, all the time, check to see if they are a First Born Child.

Others may fold and feel anxiety from these expectations. They feel too much pressure which can lead to depression, isolation, and potential drug use. Some may feel as if their siblings have it "easier" or "better" than they do, which can cause resentment. A resentment they may carry through their life, their job, and their relationships.

What do these feelings do to their need for connection? One of the common replies from the oldest child may be "They get to do it, WHY can't I?" or "They didn't get in trouble when they did the exact same thing, WHY are you coming down on me?" The response may be "Because you are the oldest and you should know better!" Think about how impactful this is to a child compared to their siblings!

A First Born child's experience may be exacerbated by the parents' capacity levels. The less capacity the parents have, the more likely they are to put pressure on a First Born Child. In the chapter "Capacity," I gave an example of how a parent might be a capacity 3 when they do not have time sharing with their children but may fall to a capacity 1 or 2, when they do have time sharing with their kids. So a single parent household may be harder on a First Born Child because a parent may look for capacity from the First Born Child.

From their parent, parents, grandparents, aunts and/or uncles a First Born Child may hear:

- Help me do this
- Take care of your sister
- I don't have time to take care of that, so I need you to do it
- Your brother can't do these things for himself yet, so I need you to step up
- Act your age!
- Show your sisters how to do it
- Be a good role model
- The other kids look up to you
- You should be able to do this by now
- Figure it out! I don't have time to show you since I am taking care of your sister

- You can take care of yourself, I have to take care of your brother
- I do everything around here, the least you could do is help me
- I need you to be a big boy (or big girl) right now and…
- You're the oldest, you should know better
- Etc…there are probably hundreds of synonyms of these statements but you get the idea

Can you identify how many of these are the parent asking for capacity?

Remember the first born child changed from an "Only Child" to a "First Born Child." I think they are less likely to have heard many of the things above when they were an Only Child. If for no other reason than the parent had more capacity with only one child to care for.

PRO TIP: Through no fault of their own, they are being treated differently. Who moved my cheese?

MIDDLE CHILD

Ever heard of "Middle Child Syndrome?" Well, this is literally where it comes from. This kid went from being born a Youngest Child to becoming a Middle Child. Many would consider the treatment of a Youngest Child preferable to that of a Middle Child. A Middle Child may feel left out or overlooked and may become rebellious. I should have put this definition last since the Middle Child often feels forgotten or left out. LOL. I crack myself up. Last week I witnessed a mom leave her Middle Child at a restaurant by mistake. Everybody thought he rode with someone else. This sounds funny but imagine the impact this has on this child's self-worth. How does this impact the child's ability to maintain healthy relationships? If he feels "less than" he may develop depression and self-esteem issues or a counter balancing "selfish sense of entitlement" may arise. Everyone is different, and everyone reacts differently, but the roots of behavior are the same.

A Middle Child may also be the most independent among the siblings because they don't get as much, if any, validation and attention from parents. They are very good mediators because they typically keep the peace between siblings. WHY? Because they are closer in age to both. They are self- reliant, flexible, empathetic, and understanding. They will have to search for their identity, and the length of time to do so will vary greatly, which can make them feel like they don't fit in.

Youngest Child Syndrome are behaviors such as social, outgoing, and charming. Very different than that of a Middle Child, right? Remember a Youngest Child, who got a lot of attention from their parents and exuded Youngest Child traits, just became a Middle Child once another sibling is born. The longer they were a Youngest Child, the harder becoming a Middle Child will be.

YOUNGEST CHILD

As I mentioned, Youngest Child Syndrome are behaviors such as social, outgoing, and charming. A Youngest Child may try to stand out from their older siblings and may develop an outgoing personality. They typically get a lot of attention from their parents and other family members. Since they get a lot of attention, they may in turn seek a lot of attention and even develop manipulative ways to get it. Watch out for Expressives and Analyticals here because they will be better at manipulating, including developing a convenient sense of helplessness so people do things for them. Also may develop a determination to "keep up with the older kids" which can increase skill levels beyond other kids their same age.

I had a friend of mine tell me: "With the first child you are so nervous. Are they breathing? Are they ok? The second child you are much more relaxed thinking "I am sure they are fine" and the third child you just leave on the floor. LOL." This says it all. A Youngest Child, especially if they are beyond 2nd born, doesn't see overly nervous and protective parents. So the Youngest Child develops a free spirited and adventurous nature. The parents may let them be more adventurous because they have more experience being parents and know how resilient kids actually are.

They may "act like a baby" and this can carry forward into adulthood. If you know an adult who is spoiled, self-centered and/or occasionally childish, check to see if they are a Youngest Child or an Only Child. Chances are they are one of these. Remember children can have gray hair.

More to consider

Twins who are a First Born Child may have it easier because they divide the load. A First Born Child, who has younger siblings that are twins, may have a harder time being a First Born Child because the parents are less likely to have capacity. A Middle Child may really feel treated like a Middle Child if the younger siblings are twins, because the twins will get even more attention than a single Youngest Child.

The impacts of Birth Order will be more pronounced if the child stayed in their role for longer periods of time. Example: if an Only Child became a First Born child at 1 or 2 years old and stayed a First Born Child for the rest of their childhood, then the traits of a First Born Child should be more prominent in that person.

And if they have shorter periods of time…

Let's say Sally was born second. Sally is born a Youngest Child. Then a sibling is born, so Sally becomes a Middle Child. Then the older sibling passes away, Sally becomes a First Born Child. Then the parents get divorced. One parent moves away with the younger sibling, so Sally becomes an Only Child (because remember I said the other children have to be in the household.) Then Sally's parent remarries with someone who has one older and one younger child and they timeshare with the co-parent 50% of the time, so Sally becomes a Middle Child 50% of the time and is an Only Child the other 50% of the time. Is your head spinning? So is Sally's! This poor thing had so many Birth Order roles that she probably exudes characteristics of each one. However! If you ask her about her Birth Order she will tell you that she was "all over the place and experienced each one" so her behavior spanning characteristics of each, makes perfect sense. Sally is probably an interesting and well rounded adult because she had to adapt so many times.

With the divorce rate around 50% we might as well throw in this scenario. Like Sally, when a child is time sharing with one parent they may be a First Born Child. When the Child is with the remarried other parent, they may be a Middle Child. Growing up and having 50/50 Birth Order like this would be mentally very difficult for a child. Especially if when they are the First Born Child, their need for significance is being filled. They are given duties which they perform well and their parent tells them how proud they are of them because of it. When they are in the other household, the First Born Child steals their thunder and they don't get the same significance. Divorced parents please consider this if Birth Orders are different in time sharing households.

The bottom line is we can see how Birth Order and the length of time in each role, impacts future behavior.

GENERATIONAL BIRTH ORDER

Yes! I said it and as far as I know, you heard it here first! I would love to do some research on this topic. Here is my question that will bake our noodles a bit more! What is the impact of Generational Birth Order?

What if you are a First Born Child, of a First Born Child, of a First Born Child? Rob, what the hell did you just say? I'm saying, what if you were a First Born Child, so was your parent and so was their parent? Does the Generational Birth Order amplify in the third (or more) generation?

OMG, if it does then just imagine the Middle Child of a Middle Child! Is that kid more likely to be an emotional train wreck?

Does an Only Child born from a First Born Child parent get coddled more because the First Born Child parent feels like they had too much pressure put on them and they didn't have a childhood? There is an upcoming chapter "Balance" which touches on WHY this may happen.

My second son is a second born Youngest Child, of a second born Youngest Child (Me, because my sister is older than me.) Did I raise him differently because I was also a Youngest Child? I lovingly told him all through his childhood that he is annoying. He really exuded Youngest Child traits of being manipulative and attention seeking in a negative way (this is WHY he was annoying.)

What about…

GENERATIONAL GENDER BIRTH ORDER

Yes! I said it again and as far as I know, you heard it here first! I would love to do some research on this topic too. What is the impact of Generational Gender Birth Order? For example: My oldest son is a First Born son, of a First Born son, of a First Born son.

I'll break this down:

My father was a First Born (of only 2 kids, both boys.) So he went from an Only Child to very quickly becoming a First Born Child, since the siblings are close in age.

My sister was born first, I was born second. So I am a Youngest Child; however, I am the first born son. No other children from my parents.

I have 2 sons.

How do we think this impacts the way my First Born son was raised and the family's expectations of him? Was my First Born son, being raised by a First Born son, with his grandfather (alive and involved in his life) being a First Born son, impacted by Generational Gender Birth Order? Were the family expectations of him different than of my second born son?

Do you see what I introduced there? Gender variant as opposed to direct Birth Order. My oldest son may have been influenced by the first born male figures in his life, while my second son may have had a different upbringing (even though by the same family) being influenced by the other Generational Birth Order and Generational Gender Birth Order. Someone do research on this please and get back to me.

If you are having an epiphany now because you feel like your life has been impacted by Birth Order, peel back the onion and really think about how it has impacted your life, your expectations, your relationships, and your behavior.

If you have multiple children, I suggest you really take a look at how you are raising your children. Specifically keeping an eye on if you are treating them differently, by Birth Order. Are you putting too much pressure on the oldest? Are you coddling a Youngest Child more than they should be or more than your other children? Are you ignoring a Middle Child more than the others? What do you think the future ramifications are?

A WORD ABOUT PARENTING

A child who is difficult to raise will need very little, if any, parenting when they are ready to leave the nest and go into the world. A child who is easy to raise will always need parental intervention. You either do it now, or you do it later. Parents of difficult children can exhale.

One of the biggest factors in Nurture is our parents. They have the most influence on us, up until a certain age. A parent's EBR (Expectations, Beliefs, and Rules…this chapter is coming up soon), value systems, morals, and behaviors are learned by the child.

Children are little sponges. They pick up on everything. If there is a family secret you are keeping from the child, odds are the child already knows.

PARENT PRO TIP: Your reactions are instrumental. When it comes to the child learning their own value system it is the parent's reaction to their behavior, other people's behavior and other events, which has a huge influence. When I say other events, an easy example might be: if the parent drops a full coffee mug on the floor, how does the parent react?

Variations of: the child witnesses their parent drop a coffee mug on the floor:

Coffee mug drops on the floor in a coffee shop.
Reaction: The parent keeps their cool in public, apologizes to the nearby customers asking if everyone is ok. They apologize to the Barista and leave a tip for the trouble. They get another cup of coffee and leave the coffee shop without further discussion. The ever-watching child learns this reaction is appropriate for this circumstance.

Coffee mug drops on the floor at home.
Reaction: The parent gasps, and sucks all the air out of the room, while the coffee cup falls to the floor. As the coffee mug hits the floor and the coffee spills, they start shrieking saying "Are you kidding me? I don't have time for this! Son of a bitch! This is not how I wanted to start my day!" Then they grab a towel, a bottle of cleaner, and continue mumbling under their breath until the coffee is cleaned up. Then they stand up, apologize to those watching for their outburst, and go about their day trying to overcome their frustration. The ever-watching child learns this reaction is appropriate for this circumstance. Since children have self-centered and narcissistic tendencies, the child may think on some level it is their fault and you are actually mad at them.

Side note: I know most people have an aversion to the term narcissist and associate it as a bad thing. As a child we are born with this ideal. It is a parent's job to teach the child to share and to think about someone other than themselves. The problem occurs when the child never outgrows this belief.

Coffee mug drops on the tile floor and cracks the tile or falls on the light color carpet and stains the carpet.

The reaction is the same as above except the parent also yells at a family member. Maybe even yells at the child. WHY did you leave your item here on the floor? I tripped over it and now coffee is everywhere. To a spouse or First Born Child: "You get in here and clean this up because this is your fault! I have asked you time and time again to clean up your items and now look what it has caused!" The ever watching child learns that this level of incident means it is ok to mistreat one's spouse or child. The child also learns that it is ok to mistreat a family member; however, it is not ok to mistreat complete strangers, because the parent reacted differently in the coffee shop. Let's also take a moment here and realize how the First Born Child felt. They cleaned up 9 out of 10 toys but left one toy on the ground and are getting yelled at for that. The Youngest Child leaves toys on the floor all the time and doesn't receive any yelling from the parent. How does the First Born Child feel here? Like they are being treated unfairly? Who moved my cheese? Are they developing feelings of animosity towards their sibling?

Parenting moment: I remember one day my son, who was 5 years old at the time, said something and sounded like a complete jerk. I couldn't believe he said what he said so I marched over to him to correct this inappropriate behavior. During my determined walk over to my son my light bulb went off and I realized, he sounded exactly like me! He learned to say this from listening to me! Oh my! Doesn't that speak volumes?! I realized it was time for some reflection of my own behavior and reactions.

Now change these scenarios to: The child drops a cup of coffee on the floor.

The child doesn't know that you have had a bad day, if the mortgage payment is going to be late or if you are stressed about your job. All they know if you freaked out on them and it must be their fault. Watch and override your reactions if they are not calm reactions. After all, what the child takes away from this is much more important than dropping a cup of coffee.

Now change the scenario to: A guest in the house drops a cup of coffee on the floor.

Reaction: The parent rushed over alarmed at the situation. They ask the guest if they are alright and if they burned themself. Once the person confirms they are ok the parent goes to get cleaning supplies. The guest offers to clean it up but the parent declines. The parent cleans up the coffee spill and gives reassuring words of affirmation to the guest saying, "It's ok, don't worry about, it certainly could have been a lot worse." The ever-watching child learns to treat strangers better than they treat their family members. The First Born Child wonders WHY the guest wasn't chastised for the way they handled the coffee mug because clearly they could have been more careful. The child goes on to think *If I had done the exact same thing my parent would have yelled at me, maybe penalized me or maybe even hit me.* How does their value system look? Do you think they are on the path to self-worth?

Children learn their value system by how we treat them. Through watching our actions (and reactions) we also inadvertently teach them.

You might be a parent having an epiphany or you might be an adult reflecting on your childhood. Either one, or both, are great to reflect on.

Story time!

I was with my son at an indoor playground. Many children were there climbing on things, bouncing on things, throwing things, and roughhousing. Apparently, my older son did something which violated the house rules. I saw one of the workers confront my son. Then they continued to chastise him and got "in his face." Then I saw my son's face change to being nervous and bordering on fearful. The next thing my three-foot-tall son saw was his 6 foot 1 inch, 200-pound Black Belt father getting between him and the worker. As I towered over the worker, I said in my dad voice "Doesn't feel good when someone bigger than you gets in your face does it? You don't EVER talk to my son like that. Now get away from him and leave him alone." The worker went about his business and left my son alone. My son looked at me with a thank you in his eyes and understood his value. Not only did he have a value but his big protector Dad was willing to take action to enforce that value.

Since you loved that one, here is another one. LOL. This story happens ten years after that last story. I met my future bride in April, and we were engaged in October the same year. Analyticals are asking "Which April?" It doesn't matter! Focus on the forest, not the tree. In December of that same year, we went to an ice skating rink during the Christmas holidays. We took her nieces and nephews and joined some friends. At the time I was very much accepted by her family, but things were still kind of new. While skating, my fiancee's 10-year-old nephew Max did something which apparently violated the house rules. I saw the same instance all over again. One of the workers got in his face. I calmly watched for a moment, just as I did when my own son had gotten in trouble, to see how the worker would handle it. The same thing happened. The larger worker got in Max's face and chastised him. Once an appropriate amount of chastising had been completed, the worker kept going and Max's face changed. The next thing both of them heard was my dad voice yelling "Hey!" They both turned to look at me wondering

WHY someone had yelled. Then I said, "He heard you, now that's enough." The worker started defending his behavior. I stood up and got next to Max. While I towered over the worker, I cut him off by saying, "I said he heard you and he won't do it again. Now get out of his face. Right now. If you get in his face again you will have to deal with me." The worker left. Max turned to look at me and said, "Thank you." He felt that I had given him a value and he knew I was willing to risk myself to enforce that value. A value that typically only a dad would defend but since his dad wasn't there that day, I did it. I went on to cement that feeling by saying "I got your back buddy, if someone messes with you they have to answer to me!" Max told that story to his mother when he got home and then told that same story a year later at a family gathering. It was very impactful for him.

I will add here that I have a very even temper. I am very calm in a crisis and I practice Equanimity (more on that later). It takes a lot for me to get upset. When I defended both of the children in those stories, I was not upset. I knew each incident was an impactful moment for the Dad/Son and Future Uncle/Nephew relationship and their value system, which is WHY I sprang into action. In the moment all I was thinking about is *say what you need to say so the child feels defended, supported and valued.*

Remember these stories for later in the book because they tie into something very interesting!

IF YOU ARE DIVORCED OR NO LONGER WITH YOUR CHILD'S OTHER PARENT…

In this chapter we discuss some of the ways dealing with divorce may be difficult for children. If you chose to have kids then you choose to do your best to give that child the best start in life they can have. That doesn't mean being rich and having stuff. I mean making sure the child does not go without, their basic needs are met, they feel loved, and they are encouraged to learn who they are. With that said let me remind co-parents of the rules:

1. Never pass messages through children
2. Never use children as weapons to hurt the other parent
3. Never withhold time with the other parent, unless it is not safe
4. Respect the other person's parenting style as long as it does not hurt the child
5. Don't speak negatively about the other parent, when the child can hear you
6. Don't use children as leverage
7. Don't compete for your child's affection
8. Encourage the child to have a good relationship with the other parent
9. Do not argue with the other parent when the children can hear you
10. Uphold your end of the co-parenting agreement
11. Reinforce to the children that the divorce is not their fault

CHAPTER 202:
Expectations, Beliefs, and Rules (EBR)

"All that we are is the result of what we have thought."

~Buddha

Remember in the Introduction when I told you I wrote the first WHY book about 20 years ago? When I went back 20 years later to update this chapter I couldn't stop smiling. This is one of my favorite chapters. Enjoy!

EBR DEFINITIONS

Expectations

An outlook, anticipation, or assumption that something will happen, or be the case, in the future. An Expectation is not a "hope." "I hope someone is there to open the door for me, because my hands are full," is different than the Expectation "I am paying the doorman very well, so he better be available to open the door when I arrive."

Beliefs

A trust, faith, or confidence in someone or something which can be based on past experiences, social norms, personal beliefs, or promises.

Rules

A more intense form of an Expectation which is explicit and understood. These are regulations, laws or principles governing conduct. For our purposes we are going to focus on our personal rules. Personal rules are how you govern yourself. The minimum quality of behavior you expect from yourself and your boundaries concerning the way you expect to be treated. Example: you are not allowed to hurt me. This is beyond an Expectation. If one violates my Expectations, I may not be happy with them. If one violates my Rules, there will be consequences.

Expectations can be:

- I Expect to have to do everything myself
- I Expect people to help me do things
- I Expect mediocrity
- I Expect to be average
- I Expect to be exceptional
- I Expect people to tolerate my behavior when it is less than
- I Expect people to have manners
- I Expect great service when I am paying for an experience

Beliefs can be:

- I Believe in this religion
- I Believe all people are good (or bad)
- I Believe I am awesome
- I Believe my family loves me
- I Believe people are helpful
- I Believe the government is doing a good job
- I Believe the government is corrupt
- I Believe everyone is out to get me
- I Believe all people lie

- I Believe every couple has problems
- I Believe everyone in a relationship fights sooner or later
- I Believe everyone makes mistakes

The last six Beliefs I listed become negative enablers. You are actually giving yourself permission to behave poorly when you Believe this. Avoid self-talk like this and you will have fewer problems, fewer fights in your relationships, and make fewer mistakes.

PRO TIP:

People rarely come to their deepest Beliefs through logic.

You can't use logic to talk them out of it.

People think irrationally as an adaptation to not feeling safe or to end suffering.

People use their Belief as a coping mechanism to handle some reality they can't deal with.

Remember our brains are wired for safety and security, not happiness.

Said another way, many times our deepest Beliefs are a coping mechanism for safety and security.

Ask yourself these questions:

- What are my deepest Beliefs?
- When did I get those Beliefs?

Did you form those Beliefs when 1) you were too young to have another opinion or 2) during a time when you needed the most safety, security and needed a coping mechanism for something you otherwise couldn't handle?

If the latter, when you were in a "bad place" (financially, emotionally, felt unsafe, needed a way to cope) did someone offer you love, compassion, and understanding if you accepted their Belief? What Six Basic Human Needs did this fill? Love, Certainty, and Connection, right? Remember if one action fills three or more Needs, it will become a habit. Don't you think the people who have gone before us knew your "lowest time" (when you lacked your Six Basic Human Needs and when you were at the bottom 2 levels of Maslow's scale: had the need for safety and security) was the best time to share their Belief?

A friend once said to me, "If you don't Believe in something, you will fall for anything." My response, "And you did."

What I think: as long as you are a good human, I don't care what you Believe.

Remember I said you won't like everything I had to say. This book is called WHY.

Rules can be:

- Do not touch my spouse
- Do not hurt me nor my family
- I must obey the law

People with a strong need for uncertainty and poor morals say, "Rules were made to be broken." Nope. Sorry guys, this is not the case.

WHY is your EBR important? Because your EBR determines:

- Your outlook on life
- The way you think you should live
- The way you think others should live
- The way you act
- The way you react

- Understanding of people
- Acceptance of people
- Tolerance of people
- Your ability to create peace

I Expect something to happen means I will be disappointed, or upset, if it doesn't happen. I Believe in something means I know it to be true because I have seen it, experienced it in the past, or have been made to Believe it is real. If it's a Rule, then the Rule needs to be followed or there will be consequences. I am trying to accentuate the level of severity of what each one means. An Expectation is the lowest degree of importance to you. Beliefs are higher than Expectations, and Rules are the highest form of anticipated results.

If you are carrying a cup of coffee and someone bumps into you spilling the coffee, WHY does the coffee spill? The answer is because you have coffee in your cup. If you had water, the water would spill. If you had tea, the tea would spill. The point is whatever you carry around with you will spill out once life bumps you. Choose your Expectations, Beliefs, and Rules wisely because life will bump into you and your EBR will spill out.

PRO TIP: Remember that analogy for the rest of your life and it will make you a better human. When life bumps into you and your cup spills, do you like what you see? If not, this is your call to action to sweep your own doorstep.

This is where we really get into it. Just to refresh our memory, Nature is the personality traits you were born with. Nurture is the environment that unique person experienced. What environment do I mean? Birth order, culture, religion, upbringing, customs, and learned behaviors. Nature will be tested here.

When nature and nurture are in conflict, there will be inner struggles. Example: I just watched the Jackie Robinson movie the other day. There is a scene where a boy, maybe 9 years old, is hearing everyone in the crowd at the Dodgers' baseball game yelling racial slurs at Jackie Robinson. The boy appears to be uncomfortable. Then his own father starts yelling the same slurs over and over and over again. At first the boy's nature was struggling because he knew it was not the right thing to do. Unfortunately, the peer pressure (nurture of his environment) took over, and the 9-year-old boy yelled a few slurs himself. I think he was trying them out to see if he preferred that, but after he yelled them he regretted it. In this case nature was tested by nurture and nurture may have won. For a moment anyway.

Examples of how some personality types and social hierarchies can violate your EBR:

Alphas are at the top of the social hierarchy. Some Alphas may be less than eloquent in reminding you of that fact if they are unevolved and very dominant.

Omegas, in contrast, are at the bottom of the social hierarchy and they don't care what people think. Their honesty and lack of social graces may come across as off-putting.

Expressives can be loud and obnoxious, especially when they feel they need to do more in order to be the center of attention. You may be at a nice restaurant having a quiet evening, but that will change when an Expressive sits down at the table next to yours. If they are not obnoxious yet, just add wine and you will hear when the filters come off. Check please!

Gammas, and their rebellious nature, are likely to rebel from social norms, which can violate other people's Expectations. Gammas are least likely to identify themselves as Gamma males. They are insecure and envious. This can lead to a delusional idea they are superior to Alphas. Voted most likely to "poke the (Alpha) bear" they can violate people's Expectations and may not even know they are doing it.

These are just examples. Every personality type or social

hierarchy can violate your EBR. The more EBR you have, and the stricter you make them, the more likely they are to get violated. Read that twice.

PRO TIP: Remember mind over matter. If you don't mind, it don't matter! The French have a saying "the less you have, the more you are free." This goes for possessions and EBR.

Amiables, that pro tip is not permission to let people violate your boundaries.

Oh, and one more thing. You show me a poor neighborhood and I will show you a whole lot of MA personality Gammas. They are lazy, nothing is painful enough for them to take action, and they feel like the world owes them something. If the world gave them a 3-bedroom house, they would complain the world should have given them a 4-bedroom house. They feel entitled. Nothing is ever good enough and they want something for nothing. The MA Gamma is an infectious WHY NURTURE, like a virus or a poison. The MA Gamma is very vocal about WHY they blame everyone else (especially Expressives and Analytical MA Gammas) because they have no accountability for their own actions. They may have a lot of capacity, but that is only because they don't have a job. WHY am I mentioning this? Not for the MA Gamma, they won't change. I am mentioning this for the people around them. If I just described some of your family members, or people you knew when you were around as a child, their poisonous personality had an effect on you. It is easier to justify, rationalize, and blame others for their lack of success, than to take action.

PRO TIP: Always remember you cannot explain to a loser WHY you are not a loser. WHY? For three reasons. 1) Misery loves company. 2) This is their Belief and one cannot change someone's Belief with logic. 3) If everyone else is a loser they can justify and rationalize their behavior.

Back to the person in proximity to the MA Gamma(s). The

good news is it never felt right to you and you were questioning WHY they acted like this. This is WHY. Their behavior fills their need for significance when people listen to them. It fills their need for connection when people listen to them. It fills their need for certainty. They may even feel like they are contributing to your life. Remember, once 3 or 4 needs are filled with one action, it becomes a habit. This is their EBR. What do we do about it? Now that we understand, we can tolerate their behavior and accept them for who they want to be. Don't try to change them, it won't work. Love them for who they have chosen to be but break away from the poisonous message they have infected you with. Change what is in your cup, take action and become a successful and good person.

SETTING EBR

One of the common themes all throughout WHY is establishing and enforcing boundaries. Setting Expectations means establishing and agreeing upon future boundaries. Example: you invite a friend over to your house and they reply, "I would love to come, but on one condition: You know we don't like the same music so I will come over if we both agree not to play any music." You say, "Ok deal." Your friend communicated their Expectations (future boundaries) in advance, and you agreed to them. Now neither of us will feel uncomfortable during our time together.

We set future Beliefs and Rules using the same technique, we just communicate their importance, and repercussions, if those Beliefs or Rules (as future boundaries) are not adhered to. Example: you invite a friend over to your house, but you know they like to carry a gun. So you call them to invite them over and you say "Hey Sally, I am having a party at my house this weekend and I would love for you to come; however, I have a strict "no guns in my house" policy (I have a Rule) so if you come over you cannot bring one." Sally replies "well then I'm not coming!" Just kidding, had to throw you a curve ball.

Answer these questions:

1. What percentage of employees steal expensive items from stores?

A. 0% C. 25% E. 75%

B. 10% D. 50% F. 100%

2. What percentage of employees take home small items from their job like pens, paper clips, and toilet paper?

A. 0% C. 25% E. 75%

B. 10% D. 50% F. 100%

Ok, Drivers don't just skip over the details, go back and answer the questions. Got your answers? Good! These are your Expectations. Rob, what the hell did you just say? I'm saying, if you answered Question #1 with 10%, then there is a 10% chance you would steal an expensive item from a store if given the opportunity. If you answered Question # 2 with 75%, there is a 75% chance you would take something from your employer that you deemed insignificant. Oops! Didn't see that one coming huh?

If I asked you the question "What percentage of people do drugs?", what would you say? Well now you might take an extra second to answer, because you understand the depth of the question. Let's pretend for a minute I asked Sally that question and her answer was 50%.

Even if Sally currently does not do drugs, if Sally thinks 50% of people do drugs then how likely is Sally to do drugs if given the opportunity? You guessed it…50%. Let's take it one step further. If Sally noticed someone acting strangely, how likely is Sally to think the strange acting person is on drugs? Um, does anyone want to guess 50% of the time? Ding, ding, ding! Winner! Sally would assume 50% of the time that the strange acting person is on drugs.

Now let's change our answer and say Sally guessed 10%. Sally will probably take a good long look at the person acting weird and try to figure out what is wrong with them. Sally will consider their appearance and mannerisms. If they do not look like a "bad" person, then Sally may not think the person is on drugs. WHY? Because Sally's Expectations are only "bad" people do drugs and "bad" people only make up 10% of the population. WHY do we know this about Sally? Because she answered 10%. So now Sally is trying to establish another reason. WHY are they acting strangely? Are they drunk? Are the sleep deprived? Are they sad? EBR affects your outlook. EBR affects how you start something, how you behave during the experience, what you expect during the experience, and your interpretation of what happened.

THE SECURITY GUARD

Let's say you pass by a Security Guard and the Guard's head is on the desk. To you the Security Guard appears to be resting. What do you make of this? Initially you may think to yourself "how lazy," or "the Security Guard doesn't take the job very seriously" or "the Security Guard should be fired for sleeping on the job." Is there anything positive we can say about the Security Guard? Not really because the lazy person is not doing the job very well. Right? Maybe. Is there any other possible suggestion for this? What if the Security Guard was really sick. Not enough? Ok. What if the Security Guard tried to call in sick but the boss said no, because he couldn't get his shift covered? What if the boss offered to give the Security Guard the next three days off to recover if the Security Guard could only make it in today? What if the Security Guard took so much pride in their work that 6 hours into the 8-hour shift the Security Guard hadn't even put their head down once, even during the slow times, even through sickness, and you happened to see the 3 minutes with their head down? What if the Security Guard was so dedicated to the job that they wouldn't think of calling in sick even through fever and chills? What if the Security Guard was so dedicated to providing for their family, they didn't want to miss a shift and have less money to provide for them? What if that shift counted in the last paycheck before their spouse's birthday? The Security Guard thinks the world of their spouse and this next paycheck means having enough money to buy something really special? See my point? You kind of feel like a bad person now don't you? You started an experience (judged the Security Guard) before knowing the reality based on your EBR. You also behaved differently during the experience and left the experience with an interpretation. Did you take this one step further and take action based on all of that? Did you call their boss and complain?

If you did you actually started a snowball effect. You started another experience (calling to get the Security Guard in trouble) with certain EBR based on your previous misinterpretation. If you did call to complain you probably started by telling the Security Guard's boss you don't appreciate a Security Guard sleeping on the job. You called with the Expectation of having the Guard reprimanded (or possibly fired.) Starting the experience of calling the boss without EBR may involve asking the boss WHY his employee might have his head down on the table while working. Suggesting he might want to ask his employee about it. This is the essence of behaving differently during the experience.

Let me ask you a question: are you prejudice? If the answer you just thought is "no, I treat everyone with different skin tones the same way," then you might want to look into it. WHY? Because the definition of prejudice doesn't mention race nor skin tone.

Prejudice definition according to Google: "a preconceived opinion that is not based on reason or actual experience."

So by definition, prejudice, or pre-judging, is no more than a form of Expectation.

EXPECTATIONS, BELIEFS, AND RULES (EBR)

Here is a fun question…

When you read about the Security Guard, and started to get a visual in your head, what color skin did the Security Guard have? Did he have a different skin tone than you? Oops.

PRO TIP: No one is born racist.

> *"Until the color of a man's skin is of no more significance than the color of his eyes, I've got to say War…"*
>
> ~Bob Marley ("War")

Oh, and by the way, what gender did you imagine the Security Guard to be? Are you sexist? Because the story never mentioned a gender. Oops.

My son read the story and added "I imagined he was skinny." I didn't think about that but I also imagined the Security Guard was skinny. Did you imagine this seemingly lazy Security Guard to be fat? If so, maybe you have the Expectation that all fat people are lazy.

So, let's start over: let's say you pass by a Security Guard and the Guard's head is on the desk. What does it mean? Maybe it should mean we shouldn't jump to conclusions based on our EBR.

While we are starting over let's ask ourselves: do you think Sally (the Sally who answered 50%) was pre-judging when she saw the man acting strangely and assumed he was on drugs? Clearly yes.

Story time

I called the Department of Corporations (I'll omit the state but it wasn't Florida) the other day to find out what I did wrong. During the call I found out I registered my company as a "corporation of the state" when I should have registered my foreign (Florida based) corporation "to do business in the state." During the call this happened: the lady who answered the phone held her hand over the phone (not realizing I could still hear her) and told her co-worker what I had done. When she asked her co-worker what I did wrong, her co-worker replied, "What an idiot!" Based on her EBR she immediately jumped to conclusions that I was an idiot, because I did not know their rules and she did. The truth of the matter is the person I spoke to a month earlier, in the same department, gave me some bad advice. This was the reason for my mistake and WHY I needed to call back and fix it. If she didn't start that experience with a certain EBR she would have behaved differently during the experience. She should know that other reasons for my mistake are possible besides the explanation that I am an idiot. She probably would have had a different interpretation of the entire experience after it was over if she started with an open mind. Oh, and by the way, do you think the employee who called me an idiot has a strong need for connection? Probably not. I would bet they have a strong need for significance. This is what she has in her cup and it spilled out.

So, what did we just learn here? That we develop certain EBR to fill our Six Basic Human Needs! Oh my, that is a game changer isn't it? So Rob you mean to tell me that I have Expectations in place, and see the world through this lens, to fill my need levels? Yes. So I subconsciously filter messages, information and new experiences to fill my needs? Sorry for the cold water but, yes.

If/then

If I have a strong need for significance, then I filter messages to identify opportunities for me to feel significant? Yes.

If I have a strong need for connection, then I filter messages to see opportunities to connect? Yes.

If I have a strong need for love, then I may not see new people objectively? Uh oh! This means I might ignore "red flags," and I might blow through emotional stop signs, because I am trying too hard to make something work with a person who is not a romantic match me for me? Yes and if you want to take a minute to reflect on how much time that has cost you, I'll wait.

Yes, yes, and yes. Once you understand your need levels, you can start identifying what Expectations, Beliefs, and Rules you have (the lens you have created to see the world), to fill your need levels.

This goes for Birth Order too. If I have "middle child issues" then I am filtering messages and experiences to validate my issues? Yes!

Let the epiphanies flow…

SITTING IN A RESTAURANT

Imagine (actually imagine this for it will make it easier for you to change each scenario in your mind) you are sitting at a nice restaurant with someone special (spouse, date, family member, etc…) and you are having a nice evening. You are sitting at the table, before your entrées have arrived, and people are walking by the table. A man walks by, touches the edge of your table and keeps going. Does this bother you or your dinner mate? Now change that to: when he is walking by he puts his whole hand on your table, without touching anything on the table (silverware, glasses etc…) and keeps walking by. Now change that to: as he is walking by he pauses, places his hand on your table for support and turns his back to you while he starts talking to the table adjacent you. Offended yet? Now change each one of those scenarios to: your entrées are on the table when this happens. Does this change the point where you get offended? In your mind was it ok for him to touch the table with his whole hand when the food was not on the table; however, you became offended when the food was on the table? Now change that to: and a man comes walking by, pauses at your table, leans his whole elbow on your table and waits there for a few seconds until he walks away. Does that offend you? Ok, let's pause for a moment.

Where was it in that story that you got offended by the man's actions, because you thought they were inappropriate? Some people were offended when the man touched the table without pausing. That couple may have commented to one other "WHY does he have to touch the table? Doesn't he have any class?" Or they may have just given each other "that glance" and the other knew that is what they wanted to say, without saying it. Others weren't offended until the man placed his entire hand on the table. Still more people hung in there and weren't offended until the man paused and used the table for support, while he started talking to the others. Some people weren't bothered by any of this except when their entrées had arrived. The point is everyone has a different "breaking point" based on their EBR. Some people finally got bothered when the food was on the table and some man was touching the table. Believe it or not some people didn't even care about their food being on the table and the man leaning on the table with his elbow! You might be saying right now "no way, everyone would be offended by that!" Nope, I promise you that you are wrong. Let's keep an open mind so you can learn to identify your EBR compared to others and not make the mistake of assuming everyone is like you. I am going to repeat that: let's not make the mistake of thinking most people are like you.

    Now let's go back to our scenario except this time I want you to change the person walking by to a woman. When does that bother you? Some people would be more tolerant of a woman making those exact same actions and would change the point when they deemed an action inappropriate. Some people may not even get offended when the woman leaned her elbow on the table but would if it was a man. Guess what! Your dinner mate got offended at a different time than you did. WHY? Because everyone is different, including having different EBR. He or she may expect you to do something about it because they assume since they are offended, everyone must be. On the other hand, maybe they didn't understand WHY you were asking the person not to do that. They may assume that since they hadn't been offended yet, then no one should be. This difference of opinion may turn into a conversation with your dinner mate (may even a heated discussion or argument) because of your actions or lack of actions. The discussion is actually over different EBR.

Let's go back another time and change the person to an elderly woman who needed to use the table for support because she was feeble. Are you offended by that? Some people say yes and others now say no. How about if the elderly woman was walking by the table, lost her balance and she had to place her elbow on the table while your entrees were on the table? Offended now? Again, some people are saying yes and others are saying no. Now you may be asking yourself WHY the people who aren't offended, aren't offended. Good question! I would venture a guess the reason they aren't offended is because of the perceived intent. They think the man intended to put his elbow there and the elderly woman simply lost her balance, therefore one should excuse the elderly woman. Some people don't care and may yell at the elderly woman. Each person has their own EBR and will react accordingly. You don't need to understand the difference. You just need to understand that the difference exists and have tolerance. Hopefully you can have acceptance and peace but we can start with tolerance.

GOING GREEK

One night I went out with a group of people to a Greek restaurant. This place was crazy. There was loud music, people happily yelling and screaming, small tables packed into a little space, and people dancing. Dancing in a restaurant! I didn't Expect this. I could tell I was going to have to leave my EBR at the door in order to enjoy this place. Keep in mind in that last discussion I would have been offended long before the man's elbow was on my table.

Willing to try something new, I waited with my group until we got a table. It was more like a picnic bench. We were packed in there like sardines, and the restaurant was non-stop action. One of the guys in my group was a regular, so he ordered for everyone.

I prefer to order my own food so once again, this is outside of my EBR. I already told myself that I wouldn't have any EBR that night and I would go with the flow. The wait staff brought drinks and then brought the food. Wow! What food! I certainly didn't expect the smorgasbord they laid in front of us. I had a 3-pound stuffed lobster in front of me, there was some gorgeous looking dish just next to the lobster that looked like duck, there was steak, and everything was delicious. The reason I know everything was delicious was because everyone was sharing all of the food. My normal EBR of an expensive restaurant, with that caliber of food, would be a nice quiet place with comfortable surroundings and an attentive wait staff. Here I am sitting on a picnic bench packed in with people. It is so loud I can't even hear them talking to me and people are dancing in the restaurant.

Here is the piece de resistance. I was leaning over my plate when I noticed something unusual out of the corner of my eye. Next to my wine glass was a shoe! So, I focused all of my attention on this shoe and low and behold it had a foot in it. I looked up to see a woman in a dress dancing on my table! She was an employee and obviously had done this several times since she danced all across the picnic table and didn't knock anything over. I grabbed my wine glass just in case, but her skills were quite impressive. Think to yourself: how many people would you expect would have been offended by the man putting his elbow on your table? Now imagine this place with people dancing on my table, stepping over my food (and other people's wine glasses) with her high heels and there was a wait to get in! I mean an hour wait or more! This place was packed. I looked around and almost all of the tables had women dancing on them so obviously this was in the EBR of the patrons of this place. It was crazy. Some people are saying "I would never go to a place like that" and some are asking, "what is the name of the place?," because they want to go!

The bill was just as shocking as the place itself. So not only were people willing to wait an hour or more to get in, but they were willing to pay handsomely for this experience. That definitely opened my eyes to the variances of EBR, within people. Can you imagine these patrons going to a Michelin star, quiet, sit down, white linen restaurant with a small jazz band playing in the background? They would probably go nuts because they would be bored to death. Need for uncertainty anyone? They would be wondering WHY someone would pay such a high price when no one was even walking on their table. By the way, the Greek patrons were sitting next to you when the man placed his hand on your table, and you got offended. They were looking at you with a strange face wondering WHY you got offended simply because someone placed their hand on your table as they walked by. Interesting right? I think so. EBR will vary greatly, it will affect behavior, it will affect tolerance, and it will affect outcomes.

We have to be realistic about how we enforce our boundaries. In the Greek restaurant it would not appropriate for me to stand up in the middle of the restaurant, ask them to stop the music, insist everyone stop dancing, and demand the employees stop walking on the tables. If my EBR doesn't fit the environment then maybe I need to consider leaving the environment, rather than trying to change it. As long as no one is getting hurt, nor doing anything illegal, then live and let live! I am going to do me, you do you, and they will do them. Vive la difference!

EBR AFFECTING EVERYDAY LIFE

The other day I was looking for my tuxedo shoes. Since I don't wear a tuxedo that often I wasn't sure where I left them. I was sure I had put them in a box and the box was in one of my closets. I guess I should say, I Expected them to be in a box and that box to be in one of my closets. I searched my main closet first because I was 90% sure they were in there. Since I didn't find the box with the shoes in it (I would recognize the box instantly so I didn't need to open any other boxes) I went to the spare bedrooms to search in there. After about twenty minutes I went back to my main closet to search some more, thinking I must have missed the box with the shoes in them. Forty unsuccessful minutes have passed and still no tuxedo shoes. I decided to look at my black dress shoes to see how they would look with my tuxedo, since I was in a pinch. As I was looking across the shoe rack for my black dress shoes, what do you think I saw? Right there in plain view were my tuxedo shoes! What did that teach me? The power of EBR. I Expected, and was so focused to find a gray box (with my tuxedo shoes inside) somewhere tucked away in the closet that I missed the actual shoes right in front of my face. Have you ever done that? Men are saying "yes." Women are saying "that happens to my husband all the time." How can we parallel this to life? If you start with Expectations, you may miss a better outcome.

When I was a child, my Father would come home from work tired. He was always tired. "Man, what a day." "Traffic was horrible." "Whew, it's so good to be home" were some of the phrases I heard all the time. So when I became a man and started working, what do you think my learned Expectations were when I got home from work? Tired, glad to be home, and talking about traffic. This went on for years until I started to understand EBR. One day when I got home from work I asked myself "am I really tired or am I just Expecting to be?" I stood there and thought about it for a minute. My conclusion was that I wasn't tired. I was just Expecting to be because of the EBR passed down from my Father. Guess what? If your EBR doesn't serve you, they probably won't serve your children when they learn them from you. Parents should pay attention here because the ever watching child is always listening. More on that later.

I also decided not to take off my dress shirt and tie, because I didn't want that to become a negative association. More about associations in the chapter Associations, Triggers, and Demons. As a prelude to that chapter: if the first thing I did when I came home was take off my dress shirt and tie, like I couldn't wait to get out of them, I would develop an Association (which would become an

EBR) that being in a shirt and tie is "somewhat painful." This may affect the quality of my work. The truth is my shirts and ties are very comfortable and there is no need to rush out of them. So I took my new attitude, shirt, and tie and went to a restaurant. In fact, I wasn't tired at all! I had the EBR drilled into my head that I should be tired when I come home from work and I should complain about the traffic. The truth is my Father drove for more than an hour to get home, so maybe he really was tired. I only drove for about twenty minutes, but I learned his EBR so I complained about the traffic.

Remember the moral of the metaphor is whatever you have inside you, will spill out when life bumps into you. If you have love inside of you, love will come out. If you have hatred inside of you, hatred will come out. If you have understanding and tolerance inside of you, those will come out. Choose your Expectations, Beliefs and Rules wisely. Because when life bumps into you, and it will, what is inside of you will come out.

PRO TIP: It's your cup! You can put whatever you want in there. If life bumps you and you don't like what just spilled out, that is your wake up call to change what is in your cup.

We should Understand, then Tolerate, then give Acceptance, and then we can have Peace.

> *"Emancipate yourself from mental slavery.*
> *None but ourselves can free our minds."*
> ~Bob Marley (Redemption Song)

CHAPTER 203:
Maslow's Hierarchy of Needs

Maslow's hierarchy of needs (MHON) is a 5 tier model of the psychology of human needs. It is typically viewed in a pyramid with the most basic of needs at the bottom. It forms a foundation on which to build and evolve. The pyramid goes up from there as we fill the more complex of needs. We find it hard to fill those needs when the lower, or more basic needs, become scarce.

How does this affect relationships?

Each person being on a different level can be reasons WHY couples may not be connecting. Let's say we have one spouse who works and one who doesn't work, or one spouse makes 80% or more of the income and the other spouse makes 20% or less of the income. The working spouse or the disproportionately higher earner probably has more stress on them because they have to succeed, gain that work, sell that deal, hit their numbers, save that working relationship, unclog that supply chain and/or meet that deadline or the family is going to have financial issues. That spouse not performing may result in not being able to pay the mortgage, less holiday spending, not affording private school, having to get a personal loan in order to make ends meet, or maybe not being able to put food on the table for their family. They are way down on the hierarchy of needs in Psychological or Safety needs.

The non-working spouse may have more time and Capacity. They may be bathing the baby at night, perfecting their culinary skills, helping the kids with their homework, and doing home improvements. They may be in the Love level, Esteem level, or maybe even in Self Actualization level. This may be the same for a lower income spouse since their job and income may not produce the same stress levels. The couple may not have the same financial repercussions if the lower income earner loses the lower income job as they would if they lost the higher income job.

See the disconnect here? One spouse has to wait two more days to find out if they are going to get that imperative contract signed while the other one is asking what color they should paint the kitchen. I remember watching a Steven Seagal movie, where he played a Police Officer, and he said "Imagine there are still people who care what color the kitchen is" or something like that. What his character was saying is that his work is so life or death, and he sees people who have real problems, that he can't imagine a life where people are in the Love, Esteem, or Self Actualization stage. This character's capacity levels may be very high, but he may spend all of his capacity at work and have little left for his family, again creating disconnect.

Keep in mind I am not discounting that being a stay at home parent nor having a lower income job may be stressful. This is just an example and not meant to minimize what someone is doing with their life. By the way, if it bothered you and if this explanation was meaningful for you, you have PRIDE issues and need to delve deeper into that. I told you that you are not going to like everything I have to say but it will be the truth!

In the chapter "Capacity," I mention the Accountant working like a dog before tax day deadline. When he is giving all his capacity to his job, he is unconsciously dropping his MHON level from one of the top 3 levels, down to the 4th level. If in the middle of this busy time he gets a health scare he may easily drop down into level 5, because his psychological needs are being tested. Dropping down in levels is another reason WHY capacity levels decrease or get strained.

In Capacity we also discussed co-parenting and spending 50% of your time with and without your children and how that situational circumstance can alter capacity levels. What having the children may also be doing is lowering you on Maslow's scale. Maybe even all the way down to the Psychological level depending on how unruly they are! An important thing to remember is, in every relationship we have to find balance or the relationship will not last. The chapter Balance is next…

SECTION 300:
YOUR WHY NURTURE

Where you are now

CHAPTER 301:
Balance

What is Balance? There is Balance in life, there is Balance in Nature, and there is Balance within you. Balance knows no time, it just knows everything in life will come into Balance. Humans have known about the importance of Balance for a long time. Chinese philosophers invented the famous Yin and Yang symbol as early as the 3rd century BCE. It signifies that Balance and harmony are achieved through the integration of complementary opposites.

If you put a glass of water into the refrigerator, what happens? The water has no way to keep itself at room temperature, so the relentless cooling system of the refrigerator takes its toll. Eventually the glass of water becomes the same temperature as the inside of the refrigerator.

Take the same glass of water out of the refrigerator and now the glass of water has no way of keeping itself at refrigerator temperature. Eventually, the relentless temperature of the room takes its toll, and the glass of water becomes room temperature.

Did I just describe anyone's life?

The environment your WHY NATURE was born into may have been as relentless as the refrigerator was on the glass of water. This nurture molded you. Remember the story of the boy, in the chapter EBR, who yelled racial slurs at Jackie Robinson? His environment (his WHY NURTURE) and his WHY NATURE were not in Balance. He tried to Balance them by giving into the environment, but it didn't feel right to him. His choices now are to give in to the relentless environment (nurture) he is growing up in or push back and maintain his WHY NATURE. It's harder for children to find the strength to push back. That statement should resonate with you if you are a parent but also as a reflection on your own childhood.

When you feel out of Balance you may not feel like yourself. You may feel like something is wrong, something is "off," or you may be feeling a need to take action. Being self-aware is ideal. Next is having a life partner who can help identify when this happens within you.

PRO TIP: This is WHY romantic relationships can be so difficult. Your romantic partner is going to put a huge mirror right in your face and you may not like what you see. Don't run away, they are doing you a favor. If you do run away, wherever you go you are taking you with you, so you are really not running from anything. You are just getting the mirror out of your face and avoiding evolving as a person.

After self-awareness and having a romantic partner's mirror in your face, the next best thing is a WHY focus group. I'll explain WHY Focus Groups later.

However, you realize "I have been a bit off lately," the good news is you have figured out you are out of Balance. Understanding is the first step. Then it is time to figure out WHY you are out of Balance. Sit down and think about it. I have been irritable, cranky, or just "not myself." I feel out of Balance. WHY? What am I missing?

The first thing to look at is your Six Basic Human Needs. Think about each one and ask yourself if you are fulfilling your needs or are you out of Balance. Once you figure it out then communicate with the people who may have been affected.

Simply say: "I feel out of Balance and this is WHY."

Examples:

- I feel like I have had too much certainty, and I'm bored with my life. (Believe it or not, this is a normal problem with rich people. WHY? Because rich people can afford Lifestyle Creep. More on that soon.)

- I have had too much uncertainty. I need to slow down and recharge my batteries.

- I feel so abundant that I feel a need (to take action) to do more for my community. (Aka filling your need for contribution.)

- I feel stagnant in my life and (need to take action) want to increase my versatility by learning new things. (Aka need for growth but this also has an undertone of boredom. So the action is getting out of a comfort zone which fills a need for uncertainty.)

Next look at your Love Languages:

I feel out of Balance because I don't feel enough connection and love. Both romantic partners should then look at their Love Languages and see if both are out of Balance. WHY both of you? Because you two have to Balance…duh! Quick prelude to the chapter "Relationships" where we discuss: you are not the problem, I am not the problem (even if one of you clearly is the problem); however, we have a problem. Also in the upcoming chapter "Winning," there does not have to be a winner and a loser. Both parties can find a win-win outcome. This is the goal here. Back to the question, WHY both of you need to look at your Love Languages? Your partner may not be doing your Love Languages enough because they are out of Balance with their life, their job, Maslow's Hierarchy of Needs (maybe someone's health has failed and it lowered them "Love" down to "Safety Needs" in this category.) Maybe, just maybe, you haven't been doing their Love Languages enough. Maybe they haven't felt love from you and in turn, whether they know it or not, they have withdrawn. Communicate and look at it from both perspectives. Amiables listen up, I didn't say make it your fault and drain yourself trying to give from an empty cup. I said Balance.

Also look at Maslow's Hierarchy of Needs. Have you gone up or down a level and this change is affecting your relationships, your work, or your life?

Are you out of Capacity or is it being drained more than usual?

Is there some change in my environment that is affecting my WHY NATURE. Maybe it's a new person in your environment whose personality type is conflicting with yours. Sometimes it so obvious, we miss it. BUT! If your mother-in-law came to live with you for the summer, then I know WHY! I am full of jokes.

We are emotionally fragile creatures and life is not the same thing every day. One day we may be happy, one day we may be sad, one day we get good news, one day we get bad news, and one day our life takes a turn for the better or worse. All of these things play a factor in how we feel, and these changes can affect our Balance.

PRO TIP: In order for a relationship to be successful, we have to compromise. Compromise is nothing more than finding Balance.

MALES

Males are fairly simple creatures but we need to watch what society has deemed "being a man." Many times, males feel like we cannot talk about our emotions. Do not harbor your emotions until you explode one day (become way out of Balance) and climb a clock tower with a rifle. This is not ok. Being vulnerable and honest takes more strength than holding emotions in. If you think "she won't respect me if I show weakness," you are correct. So show strength by learning to articulate yourself and communicate the way you feel. It's ok. It actually takes more strength to do that, with control. A woman will respect you for this. What she will not respect is when you cannot regulate your actions because of your emotions.

Getting upset and punching a wall is just a sign you are unevolved and cannot express yourself correctly. I tell my wife all the time it is harder for me to communicate with you, than to just be silent and let it go. If I didn't care, I wouldn't care. When I'm communicating, it's because I care and I am working on our relationship. If my communication stops, it's because I no longer care. Males typically become silent as they withdraw. Homosexual Expressives are yelling "not me, bitches! I'm not going out quietly!" Communicating how you feel is hard, death by 1,000 paper cuts is hard, marriage is hard, and being alone is hard. Pick your hard and find Balance.

FEMALES

So much for the "simple creatures" part. Fasten your seat belt please. If you are a female, happen to be in a relationship with one, or happen to live with one and are looking for Balance, this may be WHY. Ever wondered WHY a female can be happy one day, crying the next, and otherwise emotionally inconsistent?

Women face 4 distinct cycles, or phases, every month. Guys are saying "every month?!" Yes gentlemen, every month. There are 4 internal phases. Each phase may affect her personality, her mood, her actions, and her reactions.

Disclaimer: Ladies, I am not hating and I am not saying all of you experience this the same way. These phases can affect some females significantly, while in others these phases may go unnoticed. The phases may affect the same person more one month than it does the next. Some females are laughing right now saying "monthly?! I can have all of these emotions in one day!"

Here they are:

1. **Menstruation (Cycle) Phase** (days 1–5): This is when she gets her period. This is the rest phase. Hormone levels drop. Females may be in pain and may have low energy levels. They

may want to stay home, be cozy, feel lazy, and (due to increased hunger and food cravings) she may want to eat more.

PRO TIP: Don't take things personally during this phase. After all, if males were in pain and had low energy levels, would our responses be ideal? I don't think so.

2. **Follicular Phase** (days 6–14): Reset phase. She is more confident and social. Estrogen rises.

3. **Ovulation Phase** (somewhere around day 14 but this phase can last several days to a week): She is more energized, social, and sexual because she is fertile. Hormones peak. She is more confident, affectionate, and flirtatious. During this phase a heterosexual female may be more attracted to a man with facial hair, muscles, and masculine features. WHY? Because 4096 people ago we learned survival of the fittest. We had to run from tigers, hunt game, and brave the elements. This long embedded instinct still lingers in females today. During this phase they may search for a "manly man," the man in charge, or a dominant social hierarchy male personality. WHY? Because she wants to have strong offspring.

If you are a metrosexual man, she may be attracted to you the other three weeks of the month, but her attraction towards you is lowest during this phase.

Have you ever heard a woman say, "I don't know WHY I went out with that guy, he is not my usual type." The reason may be because her hormones were spiking or crashing and that affected her judgement during this time.

Some women know the exact day they are ovulating and some have no clue. Years ago, I had an employee who had a very tough first pregnancy. She was bedridden for months and even though I was not legally obligated to pay her while she could not work, I did. She was very thankful I did that. A few years later she came into my office and said, "I have to apologize." I asked her WHY. She said, "Because I was ovulating yesterday, had a few too many drinks and a little too much fun with my husband and I am sure here comes kid number two." Being fascinated with human behavior I asked her, "You know the exact day you are ovulating?" She replied, "Oh yes. I am so certain that when I get home from work, I am going to go clear out the spare room and make it a nursery." Nine months later, she and her husband welcomed their second child, just as she said. Wow. Talk about self-awareness.

4. **Luteal Phase** (days 15 ish–28): She is nesting. Uterine lining thickens and progesterone rises to create a comfy home for a potential fertilized egg. Her body holds onto to water and nutrients. She can feel fat and bloated. If there is no fertilized egg, progesterone crashes, she sheds her uterine lining, and her body resets back into the Menstruation Phase.

While she is trying to Balance her personality back to "her normal self" or trying to practice "Equanimity" (more on this later), just know she is dealing with all of this. I make fun of my wife because on one random day, I may tell her a joke and she thinks it's gross. The next week she will tell me an even dirtier joke, and she thinks it's funny. Female phases anyone? Am I just supposed to accept this emotional vacillation? Apparently, if you want to love a female, the answer is yes. You have to love all of her.

In case males really don't know: not all females are in the same phase at the same time. She isn't linked to the moon. However! That may not be entirely accurate either. Get this! If you live in a house full of females and feel like you are getting ganged up on once in a while, I'll tell you WHY! Because females, who stay in close proximity to one another, can actually change their cycles and sync up! Ok for real, some female named Martha tried to prove this theory back in the 1970's but her findings were not accepted. WHY? They may tell you the scientific reasons, but I think it's because smart people figured out that you can't actually tell men this and not have them freak out. I'll hold all the rest of my jokes.

Oh, and don't unbuckle your seat belt yet because it gets better! A female is born with a finite amount of eggs. She does not produce more in her lifetime. Every time she goes through her Ovulation cycle, she uses one of her eggs. Somewhere around age 50 (give or take many years) she will exhaust her eggs, and these phases will stop. Guys are thinking, "this sounds like solid news." Don't get too excited because once she has exhausted all her eggs, and these monthly phases are no longer necessary, her body changes again. Males are gripping this book even tighter now. Really? Yes. She goes through menopause. Shouldn't this be called womenopause? Not sure WHY the men are getting the brunt of that one. I'm joking. The term actually comes from the Greek word "men" which means "month" and the Greek work "pausis" which means "cessation." So menopause translates from Greek as "monthly cessation."

Fortunately women do all of this because if men were the ones who gave birth there would be six of us. (Joe Rogan joke)

Who will have the hardest time with this?

People with a strong need for certainty. WHY? Because all we are certain about is, she is going to change.

Delta men. WHY? Because they are realistic and have a more "black and white" view, when it comes to viewing the world. Someone who has spiking hormones may not be realistic on any given day and with no notice! Oh, and it's not her fault. You try dealing with hormones and see how you like it.

Analyticals. WHY? Because you are so logical. On some days of the month, you can take logic and throw it out the window.

Alpha men. WHY? Because they need to be in charge and having an emotional moving target (with occasional nuclear level explosive capability) can prove to be challenging to his charge. Phrases like "yes dear" help in these times. Speaking of nuclear explosive capability…

STORY TIME!

Once upon a time I had a French foreign exchange student. She was 14 years old when she came to live with me, in Florida. One day she came to me crying her eyes out. I thought she had witnessed a murder. She was hysterical. I kept asking her "what's wrong" in two different languages, trying to get an answer. Finally, she told me that tomorrow is her brother's birthday and she forgot to get him a card. At first I was shocked at the disproportionate (key word) level of upset this girl was, in relation to the problem. Then (typical man response) I go into solution mode. I asked her if we could send him an e-card. She burst out crying again and said "no."

I'm not used to this level of hysterical and I agree to help. I take her to the store, buy the birthday card she wants, and then we head to the shipping store. I forget the actual cost but it was something ridiculous like a $3 card and $197 overnight shipping to France. I don't know how this became my $200 problem, but since I don't want to deal with any more hysteria today (and I can't imagine what I would be dealing with tomorrow), I pay the $200. I figure this is the cost of my peace and sanity. Everyone is all smiles when we send the card on its way…or so I thought…

The next day my phone rings at 9am. It's the shipping store. The store clerk asks me "What country did you want this card to go to?" OMG, my eyes widen like saucers. "You mean to tell me the card is still at your store?!" I said. The man replies "Yes, because no one indicated what country it was supposed to go to." I can feel my blood starting to boil. I told him the hysterical nature of the 14-year-old girl I had to deal with yesterday and went on to tell him that he was going to have to tell girlzilla of the mistake. He declines and then I realize I am going to have to deal with the impending level 10 hysteria when she finds out her bother didn't get his card. After all, she was a complete and utter mess yesterday when we still had time to fix it, but today?! Today is his actual birthday and this may be a whole new level of hysteria. She is going to explode!

So, I go into her room and ask her to sit down. I told her I have bad news. She looked at me intently and I said, "There was a mix up at the store and your brother's card didn't make it to France. It is still here, in Florida, at the shipping store." As I brace myself for the explosion she looks at me, shrugs her shoulders and says "Ok!" and she walks away.

It's hard to leave me speechless but what the actual hell just happened?! Yesterday this was a level 10 catastrophe and today it's just a shoulder shrugging "Ok?!" I call my mother and tell her the story. My mother simply replies, "Welcome to hormones in girls."

I like to say "raising boys is easy. It's like having little buddies. Raising girls, is actual parenting." Speaking of parenting…

CHILDREN

When children are misunderstood or are not encouraged to be the unique person they are, they may get raised in an environment which may conflict with their WHY NATURE. Since children have a limited ability to do anything about it, they may develop behavioral problems.

If you have a child with behavioral problems the best thing you and the child can do, is become a student of WHY. This way parent and child learn WHY they do what they do, and their WHY. You both learn the child's YOUR WHY NATURE (who they really are inside) and you can figure out the best way to raise that child. We can learn WHY there is conflict in the house and everyone can work towards understanding. Once the child understands their WHY, they may alter their behavior and stop acting out.

Understanding creates Tolerance, Tolerance creates Acceptance, and Acceptance creates Peace.

"One Love, one heart, let's get together and feel all right. Hear the children crying! Hear the children crying!"
~Bob Marley ("One Love")

BIRTH ORDER BALANCE STORY

I know a person who was born a Youngest Child; however, her sister—only 18 months older than her—wouldn't relinquish her Only Child role. In order to maintain the Only Child role, she developed a convenient sense of helplessness which was enabled by her parents. So the Youngest Child was forced to be independent, similar to an Only Child role. Because of this the Youngest Child got out of Balance and felt like she didn't have a childhood. Even though "not feeling like one had a childhood" is typically reserved for a First Born Child, it happened. This continued through teenage years and made the Youngest Child feel more and more out of Balance. If I told you she played singles tennis and got very, very good at it, would you be surprised? In order to stop this dynamic the Youngest Child (once she was old enough) moved halfway across the country.

After she moved away she refused to let anyone take care of her. She insisted on becoming smarter, better, and stronger so she wouldn't need to be taken care of. Her circumstances and upbringing turned her into a strong woman. People in this position will either focus or fold. She decided to focus, become strong, and independent.

Today she finally feels like she has someone (her husband), who takes care of her. Letting her husband take care of her was a struggle. She had to allow him to do it but now that she has, this inner child has surfaced. The inner child acts like a six-year-old Youngest Child. She is rebellious, challenging, hippocratic, attention seeking, difficult, and does not listen to reason. Her and her husband have had many discussions about WHY. This alter ego inner child who was acting out was given a name. "Hippa" because she is a hippocrate. The couple is not ignoring Hippa when she comes out. The husband is not yelling at the wife saying, "stop acting like a child" or ignoring it and hoping it goes away. The husband is inviting Hippa to come out and explain WHY she is acting out.

Side note: feminine energy is beautiful but also chaotic. The husband should just put his arms figuratively, and literally, around his wife and say "let it out, let it out, let it out, I'm here for you, you are safe, let it out." Eventually this inner child will cleanse and Balance will be restored. Once this happens another level of beautiful trusting relationship will happen. This is how couples get stronger, and as we discussed earlier this is the mirror in your face that a relationship offers.

In retrospect, after she moved away Hippa was protecting the adult. Hippa wouldn't let anyone take care of her and pushed people away. She refused to settle. 30 years later, Balance is being restored.

Remember: Balance knows no time. Remember this story in the chapter "Associations, Triggers, and Demons."

IN VS. ON

Let's say you are a shoemaker and you want to start a new company, making shoes. When you start a new business you have to work "on the business" in order to get the word out there and generate new business. You may work on marketing, you may go around to places that sell shoes to ask them to sell your shoes in their store, and you may set up meetings with people who can be influential in getting your company off the ground.

Once those efforts take effect and generate business, you have to work "in the business." Once orders start coming in, it's time to roll up your sleeves and start making shoes! Now you spend all your time making shoes. Since you are not working on marketing anymore, the orders start getting less and less. Once the orders reach a dismal level, we have more time on our hands, so we start working on our marketing again. We start knocking on doors and setting up meetings with influential people. Once again the orders start rolling in, so we go back to our factory and get back to work making shoes. We spend so much time making shoes, and filling orders, that we are neglecting the marketing, door knocking and meetings, so (once again) the orders start fading away. So we start knocking on doors… and you get the point.

What are we talking about here? Balance! We have to Balance our time working "on the business" with the time working "in the business" or we will generate this roller coaster effect of income. If you have a business partner whose job is to handle marketing and sales and the other business partner is in charge of production and filling orders, we have found Balance. One person brings in all the orders, and the other person fills all the orders.

Remember the chapter Capacity? The 8th suggestion of "ways to create more Capacity" is by creating Balance. Well I ask you, how much more Capacity does the shoe business have once they Balance their marketing and production? Probably a lot.

The same thing happens with your life. We spend so much time "in our lives" that we forget to work "on our lives." We need to have a life by design. Creating Balance in your life means you work "on your life" as much as you are "in your life." What do you think would happen if you cut the people out of your life who were capacity suckers? You know who I am talking about. The people you have an unBalanced relationship with. You only speak to them when you call them. They only call you when they need something. That person. How much more time would you have without that person in your life? How many more well rested nights would that bring you? This will increase your Capacity to have more Balance in the relationships that you should be focusing on. You're welcome.

Some people give everything they have to their professional life and neglect their personal life. Meaning they get all dressed up, they are attentive at work, they are detail oriented, they remember things on their calendar, and they put a lot of effort into their work. Then when they get home, they want to "sign off," disconnect, and recharge their batteries. They take off their nice clothes, throw on old sweat pants, women may put their hair up and remove their make up, men may wash the product out of their hair, they have no attention to detail (like leaving clothes around the house), the laundry hasn't been done, their home is not clean, dishes are in the sink, dinner hasn't been planned, and you get the idea.

They give all of their capacity to work. Their relationships (spouse, kids, family) get the leftovers. Maybe they just want to chill on the couch or "just be left alone" because they need their "me" time. Putting more effort into your professional life than your personal life is not healthy (because your life is out of Balance) and your relationship probably has an expiration date. If I have just described you, then you might want to make sure your spouse is on board and they Balance you out. Said another way, look at where both of you are on Maslow's scale and figure out how to Balance each of you being on different levels.

Balancing a relationship where the two people are on different levels of Maslow's Hierarchy of Needs takes a conscious effort. Your relationship needs to Balance, in order to survive. Balance can happen from something as simple as both having a lot of understanding and compassion or it can be as complex as having frequent Strategy Sessions. More on Strategy Sessions in the next chapter "Relationships."

I asked a workaholic friend of mine "what percentage of commission do you make?" He replied "20%." I asked him "how would you feel if you found out one day you were only working for 10%?" He said, "that would be terrible." To which I replied "then I suggest you go home with some flowers and make your wife feel special before she leaves and takes half of everything you have worked for." Find Balance or find a divorce attorney. Pick your hard.

If you are a workaholic make sure your spouse understands you are putting that much effort into your professional life. You both should agree on your lifestyle, or you are making a difference in the world and your spouse is being selfless, or you are making amazing money and are setting up future generations with your wealth (just remember once again your spouse is being selfless because they are putting kids and future generations ahead of their/your relationship.) Make sure you pay attention and work on your relationship. Understand when your spouse shows signs of being out of Balance! If the non-working spouse's Love Language is Gifts, you just got off easy!

By the way, this goes both ways. What is the opposite of workaholic? An MA personality? I don't know but if you stay up late, drink too much, party too much, show up late for work, don't do your work assignments on time, and are tired at work, then your job probably has an expiration date. I am not here to judge. You do you. Just make sure your spouse is on board with the financial roller coaster that lifestyle brings or your relationship may also have an expiration date.

PRO TIP: The more severe your action to get back in Balance, the more you left your Balance unchecked. This is a sign that you are living "in your life" more than you are working "on your life."

LIFESTYLE CREEP

Lifestyle Creep is when you start making more money and new things start to show up. The old car goes away, and the new car shows up. The 2 bedroom house goes away and the 5 bedroom house shows up. When we get to higher levels of Lifestyle Creep we get a bigger house, another house, maybe a third house, a bigger boat, another car, better wine, Michelin star restaurants, more toys, take another trip, and use Lifestyle Creep to fill your need for uncertainty. Some people are saying, this sounds really good right now. Yes it does sound fun; however, the problem we don't realize is there is an end to this road. When you have a massive yacht that is the size of a floating city and are opening $20,000 bottles of DRC on a Tuesday night, you have reached the end of Lifestyle Creep. I remember an interview with Will Smith when he said something along the lines of "when you have bought everything on this Earth that you could possibly want and there is absolutely nothing left that you want to spend your money on, you realize what is left… it's just yourself." At this point there is just you. Who else has this same feeling in common? Extremely poor people. They can't afford housing, boats, cars, wine, toys, trips, and maybe not even food, what do you have? Just yourself.

Guess what we just did? We have come full circle and found Balance. Yin and Yang symbol anyone? It's the same as when we are born our parents put us in diapers and then when we are very old, we may be back to wearing diapers.

To those who are saying "I have no sympathy for the billionaire who has bought everything they could possibly buy and is bored with life," I can tell you two things 1) you don't have a lot of money and 2) you are right in the middle of that circle, feel like you are on a financial treadmill, and may be living at, or above, your means. How is my aim?

I heard an interview with a very rich man and he said, "This year my goal is for my company to do 10 billion dollars in sales, for me to do 1,000 push-ups in a row and I want to be able to run a marathon in (some crazy fast time I forget what the number was.)" Let's translate. I fill my need for uncertainty through my overachieving need for growth and I am insatiable. The problem with this is, these accomplishments are just distractions from the truth. What is the truth? He is not whole as a person. WHY? Because he hasn't looked inward yet.

PRO TIP: Fill your need levels internally, not externally. You're welcome. This goes for people of all financial classes. The poor have no choice and neither does the uber rich Will Smith.

Oh and the billionaire? Stop trying to fill your need for uncertainty with your finances. You can't do it. Stop before you have exhausted all the positive uncertainty life can afford and you venture into negative uncertainty. What is negative uncertainty? The class 4 experiences: things that are not good for you, nor good for other people. This will bring down all you have built. Don't do that.

BALANCE WITHIN YOUR WHY

WHY don't all Alphas act the same? WHY don't all Gammas act the same? WHY don't all MT's act the same?

The answer is because you are finding Balance within yourself. Rob, what the hell did you just say?

Let's use as an example: a Gamma who is an Expressive? Their Balance is so far out on the end of the limb, they don't know if they should stop or fall off. They need so much attention, think they are better than Alphas, and are overbearing. WHY? Because they are trying to Balance their personality type with their social hierarchy. The only way to do it is with excessive behaviors.

What about an Amiable who has just raised their need for significance to a 9? That is the nicest "go pound sand and leave me alone" you have ever heard in your life.

What about a socially awkward Omega (or Gamma) who has a strong need for connection? They are trying to Balance this out by signing up for dance classes, etiquette classes, and learning about fashion. WHY fashion? Because up until now their wardrobe was a hodge podge of mismatched colors and it wasn't attracting the romantic partners they are interested in.

Wait until you meet an Alpha, who is an Amiable. Wow! The Balance is something to watch. The Alpha will run you over and get what they want, while the Amiable dials down the aggressive nature and makes sure you feel happy and supported. You won't know what hit you.

What do you have inside you that you are trying to Balance? What actions did you take to create the Balance?

DON'T WISH YOUR LIFE AWAY

To close this chapter, I want to discuss one of the most important of Balances, your life. It is easy to say "Once this happens then I will be happy" or "I can't wait until this happens." If you are going to get a bunch of money one day and you think your life will be much better after you get it, then you may not enjoy your life in the meantime. Don't constantly look forward to some event at the expense of the moment. WHY? Because people who do this miss out on the precious time between now and then. Even worse it can be addictive. You may fall into the trap of constantly looking toward another event. People who do this are not happy with their lives right now. They are incomplete. They are unfulfilled. If you do this frequently then you need to figure out how to be happier now. That moment in the future, or the event that is going to happen at a later date won't make you happy…I promise. There are plenty of millionaires in therapy or taking anti-depressants. If you ever say to yourself "Once this happens then I will be happy" you are delusional. Having a baby won't make your relationship better and it won't make you happier with yourself. All it will do is temporarily distract you from your relationship with your significant other, or even worse distract you from your relationship with yourself. The real problem with people that wish their life away is, wherever they go, and whenever they get there, they will figure out they brought their incomplete selves with them.

People who have an obsession, will eventually feel their life is out of Balance. A workaholic, an Olympian who trains all the time, a professional athlete (currently or training to be), or anyone who wants to excel in a particular area and is obsessed with it. Anytime one prioritizes one thing over the rest of their lives, the more they neglect the other parts of their life. Don't wish your life away also means saying "once my business is established, I will be happy" or "once I win the gold medal, I will be happy" or "once I make the pro level team, I will be happy." Choose to be happy and grateful now for what you do have, not what you don't have.

PRO TIP: Relationship Balance comes from prioritizing your romantic partner. When couples do not put one another first, this can cause relationship problems. This includes prioritizing your

relationship over your other family and your children. Parents die and children eventually move out of the house. If romantic partners don't prioritize one another then once everyone is gone, and it is just the two of you, then your relationship will be lacking. I am not saying prioritize at the expense of the children. Give children the parents they should have, but not at the expense of your relationship. Well Rob, how do I do that? Find Balance.

A takeaway from this chapter is to remember Balance knows no time. Remember the stories I told in Birth Order? Where years later I defended my son and nephew? That Balance happened years later. Another example would be getting closure, or justice, years later for something that happened.

PRO TIP: The highest form of being out of Balance is guilt and lack of forgiveness. Always remember there are two things you can't take back 1) things you did and 2) things you said. Think before you act and if that little person on your shoulder is saying "don't do that" or "don't say that," you might want to listen.

WHAT ABOUT YOU?!

If you are reading this chapter that means you haven't put this book down. Let's work on you for a minute. Maybe you have never done this before and I want you to feel what it's like. You are halfway done and I want to take a minute to say, "I am proud of you!" I want you to take a minute to go look in the mirror, smile really big, and say to yourself, "I am proud of you!" Meaning: you are proud of you! Say "I (your name) am proud of you!" to yourself. You may be surprised how that feels. You are working "on yourself" and "on your life" and not just reacting to what life throws at you. It's ok to be proud of yourself. It's empowering and contagious! Seriously, put the book down and go do it...I'll wait.

CHAPTER 302:
Communication

Let's understand the way we Communicate. You should know me by now. I am going to pick on everyone and everything so…

Let's have some fun with the English language!

Can you read these correctly the first time?

1. The bandage was wound around the wound.
2. The farm was used to produce produce.
3. The dump was so full that it had to refuse more refuse.
4. We must polish the Polish furniture.
5. He could lead if he would get the lead out.
6. The man decided to desert his dessert in the desert.
7. Since there is no time like the present, he thought it was time to present the present.
8. A bass was painted on a bass drum.
9. The dove dove into the bushes.
10. I did not object to the object.
11. The insurance was invalid for the invalid.
12. There was a row among the oarsmen about how to row.

13. They were too close to the door to close it.

14. The buck does funny things when the does are present.

15. A seamstress and a sewer fell down into a sewer line.

16. To help with planting, the farmer taught his sow to sow.

17. The wind was too strong to wind the sail.

18. Upon seeing the tear in the painting, I shed a tear.

19. I had to subject the subject to a series of tests.

20. How can I intimate this to my most intimate friend?

There is no egg in eggplant, nor ham in hamburger, neither apple nor pine in pineapple, and no science in conscience. English muffins weren't invented in England nor French fries in France.

If we explore English's paradoxes, we find that quicksand works slowly, boxing rings are square and a guinea pig is neither from Guinea, nor is it a pig.

WHY is it that writers write but fingers don't fing, grocers don't groce and hammers don't ham? If the plural of tooth is teeth, WHY isn't the plural of booth, beeth? One goose, 2 geese. So one moose, 2 meese? One index, 2 indices? You can make amends but not one amend? If you have a bunch of odds and ends and get rid of all but one of them, what do you call it? I have no idea.

If teachers taught, why don't preachers praught? If a vegetarian eats vegetables, what does a humanitarian eat? People recite at a play and play at a recital? Ship by truck and send cargo by ship? If noses run, what do feet do? Drive on the parkway and park on the driveway. WHY isn't scrupulous the opposite of unscrupulous?

How can a slim chance and a fat chance be the same thing? A wise man and a wise guy are opposites, right? Your house can burn up as it burns down. You fill in a form by filling it out and an alarm goes off by going on. WHY doesn't "Buick" rhyme with "quick?"

COMMUNICATION

We take our ability to Communicate effectively, for granted. After reading this isn't it quite amazing that we can Communicate at all?

WHY are these all spelled the same but are pronounced differently?

- Cove
- Clove
- Move
- Love
- Glove

If these all sound the same, WHY are they spelled differently?

- Kite
- Bite
- Might
- Fight
- Height

WHY are these words pronounced differently when they all have the same "ear" in common?

- Ear
- Bear—based on "ear" this should be pronounced "beer"
- Beard—Bear'd? Did you get eaten by a Bear?
- Fear—good
- Pear—should be peer
- Hear—good
- Heard—Should be hear'd. Yes, I hear'd what you said.
- Heart—based on "heard" this should be "hurt," based on "ear" this should be "hear't"

WHY are these words pronounced differently when they all have the same "one" in common?

- Bone
- Zone
- Done
- Gone

WHY are these words pronounced differently when they all have the same "all" in common?

- Tall
- Tallow
- Allow

- Swallow
- All
- Pallet
- Wallet

Try to read this correctly the first time:

> With a bead of sweat I head out in the heat with the bread. I thought I was deaf but I heard the leaf for real, then I saw the snake taking a break and freaked when I read "brake ahead." WHY the zeal Beau, what's your deal? Leap clear off your seat and leave in peace for this realm of Earth by the beach is already heaven called a seaside.

Now read that again and realize how many times you needed to compensate for the inconsistencies in the English language with "ea" words.

WHY do we have one word which can have 3 different meanings?

Like the word "bank."

It can be a place one puts their money

Turning a plane

The side of a lake

How about some quadruplets that sound the same?

bi, buy, by, bye

cense, cents, scents, sense

praise, prase, prays, preys

Well Mr. Wright, am I right when I write about the rite of communion?

Can someone please tell me the irony of the 2nd longest word in the English language, which is "Hippopotomonstrosesquippedaliophobia?" I'm serious, it has 36 letters. What does it mean? It means the fear of long words! This is how stupid we are!

WHAT IS THE POINT OF ALL OF THIS?

The point is, language is the medium we use to Communicate and it is difficult to use. More difficult than we realize. We are compensating daily for the inconsistencies in our language. Let's add to this dialect, accents, people who speak faster or slower than you, regional slang, people who do not have the same first language as you (who are trying to speak your language) and we have a lot to contend with. Every language has the same struggles.

English is one part of America can sound very different than in other parts of America. French in Canada is different than French in France. French in northern France is very different than French in the rest of France. So different that many people in the north of France cannot even understand people in the rest of France, and vice versa.

What about Spanish? The words spoken in Puerto Rico are not always the same as the words spoken in Cuba. In fact, they can be VERY different…be careful! What about Spain? Spaniards may speak with what sounds like a lisp which is a pronunciation feature called "ceceo." The letters "z" and "c," when placed before "e" and "i" are pronounced with a "th" sound, which emulates the sound of a lisp. The English equivalent would be the word "sister" pronounced "thister." It sounds beautiful when spoken but it is very different than all other Spanish. There is an old legend that a former King of Spain was born with a lisp, so the courts, government, and eventually the people started to lisp so the King did not feel embarrassed, but there is no proof to back up this claim.

These languages were derived from Latin. So picture this: Latin speaking nomads moved away and settled in different lands. They didn't have cell phones, internet, nor a way of Communicating unless they traveled to each other's lands to visit or trade goods. Over time these isolated cultures, separated by terrain, developed their own words, their own slang and their own inventions, which they named. All along the other cultures had no idea of these changes.

Through the years the original Vulgar Latin in one area started to sound different than the Vulgar Latin or Medieval Latin in another area. Then these lands got invaded and conquered. The conquering forces brought their own language to the area which strongly influenced the way people spoke in that area. Today as much as 15% of French has Germanic influence. Some words from Scandinavia and even Dutch (from trading) are still used in French today.

The point is, these languages were not of intelligent design. They are a mix, a hodge podge, and a forced collaboration, passed down from one uneducated person to another, for centuries. Let me ask you a question: what did your great great grandfather do for a living? Have any idea? No? Well guess what, that was only 4 people ago! Imagine the mess that was passed down over the last 2,000 years! This is the language we have to work with today.

WHAT CAN BE DONE ABOUT IT?

In 1634, Cardinal Richelieu founded the Academie Francaise (French Academy) for the purification and preservation of the French language. WHY don't we have this in modern times for English and other languages? Clearly, we need it!

I would call for someone to purify the English language, and all other languages for that matter! For example: WHY, in Spanish, are there about 40 conjugations of the verb "comer?" This seems excessive. I would love for people to keep their own language so we remember where we came from; however, in order for people to unify and become one, we should all have a universal language. Maybe sign language as an example. Something everyone can learn and use to communicate.

Ok Rob, WHY are we talking about all this? The reason for this chapter is the same reason for this book. Understanding brings tolerance. Tolerance brings Acceptance. Acceptance brings Peace. We have to have quality Communication in order to have Understanding of one another.

EFFECTIVE COMMUNICATION

Rules of effective Communication: Be clear, Be concise, Be respectful, Actively listen, and Adapt to your audience.

Tone and Inflexion

Tone and inflection change the way the listener receives information. Say a sentence with your voice getting higher and it sounds like a question or weakness. Say the same sentence except at the end have your voice getting deeper and it sounds like a command, or strength.

Try this sentence as an example: "Is that it?"

When you say that with the Inflexion of your voice going up, it sounds like you are confused or asking for more. When said this way, the listener may feel empowered like they are in charge. Aka you are weak, or coming from a position of weakness, and they are strong.

When you say it with the Inflexion of your voice going down it sounds like you are underwhelmed, disappointed, or have more expectations. If you add a little extra Tone on the word "it," the listener may feel like they are in trouble. Thus giving the impression you are strong, or coming from a position of strength, and they are weak.

Need a visual? Imagine you are serving food and the person you are serving is asking "is that it?" When you imagine this scenario they probably have their Inflexion going up. Just by the Inflexion you feel as if they are weak, asking for more, and you have the upper hand/are in control.

Now imagine your boss came to you and said "Is that it?" Their voice Inflexion was probably going down and they may have added a little extra Tone. Your reaction may well be to think you didn't do enough. The boss has established the upper hand.

Use Tone and Inflexion to convey the feeling you want to convey.

Speak clearly in words that are not easily misunderstood

Incorrect word choice is another way to be misunderstood. For example, let's say you are at a restaurant and need a knife. The waiter walks up and you say:

A. Can I get a knife please?

B. May I have a knife please?

C. Will you bring me a knife please?

Of the three "Will you bring me a knife please?" is the best and most effective form of Communication.

This is WHY:

"Can I get a knife please?" literally means "Do I have the ability to get out of my chair and get myself a knife?"

"May I have a knife please?" literally means "Am I allowed to have a knife?"

"Will you bring me a knife please?" is perfect. It denotes the person "you the waiter," the action "bring," the direction "to me," the subject "a knife" and the respect "please."

Now you may be saying "All of the above will work, Rob." The guy is going to bring you a knife regardless of which one you say. Maybe. The point I am trying to make is not in the semantics of this example. When you choose your words correctly and clearly as in # 3, you are less likely to be misunderstood. This lessens the chances of miscommunication and how often the world has to compensate for our inability to command our language. The skill of choosing correct words is a superpower.

If you want to Communicate effectively do not use pronouns when speaking. Instead of saying "then she said this" say "then Sally said this." Note: this has nothing to do with what pronouns Sally identifies with. It has to do with effective Communication. Saying "Sally" instead of "she" is clearer and more effective.

When it's very important that someone understands, also say it a different way

This technique is a really good one. If done correctly and fluently, it will greatly improve your Communication skills and no one will even know you are doing it. Unless of course they are a student of WHY. If they are, they will appreciate it. Here is how it works: let's say I want you to trim a five foot tall hedge down two feet. By the way…how many people read "I want the hedge trimmed down _to_ two feet" and how many people read "I want the hedge trimmed two feet?" Now you know WHY it is important to clarify, and this technique is the way to do it!

Here is what I would say to make sure I communicate effectively: "Please cut two feet off of this hedge, so when you are done it will be three feet tall." Do you see how I just did that? I said the exact same thing in two different ways, which reduces the chances of a miscommunication. I gave direction going down (trim off two feet) and going up (it will be three feet tall when you are done.) That is literally and figuratively going both directions!

Other examples:

I want you to take all of the bottles off of that wall. So, when you are finished, there will be none left. I mention the task I want done and what the finished product will look like.

The cost of the job is eighty dollars? So, If I give you a $100 bill I am getting back $20 in change, right? I mention how much it is and how much less it is than one hundred.

You have 10 children in your class. You want me to take 6 of them to the gymnasium, and you will keep 4 of them right?

When effective Communication is very important: Ask the other person to repeat what they heard

This section is as easy as it sounds although it is very easy to sound rude and/or condescending when using this technique. A good way to effectively Communicate is by saying: "Listen, I don't want to be rude but what I just told you is very important so to make sure we didn't just have a miscommunication. Please repeat what you heard me say." You may be very glad you did. With kids, this is pretty much a must. Especially with boys.

The other day I had a conversation with my highly Analytical teenage son which went like this:

Me: Your 6-year-old cousin is hungry (basic term), will you go to the store and get her a sandwich please? (clear objective)

Son: What kind of sandwich?

Me: She likes turkey with cheese.

Son: What if they don't have turkey with cheese? (Hear the Analytical here? "What if" are two of their favorite words)

Me: Then get her chicken (clear objective). If they don't have either call me (since I know you were about to ask another "what if" question, I'll predict behavior and get ahead of it.)

Now I also know Analyticals can get paralysis from analysis, so I went on to finish the conversation by saying...

Me: Let me be perfectly clear here, do not come home without something to eat for this child. Now please repeat what you heard me say.

Son: Turkey with cheese, otherwise chicken, if neither call you, and under no circumstances come home without food for my cousin.

Me: Perfect! Thank you!

PRO TIP: Anytime you are speaking to a child about something important, it is a good idea to follow up with "Now repeat what I just said." If they can't, you know they weren't paying attention. Know your audience and your life will be easier.

The good news is, as I said in the beginning of this book, once you understand human behavior you can then begin to predict behavior. I knew based on the personality of the person I was talking to (my highly Analytical son) there is a chance he would have looked for turkey, and then chicken, found neither, and come home without food. By predicting behavior, I got ahead of this by clearly reiterating the goal.

Listen for the answer

When you expect someone to say something (EBR) it is easy to mistake what they said, for what you wanted them to say. In other words, your EBR can trick your mind into hearing what you wanted to hear. Make sure you do not hear what you want to hear. Start with a blank page in your mind when someone is answering your question and really listen for the answer.

Some people purposely try to divert the dialogue onto another topic so they can avoid answering the question. When you ask a question that someone doesn't want to answer, they may purposely try to distract you from the topic. Listen for the answer and try to determine if the person answered your question with their response. If not ask them again. If they don't answer the question the second time you ask, you may have more to discover than you expected.

I received a suit (the kind you wear, not a lawsuit) in the mail, that I had ordered online. A co-worker heard me complaining that the suit was about 2 sizes smaller than what I ordered, and it didn't fit. A few hours later we were discussing Communication skills and I told him to ask me what I thought of my new suit. So he asked, "What do you think of your new suit?" I replied "I'm pissed man. The damn thing does not fit me!" I then asked him if I answered his question. He replied "Yes." I told him that actually I did not answer his question. I actually answered a question that had not been asked, which was "How do you feel about your suit arriving in a size smaller than what you ordered?" I then told him that I love the suit and think it is beautiful. That is actually what I thought of the suit and that is the answer to the question he asked. Now had I not communicated that effectively, he would have left the conversation thinking I did not like the suit and may have shared that with other people. This is how miscommunication occurs and a snowball of problems can begin. This is a great segway to…

Answer the question, then give color commentary

You ask a question to a friend: "How do you like your new car?" Friend's response: "It is amazingly fast!" Did your friend answer the question? No he didn't. He seems to like the speed of the car, but he has not actually told you if he likes the car or not. Let's say we ask again "Do you like your new car?" His response this time: "Well the interior is kind of cheap and it has broken down a few times, which makes me angry. Also because it is amazingly fast, so it does not get good mileage and is very expensive to drive. I like the color though." Now he has answered the question. If we didn't listen for the answer in his first response we may have told other people that your friend really likes his new car. When he talks with the same people and tells them what he really thinks of the car everyone may be wondering WHY you told them what you did…including the car owner himself! Do you see WHY this method of communication is so important?

Example of "answer the question before you go into explanation"

Question: Robert, did you pick up the book from the store?

Poor Communication: I put it on the bookshelf. (This is color commentary only implying an answer.)

Good Communication: Yes I did and I placed it on the bookshelf. (This is better.)

Superior Communication: Yes I picked up the book from the store and I placed it on the bookshelf.

Answering the question first and repeating the question you answered before giving commentary, is ideal.

Listen to the specific word choices

If I say: "He said five things about that guy and he had nothing positive to say." My question to you would be "How many negative things did he say?" Five right? After all if he said five things and none of them were positive then obviously they were negative right? No. Absolutely not. Listen to what I said and the word choice I used without jumping to conclusions. Listening without jumping to conclusions is a big factor in Communication. I said "…he had nothing positive to say." That means exactly that: "he had nothing positive to say." What if he said things like: "he was very tall" and "he was punctual." Listening is a superpower.

Here is a fun one:

"What do you *think*?" compared to "How do you *feel*?"

If I ask you "what do you *think* about that car?" What type of person am I? An Analytical. What am I asking you for? A logical response. I want to know statistics, test results, and your logical point of view. All that because I used the word "think" instead of "feel?" Absolutely! An Analytical doesn't care how you feel (especially when they are low on emotion) when they are trying to weigh pros and cons.

If you answer a person that used the word "think" with "it's pretty," "I really like the color," or the highest form of miscommunication, "I really have a good feeling about it," just know they stopped listening and are probably rolling their eyes.

On the other hand, if I ask you, "how do you *feel* about that car?" What type of person am I? We don't yet know but we can rule out Analytical. WHY? Because their thought process, and decision making, is based on feelings and intuition, not logic.

If you answer me by telling me how fast the car can do the quarter mile, the fuel economy compared to others in its class, and what the average life expectancy of the car is I probably won't hear a thing you said. WHY? Because I don't care about that. Because I really want to know how you *feel* about it. Do you like the color? Does the interior *feel* cozy? Do you have the *feeling* that I am doing the right thing? If you are having a bad *feeling* about the car, I probably won't buy it. When someone starts a question with "what do you *think?*," start your response with "I *think*." If a person starts a question with "How do you *feel?*," start the response with "I *feel*."

Manners

This is part of the "Be Respectful" (self-explanatory) rule and an important part of the "specific word choice" category. WHY? Because manners establish intentions. Someone's interpretation of your intentions is more important than the words you choose to communicate with them! If people think you are disrespectful, rude or insincere, they shut down and stop listening. Manners indicate whether your intentions are to be polite or rude. Words like: Please, thank you, excuse me, Sir, Ma'am, Hello, and Goodbye.

Communicate your feelings and expectations as you go, not all at once

Don't hold in all of your feelings in until the only way you Communicate is by exploding. This is common with people who avoid confrontation, and have a problem being assertive. Amiables and Betas listen up.

PRO TIP: People who have a problem being assertive are typically aggressive with people they know, so the people they know think they are assertive with others. It's an example of Bad Pride. Just be yourself without trying to cover it up.

If you struggle with confrontation, being assertive, or maintaining boundaries consider Strategy Sessions in your relationships. Because people are not mind readers. In the upcoming chapter Relationships, I explain "Strategy Sessions."

Speaking down or poorly to someone when they have violated your expectations, is unacceptable. Speak to people nicely regardless of how you feel. Be polite and courteous even when you don't want to be. People with a need for significance and people with low capacity will have the hardest time with this but we all need to do our part to have tolerance, acceptance, and peace.

PRO TIP: People tend to get aggressive when they cannot properly articulate themselves. You wall punchers know what I mean.

Tell the truth

This one is very obvious yet extremely important. Lying is not effective Communication. I admire Knights of the old days. When you were sworn into Knighthood one of the vows you took was telling the truth. You took a vow to tell the truth even if it meant your own death! That purity is amazing. Always tell the truth to the best of your ability and understanding of the matter at hand. People may not like what you have to say, especially if the "truth" happens to be your opinion, but they will respect your ability to do so. Just to clarify: if someone knocks on your door and asks you where you hide the cash in your house, you do not have to answer the question! Use good judgment. Unless it's me, then I will use the cash to buy us a good wine, and we will both be happy!

Speak correctly

Enunciate your words. Ladder and latter are pronounced differently. Differently has a "t" in it and it needs to be pronounced. Make sure when you say the word "for," it doesn't sound like the word "fir." The word "that" also has a "t" at the end, pronounce it. People, especially intelligent people, tend to speak quickly and in doing so they tend to sacrifice correct pronunciation. At first, it will feel strange when you hear yourself enunciate but push through that strange feeling. When you take time to properly say each word, you are actually speaking at a proper speed. Speaking correctly is a superpower. When you do, you will begin to notice how poorly others speak and it is empowering. Especially for those with a strong need for significance.

I messages

I messages are a very important form of Communication. What is an "I message?" It means when you want to Communicate how you feel, start the sentence with "I."

Examples:

- I would like to go to the store, what would you like to do?
- I feel this way when this happens and I would like to speak with you about it.

Look at the difference between "I messages" and "you messages":

- "You keep doing this and it makes me mad."

When you start a sentence with "you" it is accusatory, off-putting, and you invoke someone's pride. They may feel the need to defend themselves. This leads to a debate about the subject, rather than an understanding. It can also lead to a discussion about the way you speak to people, rather than the subject at hand.

Don't anticipate

Too many times, I see people anticipating what the other person wants, and then reacting to it. Sometimes they have the first part of the conversation inside their head, overthink it (hello Analyticals), and then only verbalize the 2nd part. People are not mind readers (hello Amiables). Just like with "I messages," say what you want so it is clear.

I had a conversation with my wife this morning and it went like this:

Her: Honey, I have to go to the doctor today to have that small procedure done, but you don't have to come.

Me: So, you don't want me to come?

Her: No that's not it, I would like you to come.

Me: Then WHY did you start the conversation by telling me I don't have to come?

Her: Because I didn't think you wanted to come so I was being nice.

So, what happened here? I know my wife is an Amiable and many times I have to dig deeper into what she is saying in order to understand her message. One of the problems with Amiables and Analyticals is they anticipate what they think you want and then act on their assumption. The problem with that is people aren't mind readers. If when she said, "You don't have to come," I responded with "Ok, I'll stay home," what would have been the result? The result would have been, she really wanted me to come and I really wanted to be there to support her, but she would have gone alone. Neither of us actually got what we wanted. Read that interaction again knowing when she started the conversation I was in my secondary Analytical personality, so I had a lot of questions and needed more information. If I was in my primary personality the Driver probably would have just replied with "Ok, I'll stay home".

PRO TIP: If you find yourself asking your partner "WHY are you so difficult to speak to sometimes?" It is because each of you toggle back and forth into your primary and secondary personalities.

An "I message" is designed to remind us to get the original thought out of our head, in a way that doesn't come across as aggressive, accusatory, and confusing.

How could this Communication have happened with an I message?

Her: Honey, I have to go to the doctor today to have that small procedure done, and I would feel much better if you were there (even add the real reason being that she was a bit scared) but if you don't want to come, that's ok. This is a clear message and a good example of: "I would like this, what would you like?"

In the chapter "Relationships" I am going to mention not guessing or anticipating what the other person is looking for in a romantic partner and acting on that anticipation. Think back to this chapter when you read that because it's the same concept.

PRO TIP: If the other person doesn't understand what you were trying to Communicate (assuming they were paying attention, speak the same language, and were ready for you to say it), it's your fault. There is no debate here. If this happens this is a signal for you to work on your Communication skills.

SELF TALK

If you had someone follow you around all the time, saying negative things to you, what would you do about it? Would you separate from this person? Would you ask them to stop? Would you make them stop?

On the other hand, what If I told you that you could have one amazing friend for the rest of your life, and you can never get rid of them? How would you treat them? How would you talk to them?

Well that's you. You should be your best friend. Treat yourself well. Date yourself (if you don't currently have a romantic partner), get yourself a birthday/holiday present, and most importantly talk to yourself well.

Your brain doesn't know the difference between what is true and what you imagine. Your brain believes what you repeatedly tell it, and what you focus on. After all, you are literally telling it what to think. We need to decide who is in charge, you or your brain? The more emotion you attach to these thoughts, the more it gets anchored into your nervous system.

WHY is this important to you? Because this is the lens in which you view the world.

WHY is this important to the rest of us? Because when you see something, encounter something, or meet someone new you may not be seeing it, or them, for what they are. You may be seeing what you want to see, hearing what you want to hear, or labeling something before you have given it a chance. We cannot have true understanding this way and are more likely to miscommunicate.

Our brains are wired for survival. Remember when I said in the chapter Bringing YOUR WHY NATURE All Together, that you are the product of 4096 people? Well some of those people didn't know when they were going to eat next, some starved to death, and ran from tigers. Our brains are wired for survival, not happiness. We have to override some of the thoughts that our brain comes up with and replace those thoughts with positive self-talk. If you do not tell your brain what to think then it will go off on its own.

Self-talk becomes thoughts. Thoughts become feelings. Feelings turn into actions. Actions become YOUR WHY. Change your thoughts and change your life. If you just said to yourself "yeah but that's hard to do." That is your wake up call to change your self-talk. Replace that self-talk with "Ok, I want to be in charge and live my life by design, I can do this!" That's what I'm talking about.

If you don't actively control your thoughts, ask yourself WHY not? Seriously stop and think about it for a minute. WHY not? If your answer is, "you can't actually do that," then you are right. If your answer is, "I can do that," then you are right. You can't do it if you think you can't do it. Again, change your mind and change your life.

Speak to yourself with positive self-talk and it will reshape you. Say it with emotion and it will reshape you faster.

PRO TIP: Don't say what you *don't* want, say what you *do* want. Don't say "I will not lose." Instead say "I will win." We should not have positive self-talk from a negative point of view.

When the little runner man in your head (we are going to talk about him more in the chapter Associations, Triggers, and Demons) brings you a file that is unacceptable, you need to tell him that is not what you want to focus on.

Remember the first paragraph of this section?

If you had someone follow you around all the time, saying negative things to you, what would you do about it? Would you separate from this person? Would you ask them to stop? Would you make them stop?

Think of it this way. If we were about to have dinner and I started showing you disgusting images, you would tell me to stop, right? Then WHY don't we do this with our own brain? After all, do you want to be an emotional slave or do what to have a life by design? Most of your behavior is subconscious. WHY? Because we are not taking control.

One of the hardest things we can do is self-regulate. What is self-regulating? Think of it as the little guy on our shoulder who says "don't do that," "that wasn't very nice of you," "I like the way you did that," "that was very mature," "good approach!," or "you did a great job and I'm proud of you!" After all, the little guy should see the good, and not so good things we do objectively. Listening to your conscience is also self-regulating; however, your conscience typically only helps with morality. We want to be more active in our self-regulating, every day. Don't say things like "well with my luck it will never work." Don't put yourself down, even as a joke.

Want to know WHY The Law of Attraction works? Because you are telling your brain what to focus on. The brain doesn't know the difference between real and imagined. Visualize the outcome you want, like athletes do, and your brain can help make it happen. You literally attract what you focus on, because your brain will filter through messages to find things which validate your thoughts. Manifesting outcomes starts with self-talk.

When you talk to yourself you are telling your brain what to look for. If you are thinking about buying a red car, your brain will filter out the millions of messages it receives and send all the red cars to the front for you. If you keep thinking people are rude your brain will find all the rude people. If you keep thinking, and repeating to yourself, there are so many good people in the world, your brain will find proof of that. Your brain receives millions of messages every minute and it filters out the things you are not interested in. In short, you see the world the way your brain is trained to filter it. WHY not actively change our filters to see all the good and the beauty?

Bob Marley believed words like "you," "me," "they," and "them" separate people. Bob (and other Rastafarians) used words like I and I, in the belief that we are all one. It's not a U-nity thing, it's an I-nity thing. This self-talk makes the world a better place for I and I.

Before you go to a friend's house, self-talk and give your brain tasks to accomplish. Meaning, tell yourself what you want the outcome to be. I want to find reasons to compliment my friend, I want to notice what is different about her home, and I want to leave there tonight with a stronger bond than when I arrived. How do you think your visit would change if you guided your brain to accomplish this?

A form of Self Talk is the messages you allow into your brain

Watch what Communication you take in on a regular basis. Poor messages disguised as entertainment are something to watch in particular. Negative movies, songs, and television shows are good examples. Garbage in, garbage out.

Self-deprivation

Self-talk includes self-deprivation. When someone gives you a compliment, just simply say "thank you." Do not get into the habit of dismissing, downplaying nor ignoring the compliment. As we will discuss when we talk about "Equanimity," the compliment does not define you, nor does it need to change your state of mind. Self-deprivation is a form of bad self-talk because you are minimizing yourself. If you feel you are not worthy of a compliment, you have other soul searching to do. Don't put yourself down nor minimize your contributions in order to make someone else feel better. Don't lessen yourself to level the playing field. Amiables are most prone to this; however, I am talking to everyone. There is a difference between healthy humility and unhealthy self-deprivation.

PRO TIP: It's ok to joke about something you did but never about something you are. Example: I didn't make enough food for an event I hosted. I can't say to myself nor others "I am a bad host." I can say "I am voted most likely to starve my guests." Again, it's ok to joke about something you did. It's not ok to negatively joke about something you are. Remember there is truth in every joke!

Talking to children

I talked about this in Birth Order. It is so important, I am going to mention it again. In this chapter I talk about self-talk and how it has an effect on you. Well now I am going to tell you, the way you speak to your children, has a huge affect on them.

If you want to raise an overachiever and hyper successful child, then listen up. The number one reason a child grows up to be a hyper successful adult…the number one reason…is this:

All hyper achieving adults (from world leaders to rock stars) have one thing in common: When they were children their parents (usually the parent of the opposite sex is most influential here) had an unconditional belief in the child's ability. That's it. The way you speak to your child when they try to do something, or ask if they have the ability to do something, is key.

Examples:

Little boy comes to his mother and says "Mommy, I am going to be an astronaut one day!"

Mom's optional replies:

1. That's not very likely, honey. Only very few special people accomplish that.

2. Well, that's great honey, but maybe you should take accounting too, so you have something to fall back on.

3. You will be the best astronaut ever.

Ok let's break those responses down as to what the child heard:

1. The child heard my mom doesn't believe in my abilities. The child's reaction is to have less belief in themselves.

2. The child heard my mom doesn't believe in my abilities, so if try something in the future, I should always have a plan B. How do you think this translates to decision making and relationships?

3. My mom believes in me! I must be able to accomplish anything I set my mind to!

I said "My mom believes in me" because in the example the child was a boy. If in my example the child was a girl, the father is most influential, and I would have changed the narrative.

If you are a parent who replies with option 1, then you are much more likely to raise a loser and/or a kid who struggles with self-esteem. Hey Rob! That wasn't very nice! First of all, I said you are not going to like everything I write. Secondly, it's not mean and it's not "not nice," it's not good and it's not bad, it is just reality. Some people are losers and some people are winners. It is what it is. The way their parents spoke to them and believed in them when they were children, or didn't believe in them, played a big factor in this.

PRO TIP: Not all millionaires are geniuses, and not all geniuses are millionaires. So what is the difference between rich people and poor people? The way you think! That's it! Change your mind, change your life! Some people are saying "well Rob, it also has to do with opportunities given from birth." I'll be sure to tell that to Oprah when I meet her. Oh and if you are the one who had that thought, this is the red flag to change your self-talk.

If you are the parent who replies with option 2, then you are likely raising a wishy washy, noncommittal, and apprehensive child who will have difficulty achieving. If they do achieve, they overcame the poor start you gave them.

If you are the parent who replies with option 3, congratulations on giving your child the best emotional start a child can have. Your belief in your child's ability is huge for your child's emotional development. Again, simply have an unconditional belief in the child's ability. That's it. Now reflect back on your childhood. What did your parents reply with and how did it impact you?

CHAPTER 303:
Relationships

Let's discuss romantic Relationships first because they are one of our highest forms of connection. Initially we may choose someone because they are attractive, because they seem nice, because they may be fun to be around, or because they appear to be "normal." These are perfectly acceptable reasons to consider them for a Relationship; however, if you want the Relationship to last, we need to understand your partner's WHY NATURE and WHY NURTURE.

If your Relationships don't last and you want to know WHY, I can tell you it's because you are choosing someone based on the exterior wrapper and not understanding the depth of the person they are on the inside.

Throughout this book I have repeated "Understanding creates Tolerance, Tolerance creates Acceptance, and Acceptance creates Peace." The problem with meeting someone new is we like how they look, how they present themselves, and who we think they are. When this happens, in which stage are we in? Acceptance. We cannot, cannot, cannot skip Understanding and Tolerance and go straight to Acceptance. It is like building a house on quicksand. You have to have a foundation.

The reasons Relationships don't last is because we start with Acceptance, which many call the "infatuation phase." Once we are with them for a few months we start the "discovery phase," which means we start to Understand what is on the inside. If we don't fully Understand or do not Tolerate what we are discovering, then we can no longer have Acceptance and the Relationship stops. The Relationships that work start with Acceptance, then go back to Understanding, then create Tolerance, then advance to Acceptance and then the Relationship will have Peace.

Hey Rob! How do I know what is on the inside and if they are a good match for me? Funny you should ask! Keep reading…

PRO TIP: Choose your partner out of emotion but keep your partner out of logic. WHY will be instrumental in the logic part. Choose not to listen to this advice and you will pay the price!

The most important part of a romantic Relationship is to be yourself. When first meeting someone it is normal to want to put our best foot forward, but we should not misrepresent ourselves. This is who I am, and this is who I am not. Be genuine. If you think someone won't like you if they find out who you are, then they are not the right person for you anyway. Do not make the mistake of thinking you know what someone wants in a romantic partner (Analyticals and overthinkers listen carefully) and changing yourself in advance to be that. First of all, it's not your true self and it is exhausting. Remember in Communication we discussed "I messages?" Same principle here. If someone doesn't like who you are pretending to be, you may miss a great opportunity, because they may like the real you. If someone likes you for who you are pretending to be, and the Relationship starts under false pretense, it will have an expiration date. So just be yourself and the Relationship has a much higher chance of success.

You should not want a wife, you should want to be a husband and the wife will come. You should not want a husband, you should want to be a wife and the husband will come. Note: Throughout WHY I am using male and female Relationships in my examples because men and women have a harder time understanding one another. In same gender relationships, you should have the advantage of already understanding your same gender. Whether you prefer a different gender or same gender Relationship, understanding the personality type of your preferred partner is paramount. Tailor the message for your situation. I just don't want to type every different variable each time.

If you want your Relationship to last, and not just contribute towards the high divorce rate, then you have to love your partner for whom they are and they have to love you for whom you are. If you want to love them, then you have to love all of them; however, you may not always like what they do. Since you already know WHY you like them (aka are in the Acceptance phase), let's discuss WHY they (and you) might be challenging in a Relationship.

PERSONALITY TYPES

Their Personality Type will tell you how they are going to behave. Understand them, tolerate them when they are difficult, and accept them for who they are. When you get really good at understanding, you can begin to predict behavior. This will make your Relationship flourish.

A Driver, in Driver mode, is going to need understanding and leeway when they are less than pleasant. Review all the things Driver's do for a more complete list but just to name a few: being demanding, short, intolerant, forceful, and impatient are solid Relationship stressors.

An Analytical is going to be difficult when they are slow to make decisions, hard to carry a conversation with, when they need more and more and more information, or when they think you need more information than you do. Let's face it, you chose your romantic partner for emotional reasons and Analyitcals are low on emotion! Remember when an Analytical makes a decision, you can be sure they feel they made the right one. That's if you are still around by the time they made up their mind.

Expressives are just Expressives. If you don't have a strong Need for Uncertainty, you may want to reconsider this Relationship. If you have a problem with your partner being the center of attention all the time (even if it means going to annoying or shocking levels of behavior), you may want to reconsider this Relationship. If you have a strong Need for Uncertainty, and have found other people to be boring, date an Expressive. They are anything but boring. You better hope you don't ever change your strong Need for Uncertainty, because just like I wrote in the chapter "YOUR WHY NATURE" the Expressive won't ever change. Ever.

Note: watch out for people who fill their Need for Uncertainty in negative or unhealthy ways. Males typically referred to as "bad boys." I don't know what the term would be for females. Expressives and Gammas may fit this description. The short term dopamine hits associated with these people may fill your need for uncertainty because they are fun and exciting, but this falls into a category 4 behavior (not good for one and not good for everyone else.) As we will discuss in the chapter "The Negative Wave," it is easier to do negative things to fill one's Need for Significance and Need for Uncertainty, than positive things. Then again you already know this so I am just wasting my breath, right?

Amiables are fantastic people because they want you to be happy. They can be a pain in the butt because they won't make a decision. They are afraid if they make a decision, you may not be happy with it. Ask an Amiable what they want, and the answer may be "whatever you want is fine." It can be annoying when you are trying to make them happy. Since they struggle with boundaries you may find yourself being protective of them or sticking up for them. If you are in love with an Amiable you have a responsibility not to take more than you give, from this Relationship. The Amiable will give a lot, all the capacity they have and sometimes more. Understand your partner and identify when they are giving, at their expense, or are low on capacity, to make you happy. If you support them, identify their behavior, and validate how fantastic they are for feeling they need to give so much to the Relationship, they will love it. If you to outwork them to make them happy, they will be forever loyal.

SOCIAL HIERARCHY

Their Social Hierarchy will tell you what they need.

Alphas want to take over, probably want to be Significant and want to be treated accordingly. Validate them, don't try to cage nor limit them, don't be an anchor in their driven life, nor hold them back. I touched on Alpha Relationships in the chapter "Alphas and Sigmas and Betas Oh My!"

Sigmas are highly intuitive so be honest from the start and don't misrepresent yourself. I mean, duh, you should always do this but especially with a Sigma because they will know. If you have friends who are not actually friends, they will also know. They are charming, charismatic, and persuasive which can be alluring, but you may have to contend with this if you are a jealous person. Not because they are not trustworthy, it's because others will also find them charming, charismatic, and alluring. They need their space and can be solitary so don't expect them to mingle well in large crowds. If you, or others, are not authentic they are quick to cut people out of their life. This may include your friends, which can cause tension in your Relationship. If you are not genuine, or violate their clearly defined boundaries, they will quickly show you the door regardless of how attractive you are.

Betas are submissive and typically in the background. If you enter into a Relationship thinking they are going to change, they aren't. If you are going have an issue with people who lack confidence and have unclear boundaries, then this Relationship is not for you. If you aren't going to be happy when your partner gets manipulated and avoids conflict, then you are the problem. WHY? Because a Beta is a Beta. If you have compassion for them, love them for who they are, help them fit in, show them respect, tell them they are good enough (especially if their Love Language is WOA), and reassure them when they get jealous, they will be very loyal companions.

Deltas are your average people. You may have been attracted to them because you found them attractive, have a solid job, are competent, and realistic but you soon realized those traits come with a price. They are reserved, introverted, lack drive, lack ambition, happy to let you (or others) be in charge, can be boring and are content to be average. If these traits frustrate you, then you are the problem. WHY? Because you didn't know what a Delta is, and you entered into a Relationship with someone you don't understand. If you met a highly attractive Delta and think because they look above average, all of them is above average, you are in for an awakening. You have to separate the exterior of a person, from the interior. The outside wrapper may be beautiful, but on the inside they are very happy being average.

Gammas may have taken you for a ride. WHY? Because their extroverted, interesting, adventurous, and rebellious nature seemed alluring. Maybe they were different than anyone else you had a romantic interest in. Because they challenge Alphas, you may have mistaken them for an Alpha. Then one day you witnessed an Alpha made them fold and the Gamma showed their insecurity by avoiding conflict. If this was a problem for you, then you are the problem. WHY? Because they are a Gamma and this behavior is scripted. Gammas have an inability to compromise, so be prepared to deal with that too. Gammas and Analyticals are voted most likely to be a "conspiracy theorist." Understand your partner's social hierarchy and accept them for who they are. Gammas may suit a partner with a strong Need for Uncertainty, or another rebellious Gamma, but don't mistake them for Alphas. Misunderstanding ones social hierarchy can be a recipe for disaster.

Omegas are nerdy. You are not going to mistake them. Their confident, high self-worth, introspective and reserved nature may have attracted you, but once you found their introvert, quiet, socially awkward and emotional underbelly you may have been surprised. They are very capable people and may end up being very financially successful. You just have to love them for all that they are, and they will be good partners.

MT OR MA? UNDERSTAND YOUR PARTNER

An MT will be driven and doesn't want you to get in the way. They want you to be supportive of their drive and desire for whatever they are Moving Towards. This may include having less time for their family because they are busy achieving.

MA people lack motivation. If you feel like you have to nag your partner, or if they call you a nag, they are an MA. MA's can be difficult on a Relationship because they are less likely to pull their weight. If you find yourself making excuses for your partner's lack of results, your partner is an MA.

Pro tip reminder: the only time an MT will appear to be an MA is a young person who is still in school. WHY? Because they haven't yet found the prize they want to Move Towards which is money.

THE SIX BASIC HUMAN NEEDS

Understand where your partner's need levels are. Embrace their need levels and help them raise or lower their need levels if you see them struggling (you will see it before they do.) Remember this is the easiest category to change.

Violating someone's need for Significance is the best way to invoke their PRIDE and have them react (sometimes harshly.) This can include making fun of them, telling them they are unworthy, telling them they cannot do it, telling them they are less than, etc. If the person's Love Language is WOA, it will negatively impact them more and their reaction may be harsher. If they are a Sigma, you are likely to get cut out of their life with little or no warning. If you violate a Beta or Amiable's Need for Significance, they are more likely to internalize it and try to let it go. It will hurt their feelings but they probably won't react, or even say anything, because they lack boundaries. If a Beta, or Amiable, is your romantic partner, you may find yourself standing up for them (a lot.) If you do stand up for them, they will be loyal partners. If you don't want to stand up for them, reconsider this Relationship.

PRO TIP: Every time your partner doesn't communicate and just "lets it go" that is a paper cut. Most marriages end because of too many paper cuts. Encourage your partner to speak to you. Betas, Amiables, and Alphas will need the most encouragement, for different reasons.

Your behaviors can violate someone else's Need for Connection, Need for Certainty, and Need for Love all in one action. Examples include: everything from not making time to see them (especially if their Love Language is Quality Time) to cheating in a Relationship. Tony Robbins says "when you fill three of more needs with one action, it will become a habit." The same works in reverse. When you violate multiple Needs with one action, it will have a greater (negative) impact on the Relationship.

CAPACITY

You should understand your partner's Capacity level, and they should understand yours. If you are a C1 train wreck and your partner is a cool, calm and collected C3, then that is the Balance within your Relationship. Your partner should know you are going to need their Capacity…a lot. You should be conscious of how much of a drain you are on their Capacity and under what circumstances their Capacity begins to diminish. Once you see that happen, back off and give whatever Capacity you have, to them. If the roles are reversed, then understand in many circumstances your C1 partner isn't going to be much help to you. If the male is the C3, the woman will respect him. Women have a need to respect their partner and men want to be respected, so this dynamic works our very well. Being the superman who comes to her rescue will help fill his Need for Significance. If the woman is the C3 and the man is a train wreck C1, she will not respect him and the Relationship has a very low chance of success.

If you both are typically a C2, when you come home from work you each should discuss your current Capacity level. The script goes like this: "Hi honey, I love you so much and am so happy you are home! What is your Capacity level?" Just like that. You two hopefully add up to 100% or more. If your partner is at 10% and you can't give 90%, be smart enough to be careful around one another that night. No deep conversations and no important decisions, just love and reassurance. If you both are at 50%+ Capacity, then it's business as usual. If you are both at 80%+ Capacity, then take that opportunity to cook a new dish, try a new restaurant, file your taxes, talk about changing insurance policies, bring up important life decisions and/or take that opportunity to discuss what could be better in your Relationship. WHY? Because that night you both have the Capacity to handle tough situations.

LOVE LANGUAGES

Their Love Language will tell you the way they receive Love. The way you want to give Love is irrelevant. You are in the service industry. Give Love per your partner's Love Language. Period. If you change romantic partners, you may well be changing the way you give Love. Period. Ignore this and you will pay the price!

If your Love Language is Acts of Service and you are in a Relationship with an MA personality, you two are going to have challenges. WHY? Because the AOS person wants AOS and the MA person doesn't ever want to do them. If the AOS nags them into doing something, and the MA person finally does the task, it loses its luster and the AOS person doesn't feel loved. You two are a tough match.

If your Love Language is Acts of Service and your partner's Love Language is Words of Affirmation, then you have the opportunity to have a good reciprocal Relationship. Every time your partner does an AOS, you in turn use your words and tell them how special it made you feel and how much your partner means to you. The WOA person will keep doing AOS so they can get your Words of Affirmation! Balance achieved!

Any time your partner does something to fill your Love Language, you can take that opportunity to remind yourself to fill their Love Language.

PRO TIP: If your partner's Love Language is Physical Touch (most men have PT as their primary Love Language) and the PT person has a greater sex drive than yours, you actually have a great opportunity on your hands! If your Love Language is Acts of Service (as an example) and every time your partner does an AOS you have sex with him, guess what is going to happen? That man will be outside cutting the grass, washing your car, emptying the dishwasher, painting the house, and may become a home improvement expert. WHY? Because he wants his Love Language filled and sex is the highest form of physical touch. If you are saying "but I don't want to have sex that much!" Well guess what, he doesn't want to cut the grass either! If you both are going to behave that way then I suggest you give your local divorce attorney a retainer and let them know when your sexless marriage is over. Might as well have your Realtor on speed dial too to tell them when your dilapidated house with the overgrown front yard is for sale. Good luck! Oh, and please don't have kids.

Don't take what I just wrote the wrong way. As I mentioned before, Relationships are not tit for tat; however, you both should try to "out-Relationship the other" and do what you can to make the other person feel loved. After all, you are in the service industry, correct?

Poker players have a saying "when you sit down at the poker table, if you don't know who the sucker is, it's you." This goes the same for Relationships. If you can't see the good, along with the potentially not so good in a potential romantic partner, then you are the sucker. And just like in poker, you will pay the price if you don't throw your bad hands away. What can you do about it? Become a student of WHY! Maybe one day we will have Relationship counseling and open a poker school.

THE LAW OF DIMINISHING RETURN

In any Relationship the Law of Diminishing Return plays a factor. It is best explained with a real life example. Story time! I used to have a housekeeper. She charged me an hourly wage and cleaned my house in about 4 hours. At one point I noticed there were parts of the house (we will call them X,Y and Z) that were not part of her normal routine. One day I asked her, can I pay her for a 5th hour and during that 5th hour she would focus solely on the X,Y and Z items that were not in her normal routine? She agreed and the first time we tried this experiment, it worked out great for both of us. So great that I asked her if we could change the normal routine to 5 hours and include the X,Y and Z items every time. She agreed. In the following months she stayed for 5 hours and cleaned the house, including the X,Y and Z items. All good.

One day, I noticed the X,Y and Z items were no longer being done, yet she was still collecting for 5 hours. I asked her about it, and she said it was taking longer for her to do everything. She suggested a 6th hour, so she can do everything. Being empathetic, I agreed to the 6th hour but specified I wanted the X,Y and Z items to be taken care of. Once again she agreed.

Next thing I knew, the quality of her work was going downhill and not only were the X,Y and Z items not being cleaned, but the rest of the house was starting to suffer even though I was now paying for 6 hours. Once again, I asked her about it and she said she would take care of it. The correction lasted for a short while and then the poor quality of work returned. Next thing I knew, she approached me asking for a raise! I was flabbergasted since I thought I was already paying market rates, the quality of her work was below expectations, and I was now paying for 6 hours instead of the original 4 hours. I apologized and told her that I could not meet her request for a raise. She told me her request was non-negotiable, so we agreed to part ways.

This is the essence of the Law of Diminishing Return: over time, people become complacent, entitled, take things for granted, expect more while giving less, or otherwise lose enthusiasm for their Relationship and the effort put into the Relationship begins to deteriorate. This applies to all Relationships, romantic, business, personal, or otherwise.

At the beginning of the Relationship write down what you want in a romantic partner and how you think this person fills that role. Write down what you like, admire, and respect, about that person. Also what they do well that you want to see more of.

PRO TIP: If you can't fill out these pages in the beginning, this is not Relationship material. If the only thing you wrote down is "they are really attractive," this is not Relationship material. Every six months grab that piece of paper and see where your Relationship actually is versus how it started. I heard a fun story about a couple, who are both lawyers. Every January 1st they sit down and renegotiate the terms of renewing their marriage for another year. Cute and effective.

PRO TIP: If you do the same things to keep the Relationship that you did to get in the Relationship, the Relationship has a much higher chance of success.

Loving someone is one of the hardest things you can do because a romantic partner is like a mirror in your face. They know you better than anyone, in some cases even better than you know you. They know how to push your buttons (hmmm maybe ask yourself WHY do you have buttons in the first place?), they may be the only ones who can trigger you and with them you are the most vulnerable.

If you want your romantic Relationship to have the greatest chance of success you have to, have to, have to, learn who you are and accept yourself. They have to learn who they are, and accept themself. Then you have to understand one another (hey I know a book that can help!), accept one another, and love one another for who you each truly are. Once that is done, you are in the service industry. It is your job to see that person is loved, fulfilled, and cared for. You are not responsible for their happiness. Everyone is responsible for their own happiness. You both have to put in effort because once again to quote Chris Rock "two people can move a couch real easy." When the other person doesn't carry their weight, it is next to impossible.

PRO TIP: When you are in a Relationship you form a 4-handed circle (his two hands and her two hands) and you only discuss your Relationship with one another. There should be no outside influences unless your Relationship needs professional help.

Hey Rob! This is all great stuff but I like people with nice arms, or great legs, or a good sense of style. To that I say, ok good! I want you to be attracted to your romantic partner. What I also want is for you to stop having a new Relationship every 6 months, (wasting your life) trying to figure out your compatibility. I also want married people to finally understand one another and rekindle their Relationship. If you are currently in a Relationship, this chapter will shed some light on WHY it's working, WHY it's not working, or what changes you and your partner may want to consider.

Thinking about getting divorced? Let me tell you what is going to happen. You are going to go on the "divorce diet" and get in better shape. You are going to make some other changes to your appearance, like get a new hairstyle or finally get that mole removed (you nazty), that you have been putting off. You are going to make an effort to get out of the house to go on dates. You are going to meet people, be on your best behavior, get caught up on current events, learn new jokes, laugh at their jokes, and be really nice to a potential new romantic partner. You are going to work on your triggers, your issues, your traumas, and your demons. You are going to work on your versatility by trying new things and experiencing the things that new potential romantic partners enjoy. Most importantly, you are going to get really good at WHY NATURE and WHY NURTURE so you understand your next partner. By the time you are done with all of that effort, you are going to be an unrecognizable better version of yourself. So here is my question: WHY don't you just put all that effort into your marriage? Because if each of you were doing all of that now, you wouldn't be getting divorced. You're welcome.

PRO TIP: When do you get divorced? If someone cheated, or otherwise violated your minimum standards, then you have something to hang your hat on. When you are alone at night in your new place (listening to Jewel's "You were meant for me") wondering if you made the right decision, you will have something to hang your hat on. But! What if no one did anything "wrong?" What if you just grew apart? (Aka: Death from 1,000 paper cuts, no Strategy Sessions, and otherwise poor Communication). When is the right time to just say I have had enough and I am leaving? The answer is: when the other person stops trying. As long as the other person is trying, you stick it out and try harder. If you want to know what divorce is like I will tell you with one sentence: the other day I got home at midnight, the good news is no one gave a damn, the bad news is no one gave a damn. Whichever you focus on is what divorce is like.

I want new Relationships to succeed, I want current Relationships to finally understand each another, and I want to drastically reduce the divorce rate. We can do it!

RELATIONSHIPS WITH YOUR FAMILY, INCLUDING YOUR KIDS

These Relationships are a bit more difficult. WHY? Because you don't get to chose your family! No returns and no exchanges! What is the old saying people say to children? "You get what you get, and you don't get upset!" LOL. If you want to have a good Relationship with anyone you need to learn YOUR WHY and THEIR WHY. If you want to have a good Relationship with your parents, siblings, children, or extended family then you better get really good at WHY. WHY? Because, unlike a romantic partner Relationship, your family will always be your family. For how long do you want to struggle in your Relationship with them? When would now be a good time to learn their WHY?

Here is the hard part: children are not going to learn their WHY until they get older. So you need to compensate for their lack of understanding of their raw/unevolved nature during their childhood. The beautiful part about kids is they show their WHY NATURE in a beautiful and raw way. It can be difficult to parent, but watching children in raw form is a great learning tool.

Here is the other hard part: your parents (and those of their generation) are going to get set in their ways. They may revert back to their unevolved/raw WHY NATURE and lose their filter, just like children. You want to love them so you compensate, rationalize and put a lot of effort into making that Relationship work.

For the kids and the parents: understanding their WHY NATURE creates tolerance. Through tolerance we can have acceptance. Through acceptance we can have peace. Hmmm, I have heard this before somewhere.

The parent/child Relationship is very important. Hopefully you had children for the right reasons and both parents plan on being involved in the children's lives. We discussed parental influences on children in the chapter Birth Order, and we are going to add to it here.

You can't choose your family but since you have an obligation to give your children the best start in life that you can, listen up! Let me clarify this statement. First of all, when I say "best start in life that you can," I don't mean financially.

If you are a new parent, here is the best advice you can follow:

1. Love your kids unconditionally and provide for their basic needs.

2. Like your kids conditionally: explain to them that there is a minimum standard of behavior in life and they need to maintain that minimum in order to get attention from Mom and Dad. I am a big fan of "time outs." Don't hit your children.

3. Financially it doesn't matter what you give children. I have to watch what I say here because I don't want it to be misinterpreted. I mean: it doesn't matter if a kid has 10 toys (they will want 11) or 20 toys (they will want 21.) It doesn't matter if you have an average car or a brand new Rolls Royce. It doesn't matter if you drive somewhere to go on vacation or if you fly on your private jet, as long as you have family time. Whatever you do, kids will assume that is normal. Whatever you give children, they will want more. It's in our nature to take and be self-centered. We don't start learning sharing and selflessness until ages 3 to 5 years old. For some people, it takes a lifetime and for others it takes a little longer. Children can have gray hair. As long as the children are provided for, don't worry about "keeping up with the Joneses."

4. Know your child's WHY and use WHY to bring out the positive attributes inside them. Help them understand the personality traits they struggle with.

When I say the best start in life, I mean teaching them to be a good human.

PARENT/CHILD DYNAMICS

If you are a Delta and you are raising an Alpha, you cannot raise them by your realistic ideals. It won't work.

If you are an Alpha and are raising a Beta, you may be frustrated because their behavior is not like yours.

If you are a conservative person with a Need for Certainty and your child is an Expressive, you are going to have a tough time with their behavior. Just like I said in the romantic Relationship section: let's read this again:

Expressives are just Expressives. If you don't have a strong Need for Uncertainty, you may want to reconsider this Relationship. If you have a problem with your partner being the center of attention all the time (even if it means going to annoying or shocking levels of behavior), you may want to reconsider this Relationship. If you have a strong Need for Uncertainty, and have found other people to be boring, date an Expressive. They are anything but boring. You better hope you don't ever change your strong Need for Uncertainty, because just like I wrote in the chapter "YOUR WHY NATURE" the Expressive won't ever change. Ever.

If you gave birth to an Expressive and are not used to their behavior or don't like their behavior, there is little you can do about it. In a romantic Relationship you can "reconsider the Relationship"; however, with children you cannot. They are yours and you are stuck with them. Understand this before you have kids: you have about a 25% chance to have an Expressive and all Expressive kids are Unevolved Expressives. If you are thinking, oh not my kid! My kid will be just like me. Remember you are the product of 4096 people, not just 2 people. As I mentioned in Generational Birth Order, one day we may be able to predict the personality of your unborn child, but today we cannot.

If you are an Amiable who struggles with boundaries, your kids are going to walk all over you. If you are thinking if "I just be nicer and nicer and give more of myself then one day they will realize it and they will change." You are delusional. Children need boundaries. Even in the animal kingdom, if you don't respect yourself, WHY should we respect you? The longer you let the kids walk all over you, the more harsh your behavior will have to be to correct it.

If you are an Unevolved chest beating Alpha and think you can create well behaved kids through fear, this will backfire on you. Especially when you get old, and they get bigger than you. You cannot bypass Understanding, Tolerance, and Acceptance and go right to Peace, through fear. Fear does not bring Peace, it can only bring temporary obedience.

If you are a Gamma, you do not need to teach your children your rebellious ways. They may resent you later in life.

If your child is a Sigma, and you do not understand their Lone Wolf behavior, you may push them into uncomfortable situations. Listen to your Sigma when they tell you they are uncomfortable in social situations.

If you are an Analytical and your child is a Driver you are not going to understand their lack of attention to detail, quick decision making, and high volume of mistakes (compared to you.) The worst thing you can do is compare them to you. You can say they are a lot like you, which is a good thing or they are better than you in this category, but don't compare and make the child feel "less than."

If you are a Driver and your Analytical child takes too long to make decisions, overthinks things, questions things before they act, and needs a lot more information than you, be patient with them and explain things more thoroughly than you normally would.

If you are a submissive personality and you are raising a dominant child, encourage their behavior. Let them do what is natural to them. Do not encourage them to be in the background, settle, or take a back seat. WHY? Because not only will it not work but both of you will struggle in your Relationship.

Make your children feel Significant. At a minimum let them know they are Significant to you.

Understand the parent/child Relationship is the first need for Connection they will have. Connect with them.

If both parents are a Moving Towards personality and your child is a Moving Away personality, good luck! Just kidding…sort of. You may not understand the MA child's lack of drive and having to push them to get them to do things. Just remember they are not you. Some people don't move their ass until they feel a flame three feet high.

Think about how many kids you want. If you only want one, then you should understand the dynamics of raising an Only Child (definition is in the chapter Birth Order.)

If you want a second child, realize and understand the dynamics of changing your Only Child to a First Born Child (again definitions in Birth Order.) Be conscious about treating the First Born Child differently, once their sibling is born. Reminder: the longer the child was an Only Child, the harder the transition to a First Born Child will be.

If you want a third child, then realize and understand you are changing your Youngest Child to a Middle Child. If your Middle Child is an Expressive, their behavior will be more impactful on the family. Remember this when you read The Negative Wave.

I've said this before but it is worth saying again. Children are going to be the most unevolved and raw form of their personality type. Watching children will teach you a lot about WHY people do what they do, because they are unfiltered.

Whatever you do! Do not push children into being you or like you, when they are not. As a parent you have to understand what is unique and special about them and encourage them to flourish for who they are. Don't live vicariously through your children. Their life is their life, not your second chance.

Understand the onus is on you to raise the child, since you are the adult. The child did not ask to be here, therefore they owe you nothing. Read that again.

If you don't want to understand these behavior types and just want to "wing it." I wish you the best but you may have a hard life. A life by design has a much greater chance of all parties being happy. By the way, this book makes a great gift for struggling parents (or anyone who struggles with Relationships for that matter!)

I said in romantic Relationships "You should not want a wife, you should want to be a husband. You should not want a husband, you should want to be a wife." The same applies here: you should not want a baby. You should want to be a parent. If you don't want to be a parent, do the world a favor and get a dog instead. Please.

Analyticals, people with anxiety issues, new parents, and pregnant people may be freaking out right now but you should understand one thing. You have time. Plenty of time. It is not too late to reconnect with your child and it's ok to make a few mistakes. Kids are more resilient than we give them credit for. Love, understanding, and compassion go a long way.

OTHER RELATIONSHIPS (NOT ROMANTIC, NOT FAMILY)

The messages above apply here but the good news is these Relationships are probably disposable. You can find a new boss, new employee, new coach, new student, new running mate, new team mate etc. If you want the Relationship to last then understanding their WHY, and them understanding your WHY, is very important.

Three things I want you to know when it comes to Relationships:

1. In any Relationship, one has to have a value.

2. In order to have a good, great, smooth, trusting, or exceptional Relationship the parties in the Relationship have to understand, tolerate, and accept one another. Then you will have peace.

3. We have to establish, communicate (remember "I messages" from Communication), and enforce our boundaries. Boundaries may include the minimum level of treatment we expect, the job description, the amount of pay we expect, what is expected of us in the Relationship, or the expected duration of the Relationship.

Without these 3 things in place, the Relationship probably has an expiration date.

My philosophy when it comes to Relationships is simple. No matter what type of Relationship I am in, I will out work you. I will strive to be the better spouse, the better sibling, the better employee than we agreed to, the better boss than you expected, the better parent than you are a son, the better son than you are a parent, or the better coach than you are a student. Every Relationship I treat the same way. If you can say you out Relationshiped me (yes I just made up a verb), and you are right, I will have a problem with me. Can you tell I am an MT?

Oh, and I saved the best for last.

PRO TIP: In any Relationship, the one who cares the least is in control. This really sucks, but it's true.

STRATEGY SESSIONS

If you want to strengthen a Relationship (any Relationship), or raise the chances of it succeeding, it is a good idea to have a Strategy Session. We talked about this in Balance for people who are in different areas of Maslow's Hierarchy of Needs. For those people, Strategy Sessions may be a necessity; however, Strategy Sessions are a good idea in any Relationship. Strategy Sessions create a Relationship by design, with great Communication.

What is a Strategy Session?

Once per month the parties sit down and objectively review their Relationship. My wife and I do ours on the last Saturday of every month. Whatever day you choose is fine, but it has to be on your schedule and non-negotiable. Set a time and location where all parties are free from distractions and take the meeting seriously.

A Strategy Session is an unemotional time where each of you bring pertinent information to your meeting. Think of it as a therapy session but both of you take turns running the meeting. Take turns going first every other month so one doesn't feel they always get attacked first. Again, this is an unemotional meeting to discuss three things:

1. What we are doing well.

2. What we could be doing better. Try to balance 1 and 2 out. If you can't that is a sign you are focusing too much on the good or the bad.

3. Paper cuts.

What is a paper cut? Example: my wife and I are out to dinner and she says something (or does something) that I don't like, doesn't sound very nice, or just rubs me the wrong way. Since we are out to dinner and having a nice time, now is not the time to bring it up because I don't want to derail the happiness of the evening. So I just make myself a note to bring this up at our next Strategy Session. Of course this could go the other way as well. Maybe I said something, or did something, she didn't like and she would make a note to bring it up at our next Strategy Session.

PRO TIP: This does not replace fluid communication throughout the month. If there is an immediate problem, discuss it. If you and your partner had a fight last night and are waiting until morning to discuss it (when cooler heads will prevail), then just discuss it in the morning. Don't wait for a Strategy Session. It is important to remember not to assign blame, even if it is clearly one person's fault. You are not the problem, I am not the problem; however, we have a problem. We are not trying to win, so our partner can lose. More on this in the chapter "Winning."

Throughout the month write down paper cut items, that are not immediate problems, which need to be discussed. Have the topics ready for your Strategy Session. Come to the meeting prepared and put effort into the meeting. On the day of the Strategy Session, before your meeting, read what you wrote. If you still feel the same way as when you made the note, then bring it up. If not, let it go. I did not say, let it go because you want to avoid confrontation. There is a difference. If the problem is truly no longer a concern, then put it to bed. If you still feel this way, then put your big boy pants on and speak about it. This is supposed to be an unemotional safe space to bring up paper cuts.

During these sessions we will learn our partner didn't know we felt like that, or they meant something a certain way and we received the information differently. This is cleansing for a Relationship and makes it stronger. Relationship deaths are typically caused by 1,000 unhealed paper cuts. Communication is key. This is a great Strategy to bring your Relationship back into Balance. We are not dredging up the past. Once something has been put to bed, we let it stay there. If it hasn't been put to bed, then keep discussing it. If these turn emotional then you have let something important sit too long and it has entered your nervous system. If one or both of you are getting upset, and having visceral responses from these conversations, then you are letting problems sit for too long. Remember, problems get discussed right away. Paper cuts can wait for a Strategy Session.

CHAPTER 304:
Associations, Triggers, and Demons

What is an **Association**?

An Association is when our mind connects (now) experiences with past memories. Example: Every time I smell chocolate chip cookies, I am reminded of being a child in my grandmother's house.

What is a **Trigger**?

A Trigger is an Association that evokes strong emotion(s) or psychological reaction. These are typically from significant events or traumas.

What is a **Demon**?

A Demon is a Trigger, driven by guilt. When you did something (or didn't do something, like warn someone) you feel guilty about, deeply regret, wish you could take back, or otherwise wish didn't happen, that is a Demon. The guilt haunts you, plagues you, and inhibits your ability to move forward.

WHY are we talking about Associations, Triggers, and Demons? Because they affect our mental health. Because they are an important part of how we receive, and react to, information. You are more likely to interpret behavior the way you expect it to be, rather than objectively. The goal of this chapter is to understand our Associations, Triggers, and Demons so can receive information objectively, interpret it for what it is, and then react. We want to have emotions and experience life; however, we do not want to be an emotional slave.

Think of it this way: your brain is a big file room and there is a little man inside. His job is to run into the file room, access files and bring those files to the front room, we will call the viewing center.

IT GOES LIKE THIS

Ok team, we just received a signal from nose that chocolate chip cookies are near. Runner go! The little runner man runs in the back of your brain and grabs the "chocolate chip cookie" file from the memory room. He runs back to the front room viewing center and opens the file. Now the viewing center looks inside the file and there is a picture of you in your grandmother's house. Association complete.

Ok team, another incoming signal. We have a man approaching wearing all black, he looks shady, and he is walking straight towards us on a collision course. Runner go! The little runner man runs back into the file room and grabs the "shady man wearing all black" file and brings it to the viewing center. When the file opens we see images of news reports. One dated 6 months ago, one dated 7 years ago, and one dating back to our childhood. There are news reports attached to the images. In all the reports, the victim didn't do too well. Now our eyes bug out…victim?! What do you mean victim?! The viewing center sends a signal to activate response mode. In response, we hide our belongings, veer our course a little to the right, walk in the well lit area, and look around to find escape routes. The viewing room ques the adrenaline rush and our hands start to sweat. Entering fight or flight mode we send the runner back to grab the "Karate" file. When the runner returns with the file, the viewing room has sounded the alarm. Red lights are flashing and there is a buzzer which sounds like an old alarm clock. The viewing room peers into the Karate file and sees all the pages are faded, illegible, and we can't remember a darn thing! After all, this file is old. The shady man wearing all black walks by and we notice he is wearing a hoodie from our favorite musical band. We think "hey, that guy may not have been so bad after all!" Then we turn off the alarms, turn off the red flashing lights, and consider revisiting Karate class.

ASSOCIATIONS ARE PRE-CONCEIVED NOTIONS

- Chocolate chips cookies = Grandma's house
- Shady people = fight or flight mode
- Smelling jasmine = Mom's old perfume
- Hearing a song from high school = memories of being carefree and hanging out with your friends
- Seeing a dog = getting scared because all dogs are going to bite me
- Hearing about a car crash = remembering when you were in a car accident

Whatever you focus on, your mind will find evidence of it for you, validate it, and make it real. I am not saying some of these things are not real. A shady looking person might actually have bad intentions. Maybe your mom used to wear perfume that smelled like jasmine and clearly your grandmother made some really good cookies; however, not all of our Associations serve us.

Let me ask you a question. If I start speaking to you in a language you don't understand, WHY don't you understand it? The answer is because you have not Associated those sounds with what they mean. In an effort to understand, your brain is now trying to pick up ancillary clues. You are listening to tone, voice inflexion, watching facial gestures, hand gestures, and other context clues, to try to figure out what these words mean.

- If someone laughs and points at you while raising their voice, what does that mean?
- If someone is yelling at you and clenching their fist, what does that mean?
- If someone looks at you with a frown and is shaking their head no, what does that mean?
- If someone is smiling at you and nodding their head yes, what does that mean?
- If someone gives you a hug, what does that mean?
- If someone gives you a kiss, what does that mean?

Answers: it doesn't mean anything! It only means the meaning you have attached to that behavior.

When someone does something or says something (we are considering tone, mannerisms, and inflexion… Sigmas are really good at this), our little runner man goes to the file room, grabs that file and we Associate meaning to that action or those words. The problem is they may not have meant it that way, didn't realize they were doing it, or they just weren't considering you at all when they did it. We have to understand while there are a lot of actions which many people can agree on their meaning, but that doesn't mean everyone thinks the same way you do, all the time.

Creating Association

One of the most famous studies on Association was Pavlov's dog. Pavlov rang a bell every time he was going to feed the dog. Eventually the dog would salivate just when it heard the sound of the bell. The dog associated the bell with being fed and didn't even need the smell of the food to begin salivating. This is the essence of Association. Before Pavlov created this Association within the dog, what do you think happened when the dog heard a bell ring? Nothing. Now what does it mean to the dog? Dinner! So much that the dog's brain told the dog's body "get ready to eat, I just heard a bell ring." To the point the dog salivated without there being any food. The dog "linked" the bell to food.

We are not unlike Pavlov's dog. There are certain things that happen in our lives that are our bell and consequent salivation. If you play a word game where someone says a word and you say the first thing that pops into your mind it will shed light on your Associations. If I say dog, you may say pet, if I say bridge, you might say water, if I say Golden Gate bridge you might say San Francisco, if I say leaf you might say tree, and so on. You might be surprised what you learn about yourself.

Marketers know repetitive advertising of shapes, colors, symbols, and slogans make a product a household name or "brand," as it is called. WHY do you think marketers pay celebrities to endorse products? Because seeing the celebrity invokes certain feelings within you. The goal of advertisers is to make a symbol or slogan invoke emotion and have you remember it. If they can successfully create an Association you will remember their product, which will increase sales. This is how emotionally fragile we are. Marketers call us "sheeple."

If I say Eiffel Tower, you might say Paris. If I show you a leaning tower, you might say Pisa. If I show you Big Ben, you might say London. If I say Space Needle, you might say Seattle. If I say Statue of Liberty, you might say New York. The pride you get when you look at your country's flag is an Association. The colors Associated with your state, country or your school and the slogan Associated with them i.e.: "These colors don't run," may create feelings within you. These feelings are a result of the meaning you have attached to seeing those symbols or hearing those slogans. We talk about this more in the chapter "Tribalism," that people are using our need for tribalism to create these Associations. Just remember to be careful of those who would use Association and Tribalism to negatively manipulate you, especially when it is disguised as entertainment. Note: symbols do not have to be major landmarks to create Associations, they can be any size.

Speaking of creating Association. What do you think happens if one parent always reprimands the children? The children are going to link Associations to this. One child may link up bad Associations and create a better relationship with the other parent. Another child may link Associations of respect to the parent who sets boundaries and a lack of respect to the parent who doesn't enforce boundaries. Did your parents do this with you? By the way, it is a good idea for both parents to discipline the children. If your co-parent is an Amiable, they probably won't do it (they struggle with enforcing boundaries) and you will become the enforcer. Maybe I should have put that part in the Relationships chapter. Oh well, you got it now.

Changing Association

Story time! I have a cat that did not like to be picked up and held. He Associated being picked up with something negative so he would complain and struggle to be put down. So, I decided to change his Association. Here is how I did it. When he was a few feet from his food I would pick him up and quickly put him down right by his food bowl. Once he got comfortable with that distance of travel, I would try it from farther away. I would repeat this process, each time getting farther and farther away from the food, until I could carry him a long distance to his food, without him complaining or struggling. I successfully changed his Association of what being picked up means. He now links being picked up with eating, which to him is a good thing. I replaced whatever negative Association he had with a positive one. Now I have one fat little friend! I can pick him up whenever I want, without him being upset, even though the end result isn't bringing him to his food. His Association has changed positively. First there was Pavlov's dog, and now there is Rob's cat!

You can do this with yourself, or with other people, the same way I did it with my cat. So how do we change an Association? This book isn't called HOW, but I'll be nice and give you another freebie. Example: let's say you move from one house to another and want to quickly make that house a home. You can take something from the original house, which made it a home, and apply it to the new house. Let's say the smell of freshly brewed coffee in the morning was a fond memory in the original house. Brewing up a fresh pot of coffee the first morning you are in your new house will probably bring back the same feelings you had in the original house and help make the new place feel like home. You are now transferring that Association to the new house.

TRIGGERS

Practicing equanimity helps with patience, understanding and not being a slave to one's emotions. Once you get good at it, the road from feeling content to being upset is a long road. However! There is a direct bypass from zero to upset, mad, or really pissed off and they are called Triggers! Do not pass GO, don't collect $200, just go straight to emotional jail!

When it comes to Triggers, think of it this way. You have a big red flashing button on your back and people who know you best can come along and press that button whenever they want. Once the button is depressed, you may go from content to mildly ticked, to upset, or even all the way to ready to start smacking people! Strangers, and people who don't know you as well, may inadvertently push that button but it is not intentional because they don't know what Triggers you. However, they can guess!

I was watching the Jackie Robinson movie the other day and, in the movie, the coach of the other team kept yelling racial slurs at Jackie. He didn't know Jackie at all, but he wanted to get under his skin and took a good guess that continuing to yell racial slurs was a good way to do it. Jackie handled it very well, but it was starting to affect him. Sometimes Triggers are more easily guessed, like calling a short person "short."

My 16-year-old son hasn't had his growth spurt yet and when he can't reach something, you can see that big red metaphoric Trigger button flashing on his back. Of course his older (and taller) brother takes every opportunity to tell a short joke in that moment and give him a hard time. It doesn't affect my 16-year-old son as much as racial slurs may have affected Jackie Robinson because my 16-year-old son knows being short is temporary. Jackie cannot change the color of his skin so his Trigger may have a deeper reaction.

So what do I do about Triggers? How can I make people stop pushing my buttons?! The answer is: remove the buttons. It is YOUR JOB to do "the work." Work on yourself and realize what your Triggers are and WHY. Someone calling you a racial slur is a reflection of them, not you. They need light and love. They need tolerance. Obviously because they don't have any to give.

REMEMBER THIS PRO TIP: HURT PEOPLE HURT PEOPLE

When you realize someone who is trying to emotionally hurt you is actually the one who is damaged, it changes the dynamic. They themselves have issues, Demons, and Triggers. They feel "less than," or inadequate and need to bring you down in a feeble attempt to level their playing field. People who are happy and whole, don't do that.

Realize your WHY when it comes to Associations, Triggers, and Demons. Did someone pick on you when you were a kid and now you are a bodybuilder? Did you compensate for a Trigger or overcompensate for a Trigger? Did someone make you feel unsafe, or hurt you, and now you teach safety classes? Once you connect those dots, you may be surprised. Some people are realizing their life's goal or mission, was based on a Trigger.

You have to let the Triggers go. Unprocessed emotions stay in your nervous system. Triggers can carry visceral responses. If hearing about a car crash makes your palms sweat while you remember a car accident you were in, then these Triggers are rooted into your nervous system. We have to clear the negative Associations. You have to work them out, come to terms with them, and make peace with them. You have to do "the work" on yourself, for yourself. Once you do, you are on the path towards inner peace and being whole. Oneness.

DEMONS

Many feel the only way to clear a Demon is for you to forgive yourself. Forgiving oneself may be predicated on the forgiveness of those we think we wronged. This becomes an even bigger problem if the one who was wronged, is no longer around to forgive.

Why are they so impactful?

Demons can affect our ability to fill our six basic human needs.

We may no longer feel we can be significant. It can lead to self-degradation or purposely humiliating oneself.

Demons can affect our ability to connect with ourselves, and other people. They can even make us push people away.

They can inhibit our ability to love ourselves and others.

We may not want to grow, nor contribute.

Again, these are needs, not wants and desires. When we don't fill our six basic human needs, it becomes emotionally damaging.

Even worse our certainty, uncertainty, and connection may be filled by the singular action of going to a dark place and reliving the moment which is known as "when the Demons come."

Imagine a lone wolf sigma with Demons. Think they may be more likely to seek isolation?

If you are not a religious person, then your guilt is all your own.

If you are a religious person then I am reminded of the words in the movie "Kingdom of Heaven." In the movie the king said "Your soul is in your keeping alone. When you stand before God you cannot say 'but I was told by others to do thus, or that virtue was not convenient at the time.' This will not suffice." We must always remember there are two things you cannot take back, things you did and things you said. It's a good idea to watch the things we say and the things we do, because Demons can be relentless.

At the end of the day, whatever you believe, I am reminded of the immortal words of Bob Marley "only you can redeem yourself." Maybe listen to "Redemption Song" and see what you come up with.

What do we do about Demons?

Seek help and find forgiveness. You have to clear your guilt.

"Therapy is a good thing. It does not make you weak. It does not make you broken. You are not alone. Please do not keep it to yourself. Talk to someone. Talk to your parents. If you can, talk to a therapist. Your life is always worth living. Stay with us. Don't take your light from us. We need you."

~Dan Reynolds (from Imagine Dragons)

Ok, I may have teared up when I wrote that quote. Keep up the good work, Dan. I love your music and your message. Thank you for being a good human and helping people. Now it's my turn to help with your message. Now I'm signing "It's where my Demons hide, it's where my Demons hide."

Story time!

I had a Trigger once. When I was 11 years old, I played baseball. In those days they assigned teams differently. Players stayed on the same team for two years. Half were 11 years old, and the other half were 12 years old. The next year, the 12-year-olds became 13, and moved up to the next division. The 11-year-olds became

12-year-olds. They stayed together and were matched up with a new set of 11-year-olds.

So when I was turning 11, I was assigned to play with the Cubs. I was the best player on my team and one of the best in the league. When it came time to pick All Stars, the coach told me he wasn't going to pick me for All Stars. He could only pick 2 players and he was going to give both slots to 12-year-old kids, since it was their last year in this division. Conveniently, one of them was his own kid. When I went to All Star practice, the other kids asked me WHY I wasn't in uniform. I told them coach didn't pick me and they were all shocked. This was very emotionally impactful for me.

The next year I turned 12. I played with the Cubs again and had the same coach. All season I continued to show I was the best player on the team and one of the best in the league. When it came time for All Stars, the league decided to give the first place team's coach 4 slots to choose from his team, 3 slots for the 2nd place team, and so on. Well, my team came in last and the last place team got zero slots. So I missed out on All Stars again. Once again, I went to All Star practice and the players asked me WHY I wasn't in uniform and I, once again, had to say I was not given a chance. This was very emotionally impactful for me. Again, I was 12 years old.

Let me tell you what this did to that 12-year-old boy. He developed a Trigger. A big one. For the next several decades, when I was promised something, I made sure I got it. Whenever I was promised something and I did not receive it or someone didn't hold up to their promise, they got a disproportionate reaction from me. Sometimes threatening a relationship, threatening to quit my job, and even bordering on hostile. This went on for decades. I carried this Trigger with me not knowing what a Trigger was, nor that I should do something about it. That 12-year-old had a vengeance to the world and he was ready to pounce at the opportunity.

Then one evening (when I was in my 40's) I came home while

my 12-year-old inner child was Triggered. I was upset. Really upset. The reason I was triggered is not important, just know this Trigger is now over 30 years old (and Triggers don't know time.) I was home by myself. I sat on the couch in the dark. I wanted to clear this Trigger so I started talking to my 12-year-old self. WHY are you so upset? So disproportionately upset? I don't understand. Talk to me. I imagined my 12-year-old self standing in front of me in my Cubs uniform. I could see him as plainly as I could see my current self. He was there but he wasn't there. He yelled at me. I didn't expect that. He said "I should have been on that team when I was 11! I earned it! The 12-year-olds didn't deserve it, I did! And that damn coach gave it to his son!" He went on to yell "I believed the coach, a person of authority, when he told me I would be on the team next year. Then I didn't make the team again! I deserved to be on that team again. I wanted to be on that team. I was one of the best in the league!" He was so upset. What came next really got to me. He yelled, "And nobody would help me! Nobody fought for me, nobody stood up for me, not the coach, not mom, not dad...nobody!"

Oh my, I didn't know that was in there. I was shocked. I said to him, "I understand you are upset and yes, you deserved to be on that team. What they did to you was not right. But let me tell you the results. Years later, when you go to high school, you walk off the baseball field and stop playing." The 12-year-old was shocked. I continued to tell him "You don't end up being a professional player. So had you made that team, it wouldn't have changed your outcome. Let me tell you what you did though. Because you were not on that team, some other 12-year-old was, and he needed that spot. It changed his life because he believed in himself. It gave him the self-worth he needed to have a better life." The 12-year-old stopped yelling. He smiled and then he disappeared.

Now reflect back to the stories I told in Birth Order. Let's also remember when I wrote "Balance knows no time." I now understand WHY I got in those worker's faces when they made my son, and my nephew, feel "less than." No one stood up for me when I was 12. When I couldn't stand up for myself. But the day my son and nephew needed me was not that day, and damn it, that day I had the ability to stand up for someone who couldn't defend themselves. I am no longer that 12-year-old defenseless boy. I am a tall, muscular, and highly trained Black Belt and those guys yelling at my son and nephew just called down the thunder. I think I forgot handsome and very humble in the last sentence, but we can just move on.

When I sat on the couch and had it out with my 12-year-old self it was very emotional and I didn't want to do it, but I did. That is one example of how I did "the work." My Trigger is not there anymore.

TYING IN COMMUNICATION

We discussed this in Communication and it's worth revisiting here. Your brain doesn't know the difference between what is true and what you imagine. Your brain believes what you repeatedly tell it and what you focus on. The more emotion you attach to these thoughts, the more it gets anchored into your thoughts.

WHY is this important you to? Because this is the lens in which you view the world.

WHY is this important to the rest of us? Because when you see something, encounter something or meet someone new you may not be seeing it, or them, for what they are. You may be seeing what you want to see, hearing what you want to hear or labeling something before you have given it a chance. We cannot have true understanding this way.

The way you speak to yourself, is what your brain will believe. After all, you are literally telling it what to think.

One of the hardest things we can do is self-regulate. What is self-regulating? Think of it as the little guy on our shoulder who says, "Don't do that," "That wasn't very nice of you," "I like the way you did that," "that was very mature," "good approach!," or "you did a great job and I'm proud of you!" After all, the little guy should see the good, and not so good, things we do objectively.

Thoughts become feelings. Feelings turn into actions. Actions become YOUR WHY. Change your thoughts and change your life. If you just said to yourself "yeah but that's hard to do." This is your wake up call to change your self talk. Replace that with "Ok, I want to be in charge and design my own life, I can do this!" That's what I'm talking about.

If you don't control your thoughts. WHY not? Seriously stop and think about it for a minute. WHY not? If your answer is, you can't actually do that, then you are right. If your answer is, I can do that, then you are right. You can't do it if you think you can't do it. Change your mind, change your life.

Speak to yourself a certain way and it will reshape you. Good or bad. Say it with emotion and it will reshape you faster.

When the little runner man in your head brings you a file that is unacceptable, you need to tell him that is not what you want to focus on. Think of it this way. If we were about to have dinner and I started showing you disgusting images, you would tell me to stop, right? Then WHY don't we do this with our own brain? After all, are you an emotional slave or do what to have a life by design? Most of your behavior is subconscious. WHY? Because we are not taking control.

Want to know WHY The Law of Attraction works? Because you tell your brain what to focus on. The brain doesn't know the difference between real and imagined. Visualize the outcome you want, like athletes do, and your brain can help make it happen. You literally attract what you focus on because your brain will find things to validate your thoughts.

SECTION 400:
YOUR WHY NURTURE

What you might not realize

CHAPTER 401:
Are You Smart Enough to Feel Stupid?

Let's have some fun and take the smart person challenge…

You have 10 seconds to answer this: List what you had for dinner the last 5 nights in a row.

Tick tock, tick tock, tick tock. Buzzer sound! Time is up. How many did you list? Did you get complete stage fright and couldn't think of even one of them? Not even what you had for dinner last night?! Did you remember what you had for dinner last night and then had to look at your calendar to confirm today is Tuesday? Once you confirmed today is Tuesday you asked yourself, what did I do on Sunday? Hmmm…

1 or 2 out of 5, is a failing grade.

Ready for Test #2?

10 seconds to answer: List the eight main teachers you had from 1st grade thru 8th grade.

Tick tock tick tock tick tock. Buzzer sound! Time is up. How many did you name? Did you get all 8? Did you get any?

You can't do it, can you?

Ok Rob, WHY did we take those tests?

We have just confirmed both your short-term memory and long-term memory aren't that great.

Let's move on to something that doesn't involve memory.

Don't think of an elephant. Try really hard. Don't think of an elephant.

Tick tock, tick, tock….

Let me guess, the ONLY thing you can think of is an elephant, right? Great job, smarty pants! We just showed we can't consciously control our own thoughts!

Want to know what prompted this chapter? I had a bad dream last night. In my dream it was the holidays and when it came time to pass out presents, I realized I had forgotten all the presents I was going to give. I my dream, I felt horrible and was trying to compensate for this. You dream analyzers can go nuts here but my point is, consciously and unconsciously we are not smart enough to control what our minds think about. My mind tortures itself while I am sleeping. Do you ever have bad dreams? Restless thoughts while you sleep? You understand that is your own brain torturing you, right?

In the chapter "Associations, Triggers, and Demons" we talked about the "Little runner man." He is the manager of the file room inside your head. Let me tell you something, he gets bored and I think mine drinks too much. I imagine mine looks like some crazy scientist, who hasn't slept in 3 days, with big hair and eyeglasses falling off his face. When I don't tell him what to do, he goes into the file room and starts grabbing random files. Apparently when I fall asleep, he starts drinking. A few too many drinks later he runs back to the file room, grabs random files, opens them without his glasses on, and then throws them on the floor. He is stepping on them as he grabs another random file, then he loses his balance and as he is falling, some file from my childhood goes up in the air, hits the ceiling and the pages come down like falling leaves. These become my dreams. In the morning the inside of my head probably looks like the aftermath of an outdoor concert, like Woodstock. As I am waking up, the cleaning crew is starting to tidy up while Jimi Hendrix is still playing and it's starting to rain. No wonder I wake up groggy and hit the snooze button.

I mean what the actual hell? How can I be in the house where I lived when I was 8 years old but driving a car I bought last year, while talking to my dead Grandmother, and people are chasing me? I'm saying this half joking, but it's true! My own brain was torturing me last night with these random thoughts, and timelines, that don't make sense. Evidently this is how dumb I am because I can't even control my own thoughts! It's time we focus attention here and let The Litter Runner Man know when he brings us files that are unacceptable.

Some of us torture ourselves while we are awake. Anxiety anyone? Am I smart? Am I dumb? You may be smart in relation to the rest of us; however, we have to realize that as a species we are very low on intelligence. Seriously, if aliens landed and we compared intelligence, humans would have more in common with a bucket of shrimp. Still don't believe me? Try this test. Recall the address for every home you have had in your life? Can't do it can you? How about this? Tell me the phone number of all the phones you have had…cell, work, and home. Can't do that either? Hmmm. Ok smarty pants, I'll make it easier for you. Think of a place you drive to regularly that has at least 10 turns. If you work at an office every day, that's perfect. Name all the streets you drive on. Can you do it? Oh and "that street where Sally lives" is not a qualifying answer.

Oh and one of my favorites. Remember the last time you asked someone for a phone number, called that number, and started talking only to get disconnected and had to call back? Did you remember the phone number or did you need to ask for it/check it again? You checked it again because you didn't even remember the number someone gave you 44 seconds ago!

How about this? Have you ever been mid-sentence, get distracted and then ask the person you are with, "what was I just talking about?" and neither of you can remember? Then you both had to retrace your steps to get the thought back? Ummm (retracing usually starts with an audible pause) you mentioned your favorite sports team, then we talked about rising interest rates and then you said you wanted coffee and OH YEAH I remember! LOL. We have all had this happen. WHY? Well it isn't because we are a super smart species!

Ok enough torture. WHY am I accentuating this? Because we need to know exactly who we really are and then back that down with a bit of humility. Be smart enough to know how smart, and not smart, you are. Know what you are good at, and what you aren't so good at. Evidently mine is ending sentences with a preposition.

We are smart in many ways; however, we are so dumb, impressionable, naïve, ignorant, and easily manipulated in many other ways. Evolved people, who don't have bad pride, (more on those in chapters coming up) understand this and embrace it. They know their strengths and they know when others are better suited for the task at hand.

Marketers manipulate us all the time. They call us Sheeple. Yes, people who get led around like sheep. I'll give you an example of how it works on me: when I hear the roar of a powerful gas engine and throaty exhaust, my unevolved inner child comes out. I am thinking "yeah listen to that power!" If I had that power, I would be significant! I like to be significant! People would look at this car and ask "is that your car?" and I can proudly answer "Yes! It is my car!" My inner child is metaphorically tugging on my shirt saying "this sounds amazing! Can we buy it? Pleeeeeeeeaaaaaasssseeeeee!"

"Buy American" used to be slogan to help our economy. It used to mean if you are deciding between two products where one product is made in the US and the other product, of equal quality and value (key phrase), was made outside of the US, then buy American and support domestic companies. Unfortunately, too many domestic companies (who make products more expensive and lower quality) cannot compete with foreign companies, so they resort to manipulative marketing tactics like saying "buy American."

Other ways marketers manipulate us. There are many but just to name a few:

Scarcity: "only 2 left"

Social proof: reviews, testimonials, other people using the product, and celebrity endorsements

Anchoring: Showing the product's value of $100, and then literally slashing the price to $49.

Subliminal association: using colors, music or images which trigger feelings within you

Nostalgia: tying products into your childhood

Emotional appeals: while viewing the product they trigger feelings of love, happiness, family (connection), or status (significance.) Also uncertainty, and the appeal to have safety and security (certainty) through fear. Remember our brains are naturally wired for safety and security so this is one of the easiest manipulations.

This is WHY the manipulation I despise the most is when marketers sell items using fear. "If you don't buy this educational toy, your kid will grow up and live under a bridge!" And "keep your family safe by having this product!" And "you are at risk unless you buy all three of these!" and "don't put yourself at risk take control of your life with my product!" Understand when marketers are using fear, along with other primal emotions, to create urgency. Jeez I didn't know I needed a pair of gloves in a hurricane but ok, I'll buy them to keep me safe! Que the eye roll…

Speaking of being manipulated. Let's talk about cause and effect. When something happens there is a ripple effect, or a counterbalance, to that happening.

What do you think of the women's lib movement? What was it about? Liberating women? Maybe. Let's look at the cause and effect, and the ripple effect, it had.

This is how it was sold to the public: Let's do something noble and liberate women! Let's give women access to jobs they don't otherwise have access to. Let's pass the Equal Pay Act of 1963 and make it illegal for a woman to get paid less than a man, for doing the same job. Let's make an Equal Employment Opportunity Commission (EEOC) in 1965! Title 9 of the higher education act of 1972 made it illegal to discriminate based on sex, which includes sexual harassment or unequal opportunities, in any education program or activity which used federal funds. These are all amazing things, and they needed to happen.

BUT!

Was there an ulterior reason to push for this? Here is the cause and effect, and ripple effect, it had:

1. Before this we could only tax half the population

2. We can boost the Gross Domestic Product (GDP)

3. We can boost the economy because twice the income means a lot more consumption of goods and services.

4. More spending on goods and services creates more jobs, which further stimulates the economy.

5. We can raise real estate prices because now two income families suddenly create more demand for more expensive houses

6. We can control people much more easily. Because we can break up your family. Both spouses go their separate ways in the morning, come home tired and now one parent doesn't stay home with the kids. Kids go to school earlier in life and are being taught by "the system," the government, television, and other outside influences. Once you read the upcoming chapter "You are a slave, Neo," this will mean more.

7. The marriage rate has steadily declined since the women's lib movement. Before women's lib married people only had one house, one car, and one insurance policy. Two unmarried people have two houses, two cars, and two insurance policies.

So, if you were a wealthy person and wanted to become wealthier, what a good idea it would be to buy a lot of real estate before it was going to go way up in price. Maybe invest in car companies when they are about to sell more cars. How about invest in insurance before they are about to sell more policies. Once you have all of these holdings would it be a good idea to then roll out women's lib? Do a bit of research and you will see the main catalyst for women's lib was one of the richest families in the world. If you could do something good for people, be seen as great people for supporting it, and multiply your wealth in the process, would you do it? Many would say sign me up! I'm not saying that family had any ulterior motives, maybe all of that was strictly coincidence.

Did someone else realize this cause and effect and do it again?

The NFL did something similar. The NFL emerged from the NFC and AFC merger in the 60's. After the merger, the NFL was twice the size and had twice the fan base. Now it's time to grow our fan base even more. How do we do this? Besides a larger population from one decade to the next, let's expand our reach. NFL Europe was born. But….it didn't do too well. Well then let's take games to Mexico and play there. Once again, "American football" didn't really sweep the new nation. So, what next? What country do we go to where American football might be accepted. Then some genius spoke up and said, we have twice the fan base right here in the United States! I remember when I was a kid, watching football with my father. My mother was typically cooking in the kitcheng. When my mother would come into the family room during the game, she preferred to read a book rather than watch the game. She had no interest in (her words) this "barbaric sport where big smelly men talked about big smell men."

Then one day, the reporter on the sidelines wasn't a big smelly man. The reporter was a well- dressed woman. Then more women showed up. All of a sudden the talking heads on tv had an extra seat as the show added a woman to talk about the game. She spoke well, her insight into the game made sense, and she didn't mention how cute the Quarterback is. Hmmm, honey come look at this! There is a woman on tv talking about the game. Women began to watch. The NFL had figured out how to double their audience and boost their revenues. Next thig you know "women's cut jerseys" entered the market. One could buy their favorite team items, not only in team colors but in pink as well! Wait a minute though, because merchandise is only about 10% of the NFL's revenue. How do we grow this even more? Advertising! 20%–25% of their revenue is advertising. Now twice as many advertisers swarmed to the television networks. Doritos is now selling to twice as many people because not only are Dad and Son watching, but Mom and Daughter as well. Hey Revlon, we have women watching football. Want to advertise? You do? Well, that's great. Now we have twice as many ads while the ad costs have doubled and tripled in price. WHY? Because we used to only sell ads to companies who sell men's items, now we sell to companies who sell family items and companies who sell female items. What was the ripple effect? The first ripple effect is in 2010 the cost of a 30 second Super Bowl ad, was about 3 million dollars. How much were the ads in 2025 after their version of women's lib movement? High demand Superbowl slots went for about 8 million dollars. How many 30 second commercials did they play, which were worth as much a 5 million dollars more than in 2010? Nay sayers are saying, "that is the tv networks who made that money!" Yes, but the tv networks pay the NFL for the rights to air their games.

But wait! There's more!

In 1999, the Washington Redskins (now the Washington Commanders) sold for 800 million dollars. Jerry Jones purchased the Dallas Cowboys in 1989 for 140 million dollars. Since then what happened? In 2012, for the first time, a female became an official referee during an NFL game. In 2018, for the first time, the NFL had an all female umpire crew call a game. As of 2024 the

Washington Commanders are estimated to be worth 6.3 billion dollars. As of 2024 the Dallas Cowboys are valued at 10 billion dollars. I am not saying this is all from their version of women's lib, but it helped a lot.

What is the point here? The point is not everything is being done at face value. Be mindful of what you become a part of, believe in, or subscribe to because short term gains, may have long term ripple effects we were not anticipating.

Social media platforms are very popular (short term goals) and now people who might be interested in manipulating us have tons of information about who we are, what we do, how we shop, what our interests are etc. (long term effects.)

I want you to be a good human and one of the ways we do that is by being mentally healthy. I want you to be Smart Enough to Feel Stupid. Pay attention to marketers, manipulators, unhealthy tribalism, purposely invoking your bad pride, and people who bend the truth. An example is a politician saying "violent crime went down 25% last quarter" while they are leaving out that violent crime doubled in the previous 2 years." Get the whole story, be a free thinker, and remember when the product isn't obvious, you are the product.

So, Are You Smart Enough to Feel Stupid? I hope so…

BONUS SECTION

Remember people fall in love in three stages:

Stage 1: Attraction. Someone is attracted to the exterior version that you show the world. This is the easy side. Some people use this phase to charm you.

Then they unpack the crazy….

Stage 2: Through the normal course of life, you show them your flaws, your insecurities, and the side of you that you shield from the world.

They either choose to love this side or they run away. Some people wait so long to "unpack the crazy" and are on their best behavior for years. They think that if you know who they really are too quickly, you won't like them. They are hoping that by the time they show you this side of them, you are already so vested in the relationship that you will stick it out.

PRO TIP: You can't "stick it out" and tolerate this. You either have to choose to love this side of them and embrace it or the relationship won't last. If you choose that then here comes…

Stage 3: Your partner starts to know you better than you know yourself and they put a big mirror in your face. This is uncomfortable for people who don't want to grow, don't want to evolve, and don't want to clear their triggers, associations and demons (more on this in the chapter "Triggers, Associations, and Demons".) For some people, having this mirror in their face is unbearable so they leave the relationship.

Relationships are a beautiful garden and the gardeners with the dirties hands create the most beauty.

PRO TIP: Students of WHY will know their potential partner's WHY NATURE, will understand if their personality type is a good match before they waste months or years of their life.

PRO TIP: AI robots are going to be a big problem for human behavior. There is going to be a sizeable amount of the population (mostly made up of MA personalities) that are going to choose an AI human looking bot as their life partner because the person doesn't want to grow and evolve. They would rather just have an AI bot accept them for who they are, rather than doing the work to be an emotionally healthy human. Human relationships are harder but worth the effort.

This section is not for everyone but for my friends who need it, let me tell you emotional abuse is not ok. I want to list some behaviors that qualify as emotional abuse. If these resonate with you I implore you to seek help from a friend, family member or a professional.

Emotional abuse:

- Being ignored or given "the silent treatment" by your parents/family members
- Being made to respect your parents with yes sir or yes ma'am (key phrase now) to a degree they didn't enforce with others
- Feeling unsafe or unwelcome in your own home
- You are/were made to feel wrong no matter what the situation (gaslighting)
- You approach someone with concerns or feelings and are made to feel like it's always your fault (gaslighting)
- Having low self-esteem as the result of the way you were treated as a child
- Feeling like you had to walk on eggshells, shrink yourself or avoid conversations so your family member didn't get angry (again)
- You were told your self-care was selfish
- Being told you didn't matter or your opinions didn't matter and you didn't have a voice
- Blaming yourself for a family members inability to show you love
- What you felt to be painful became a debate and eventually your feelings were invalidated
- Being raised in a combative environment
- Being loved came with unjust conditions

- If you are now "low maintenance" because your needs were neglected

- If you fear having emotions because your emotions were invalidated or you were made to feel wrong when you showed emotion

- If you are funny because you learned humor was a way to deflect pain, anger or an unsafe environment

- If you are strong or independent because you were not supported

- If you are a perfectionist because you were not allowed to make mistakes

- If you overexplain because you were oppressed

- Saying you are fine when you are not because you don't have a safe space

- Being made to feel guilty when you did nothing wrong

- You can't accept compliments because you were made to feel unworthy or insignificant

- You don't like to ask for help because you always had to be the strong one and you think you can't show weakness, ever

- You feel like If you became your true self, you would disappoint a lot of people

- If you are empathetic because you had to be in tune with their emotions in order to survive

- You feel bad when you say no—Amiables pay attention here

- You feel like a scared child even though you are an adult

You may not know it but I am also a poet! One day I wrote the poem "At Some Point" while I was thinking about my friends who experience emotional abuse. I'll share it with you:

At Some Point (2022)

At some point
Maybe I'll know who I am
Maybe I can go on
I don't think I can
My family
Fights all the time
They just ignore me
I have nothing to call mine
Go to bed little one
Dream if you dare
Some of mine are ok
Others I cannot share
I see you often
For more than a while
Please look through me
Past this fake smile
I was right next to you
I sat next to you in that chair
At some point
Please feel me
Deep in despair
Everyone enjoying life
WHY am I here
I think about what to do
Now it's me I fear
I looked until I found it
So loud like a storm
It's been hurting for hours
The barrel is still warm

Not everyone is going through the same things and some people are just trying to get through the day. If you have the capacity to help other people, please do. Selflessly take a look around once in a while and give your capacity away. Especially during holidays. Holidays can be emotionally difficult. People who recently lost a loved one, are recently out of a relationship (your divorced friends may not have anyone to spend the holidays with) and are otherwise emotionally struggling, are sitting right next to you.

> *"It's OK to be not OK. It's just fine to be out of your mind. Breathe in deep just a day at a time."*
> ~Imagine Dragons (*IT'S OK*)

CHAPTER 402:
The Negative Wave

WHY do we let Negative impact us more than positive? This is something we need to search within ourselves.

it is easier to do Negative things to fill one's Need for Significance and Uncertainty, than positive things.

As I mentioned in personality types, an expressive may figure out Negative things get attention quickly and are easier to do.

"It takes 11 correct inputs to equal 1 incorrect input."
~Albert Einstein

Do you have to remind yourself to think positive? Do you have to consciously have to think of the glass being half full instead of half empty? Do you want what you can't have? Do you have to remind yourself to be grateful for what you have? Do you find yourself not wanting, or taking for granted, something that was or is too easily attained? Ever heard the phrase "Life's a bitch and then you die?" Do you want to know WHY? Hey, excellent question! It is a concept in our world which I call "The Negative Wave." It goes through our subconscious mind similar to the way a group of fans create a wave in a stadium (by timing when they stand up.)

How long does it take for a painter to create a masterpiece? Philosophically one could say a lifetime, but I also mean literally. How much skill must he have acquired? How long must she have trained in order to create it? Now I ask you, how much skill does it take for someone to damage it or destroy it beyond repair? How much time does that take? Perhaps just seconds, right? How long must the destroyer have trained in order to accomplish this task? They were born with this "ability" right? They did not have to train nor practice in order to destroy it.

How long does it take to build a house? Months and maybe years. How much skill is required for a builder to accomplish this? Plenty and it was acquired by years of training, passing tests, and getting licensed if it is to be done correctly. How long does it take to burn it down? Minutes. How much skill does it take to throw gasoline on it and light a match? None.

How long does it take to create a human life? It might take years for a couple to successfully get pregnant; however, once conceived it takes 9 months (ish) right? How long does it take to take a life? A split second.

How long does it take to fill a tire with air? A minute or more. How long does it take to stab it with a knife and deflate it? 1 second.

Which one is faster?

Erecting a fence or knocking it over?

Building a car or crushing it?

Building a trusting relationship with someone or violating that trust and losing that relationship? It may take years to gain trust; however, that trust may be lost in a moment.

How long does it take to build a country with a strong economy? Centuries. How long does it take to invade and conquer it? Days or months. No where near the same time.

I could go on for hours with examples but…are you seeing a pattern here?

Sorry if I am starting to bum you out but I told you that you wouldn't like everything I had to say.

In order to understand our WHY we have to understand the positive and the Negative that impacts us.

The point I am trying to make is that it takes much more time and skill to create and build, than it does to destroy. What we consider positive is time consuming and usually takes skill acquired from training. What we consider negative is much faster and easier. A master may train for years in order to create something. A ding dong only takes seconds, with no training at all, to mess it up. This is the essence of The Negative Wave. I want you to understand WHY you are the way you are and this is a major influence. You can't show me a Negative baby but I can show you plenty of Negative adults. WHY? One reason is because The Negative Wave influences the way we think. In Birth Order we talked about how a middle child may act, out when they become a Middle Child. It is easier to do it Negatively, than positively. Careful!

If you have to remind yourself to look at the glass half full instead of half empty, this is one of the reasons. One reason is: life can feel like it is subconsciously stacked up against you. I love positive thinking but if you have to remind yourself to do so, this may be WHY.

Ok. Are you intrigued? Well, here is the rest. Let's talk about life expectancy. For the purpose of this explanation, I will use as an example a pillow, a car, and a piece of silver. WHY? Because these examples are nothing alike. When a pillow is new it is nice and fluffy. After months of using it, exactly what it was intended for, the pillow becomes smaller, less fluffy, and eventually flat and uncomfortable. A new car is shiny, blemish free, it has that "new car smell," and it is hopefully reliable. After years of use, even with maintenance (which just delays its decline), the shine starts to wear off, it gets scratched from road debris, wind and things hitting it and eventually the "new car smell" goes away. You can repaint it or restore it but the point is you can only put it back to new condition and the process starts all over again. What about the Silver? Whether it is used or not, it will tarnish and will need to be polished. When polishing it all you are actually doing is trying to restore it back to the way it was. Are you making it better than when it was new? No. The point is they all do not get better after they are created. Not only do they not get better they slowly decline. Ever wonder why the standard financing on an American car is 60 months? It is because years ago the average life expectancy of an American car was 60 months! Right when your car was all paid off it was time for it to be replaced. Then it's time to march right back into the dealership, get yourself a brand new car, and of course a brand new set of payments. Do you think wine is better? Wine is like people. It takes a while to get to its peak until it begins to decline and eventually dies. You (like wine) are either growing (wine's equal is maturing and evolving) or dying. Regenerating or degenerating. That's it. I don't want to sound gloomy here, but it is true. Go ask a doctor or wine connoisseur (respectively) if you don't believe me.

Here is another example of the Negative Wave that will surprise you. Decades ago, when I started my first business, I was highly focused on what I could do in order to grow my business. Ask any successful business owner how important things like marketing and customer service are, and you will get a very enthusiastic response because is very important. You must advertise your product and take care of the customer, in order for your business to stay alive and grow. Are there exceptions?

There are two exceptions to this rule: A Psychologist and a Police Officer. WHY are these exceptions to this rule? Because their goal is actually to put themselves out of business! What do I mean by that? The number of police officers needed in a city is determined by the amount of crime in that city. A police officer wants to stop crime. However if crime stopped, they would put themselves out of a job. A psychologist strives to "cure" their patient. Once the patient works out their issues, they don't need their psychologist anymore. The goal of psychologists is to mentally adjust all of their patients which would put them out of a job. It gets better! What is the direct relationship between a psychologist and a police officer? They both deal with human behavior! If I really tried to put my company out of business, I am sure I could be packing up the office by the end of the month. A psychologist's, and police officer's, goal is to put themselves out of business by ridding themselves of customers, yet they can't do it! I can't think of any profession, not dealing with human behavior, that actually tries to put itself out of business and can't do it. Amazing. A little scary too, isn't it?

Now WHY is this important to understand? Because it affects the way we think and behave. This is WHY we have self help tapes trying to get us to think positive and approach life from a good place mentally. Their intended purpose is to counter act the Negative Wave. There is no such thing as "stop thinking so positive" tapes are there? No. WHY? Because we have enough of that from the Negative Wave. The next time you encounter it I encourage you to identify it and make sure you control your thinking so it doesn't control you. Understand it is contrary to our basic human need for growth and contribution. Make it your goal to not be discouraged or overwhelmed by it.

PRO TIP: One of the reasons for The Negative Wave is our minds are programmed for safety and security, not happiness.

Now that we understand The Negative Wave it is important to understand our behavior. Sometimes we lose perspective so this is an easy way to get it back. When you, or someone else, behaves a certain way, or performs an action, and you are trying to figure out how you feel about it or perhaps what their intent was, see where it fits on this scale.

CATEGORIES OF A BEHAVIOR

CATEGORY 1
Good for you, and Good for others

These are positive, quality, impactful, thoughtful, loving, helpful, and sometimes selfless actions.

CATEGORY 2
Good for you, yet Not good for others

These are selfish, thoughtless, and self-centered acts. They only serve you and may be at other people's expense or done with an indifference to other people's needs.

CATEGORY 3
Not good for you, yet Good for others

These are selfless acts at your own expense. Giving from an empty cup, donating too much of your time when you should be taking care of yourself. Neglecting oneself.

CATEGORY 4
Not good for you, and Not good for others

These are destructive, sabotaging, vengeful, undermining, evil, and possibly illegal acts. They are meant to do harm to yourself, which is not good for others. Or they are meant to do harm to others and if discovered, you will have negative repercussions.

CHAPTER 403:
You Are a Slave, Neo

"Today, they say we are free, only to be chained in poverty."
~Bob Marley

"There are no chains around my feet, but I am not free. I am bound here in captivity."
~Bob Marley

Unfortunately, slavery existed in America before 1865. In fact, the United States had a civil war because half the country felt so strongly about owning slaves.

What is a slave?

Dictionary definition: A person who is the legal property of another and is forced to obey them.

Slaves aren't cheap. Even if you kidnapped someone against their will and forced them into slavery, you have to house them, feed them, give them drink, clothes, shoes, and give them medical attention when needed. You have to pay to transport them back and forth when they are needed at a different location. You also have to spend money on ways to keep them from escaping. Shackles cost money. Especially when they break and have to be replaced. You may have to spend money on whips to get them to keep working. An owner may have to pay someone to protect himself when they are around their slaves just in case they revolt. An owner may have to bribe someone to get information on how they plan to escape. You may have to buy a slave from another owner. Maybe you give one slave better living conditions and less work if they oversee the other slaves. Of course, better living conditions costs more money and having one less full time worker who is now a "manager" of sorts costs money in the form of less production. In short, slaves aren't cheap. Slaves have their dreams crushed, they cannot build wealth, and they don't have the freedom to do what they want to do. A slave owner may feel bad treating people this way…maybe.

BUT WHAT IF THERE IS A BETTER WAY…?

What if we can make slaves that didn't know they were slaves?

Oh, come on, Rob, how can someone do that?

Pay attention…

Ask yourself these questions…

- Are you living in your dream house or are you living in what you can afford and are settling to some degree?
- Are you driving the car you really want to drive or are you driving what you can afford?
- Are you really happy with your medical care or do you pick and choose when you go to the doctor because it's expensive? Do you see what doctors are "in network" with your insurance so you think you are "choosing" a doctor?
- Are you doing the job you truly love or are you keeping your current job because it pays well? Maybe asked another way:

have you been "promoted" to the point where it would be too hard to leave/replace that job?

- Would you be happier doing something else but can't afford to make the transition because you have bills to pay or ties to a certain area?

- If you lost your job tomorrow, for how long could you afford to pay your bills? Could you retire or would you, sooner or later, have to find another job?

- Do you travel as much as you want, in the manner you want?

- When you were born were you branded with a number which can be used to keep track of you, for the rest of your life? If you said no I'll give you a hint, it's your social security number.

- Are you doing what you really want to do with your life?

Some of you are having an epiphany right now. For those that take a little longer, I'll continue…

BUT WHAT IF THERE IS A BETTER WAY? What if we gave our slaves a small wage? As the slave owners began to protest a voice rose up to say, "We will give them a small wage but they will be responsible for their own housing, travel, medical care and other expenses. As the crowd began to quiet down the voice continued, "We will even institute a 'minimum wage' so 'owners' don't take advantage and the people feel protected by their government. This will make them not want to leave the area in which they are governed." The slave owners asked, "What will we do when they are too old to work?" The voice replied, "We will make a fund to help pay them when they are too old to work." An owner spoke up and asked, "WHY would we make a fund?" We will do that because the old people who are homeless, can't afford to eat, and don't have medical care will frighten the workers. Again, they have to feel like they are supported and protected by their government. We can't call them workers though. It sounds too much like slave. The owners spoke up and said we can call them whatever we want since they are in our employ. That's it! We will call them employees!

As the owners bought into this concept the voice rose up again to say "BUT WAIT! THERE'S MORE! It gets even better!" We will make the workers, I mean employees, contribute to this retirement fund for their entire lives so in reality, when they retire we are just giving them back the money they paid in! We will encourage them to have families because then we will have more employees paying into the fund. Then! The voice continued, we will "borrow" against the fund even to the point of making it unstable." An owner asked, "Well what do we do if the fund goes bankrupt?" The voice responded "Duh! We own the mint! We will just print more money and not tell them where it came from. Did you forget that it only costs us 15 cents to make a $100 bill?" That is true by the way. In the year 2024 it costs the Bureau of Engraving and Printing (the people who physically print the dollars in the USA) about 15 cents to make a $100 bill. How is that for a return on investment!

Ok but wait, with more dollars floating around it is more likely that more people will get their hands on the money. Won't they become rich then? Of course not! The prices of goods and services will inflate and that will make it harder for the workers to buy the same goods and services with the same money. We will even call it inflation and make it sound like a normal thing! The employees won't even notice because by then they will be so engrained in the "system" they won't care. As long as they get paid and feel supported by their government, they will think they are free. The plan is fool proof.

By the way, I will digress here for a paragraph or two since we are talking about money and governments. There is something else you need to understand, Neo. Let's say you want to buy something which costs $50. If you pay cash with a $50 bill, you get your product (or service) and the merchant gets your $50 bill. Then when the merchant takes that same $50 bill and buys something with it, they get a good (or service) and the new merchant/seller has the $50 bill. The cash bill is worth $50.

Now let's change that scenario to paying via debit or credit card. When one pays via card, the merchant gets charged a "transaction fee." Transaction fees vary in amount but they can be as high as 3.5%. Let's just say for easy math the transaction fee on the $50 transaction is $1. So as in the above scenario, you go to buy something for $50 and pay via credit card or electronic transaction. The merchant pays the $1 transaction fee and pockets $49. Then the merchant goes to buy something for $50 and his seller gets charged a $1 transaction fee. Once that $50 has changed hands 50 times the bank issuing the card has effectively taken the $50! They have devalued the "electronic $50 bill" one transaction fee at a time. Why do you think banks have been pushing people not to use cash? Aren't there transaction fees (which dissuade you from taking cash) at many ATMs? How easy is it to use a check card? Do you get miles or points or "cardholder benefits" for using your credit cards? Don't these things dissuade you from using cash? Cash can be stolen. If your credit card is stolen, you are not liable for anything! Magical isn't it? WHY are you not liable for anything? Because you using your card is worth so much to them they can afford to eat the fraudulent transactions! Feel manipulated?

Back to the story

The employees that do the best work will get more wages. We will give them free schools so they can learn to be better employees. We will do this but only up to a certain point. We will only give them enough schooling for "free" (they will think it is free but really we are going to tax their paycheck and the things they own to pay for it. If they want other services, like parks and monuments, we will just tax them more to pay for that too) to make them smart enough to either want more schooling or at least not make themselves homeless. If they want more schooling, we will call this college and make them pay for it. If the college idea goes really well, we will even give them loans to become students and charge them interest on those loans! After all, more money should be here at the top in the oligarchy.

The best slaves, I mean employees, will get paid more so they can afford better housing, transportation, food, and even travel. A slave will only be able to escape if they make enough money to pay off their house, their transports, and all their bills plus have enough money to live for the rest of their life. An owner asked, "what do we do with those people then?" Don't worry, they will come to us and become part of the oligarchy. They will then protect the system out of fear of working again.

How else will we make this plan happen?

We control the news so we will make blacks hate whites, whites hate blacks, and everyone will be anti-Chinese. In fact, we will pass "The Chinese Exclusion Act" in 1882, "The Scott Act" in 1888, "The Geary Act" in 1892, and in 1902 this will be expanded to cover Hawaii and the Philippines. The Chinese will in turn make the anti-American act in 1905. All won't be repealed until 1943 but only thanks to World War II.

All that propaganda will make employees afraid. Employees will be so focused on hating one another, their Tribalism (next chapter) will bring them to love their government. Said another way: while we distract workers to look left, right, and behind themselves, they won't be looking up. Employees won't even notice we are the ones who really have their thumb on them, keeping them in place. The perfect time for this propaganda is right before we are up for reelection or when worker confidence is at its lowest. After all if we are in the middle of a fight, especially if we think we are winning, that is not a good time to change a regime. Has a government ever staged an aggression toward their own country right before an election? I am sure this has never happened, right?

Employees will think they have freedom of speech, but in reality we will own the news distribution and will sensor what they see. We will post in the news how many crimes black people commit so the white people are afraid. After all, fear makes people consume and white people love to panic. Don't believe me? After Rosa Parks wouldn't move to the back of the bus the following year gun sales went through the roof. Guess who bought them all? Scared white people! They were so afraid that this was the beginning of an "uprising" that they went out and bought a ton of guns. Want more proof? The horrible Columbine High School shooting was April 20th, 1999. It's no coincidence that in 1999 more guns were manufactured than in the previous 3 years. After the Sandy Hook Elementary school massacre in December 2012, gun manufacturing rose from 8.5 million units in 2012 to 10.9 million units in 2013. After a deadly mass shooting in San Bernadino in 2015, gun sales went up about 85 percent in the following 6 weeks. White people love to panic.

If you haven't made enough money to get out of the system, then you are still a slave of the system.

The French have a saying "the less you have, the more you are free." That is so true…

Someone said to me: "Actually, George Washington was friends with his enslaved valet, William Lee."

Me: "Did you hear yourself? He obviously wasn't friends enough to set him free."

After they said that I did some checking to see what American Presidents owned slaves or supported slavery. After all, in order to know who we are we must know where we came from, right? This is not my opinion so don't be mad at the messenger; these are just facts. I especially love the hypocrisy of the people who owned slaves, while opposing slavery.

I just read this information on Wikipedia:

George Washington—1st President of the United States: Washington was a major slaveholder before, during, and after his presidency. His will freed his slaves pending the death of his widow, though she freed them within a year of her husband's death. As president, Washington signed a 1789 renewal of the 1787 Northwest Ordinance, which banned slavery north of the Ohio River. This was the first major restriction on the domestic expansion of slavery by the federal government in US history.

John Adams—2nd President: Never owned slaves

Thomas Jefferson—3rd President: Jefferson fathered multiple enslaved children with the enslaved woman Sally Hemings, the likely half-sister of his late wife Martha Wayles Skelton.[6][7] Despite being a lifelong slave owner, Jefferson routinely condemned the institution of slavery, attempted to restrict its expansion, and advocated gradual emancipation. As president, he oversaw the abolition of the international slave trade.

James Madison—4th President: Madison occasionally condemned the institution of slavery and opposed the international slave trade, but he also vehemently opposed any attempts to restrict its domestic expansion. Madison did not free his slaves during his lifetime nor in his will. [8] Paul Jennings, one of Madison's slaves, served him during his presidency and later published the first memoir of life in the White House.

James Monroe—5th President: Like Thomas Jefferson, Monroe condemned the institution of slavery as evil and advocated its gradual end, but still owned many slaves throughout his entire adult life, freeing only one of them in his final days.[9] As president, he oversaw the Missouri Compromise, which admitted Missouri to the Union as a slave state in exchange for admitting Maine as a free state and banning slavery above the parallel 36°30′ north. Monroe supported sending freed slaves to the new country of Liberia; its capital, Monrovia, is named after him.

John Quincy Adams—6th President (son of the 2nd President): Never owned slaves

Andrew Jackson—7th President: One controversy during his presidency was his reaction to anti-slavery tracts. During his campaign for the presidency, he faced criticism for being a slave trader. Jackson did not free his approximately 150 slaves in his will. When Jackson died he was in the top one percent of slave owners in the U.S. Unlike the prior slave-owning presidents, he did not inherit any of his slaves, but rather built a fortune in human chattel from scratch.

Martin Van Buren—8th President: Van Buren's father owned six slaves.[12] The only slave Van Buren personally owned, Tom, escaped in 1814, and Van Buren made no effort to find him.[13] In December 1824, A. G. Hammond of Berlin, New York, located Tom in Worcester, Massachusetts.[12] Van Buren tentatively agreed to sell him to Hammond for $50, provided Hammond could capture him without violence.[12][13] Hammond could not make the guarantee,[13] and was disinclined to pay because New York's gradual emancipation law guaranteed that if he was re-enslaved, Tom would be freed in 1827.[12] Tom remained free, as Van Buren probably intended.[13][a] Later in life, Van Buren belonged to the Free Soil Party, which opposed the expansion of slavery into the Western territories.

William Henry Harrison—9th President: Harrison inherited several slaves. As the first governor of the Indiana Territory, he unsuccessfully lobbied Congress to legalize slavery in Indiana.

John Tyler—10th President: Tyler never freed any of his slaves and consistently supported slaveholders' rights and the expansion of slavery during his time in political office.

James K. Polk—11th President: Polk became the Democratic nominee for president in 1844 partially because of his tolerance of slavery, in contrast to Van Buren. As president, he generally supported the rights of slave owners. His will provided for the freeing of his slaves after the death of his wife, though the Emancipation Proclamation and the Thirteenth Amendment to the United States Constitution ended up freeing them long before her death in 1891.

Zachary Taylor—12th President: Although Taylor owned slaves throughout his life, he generally resisted attempts to expand slavery in the territories. Taylor opposed the Compromise of 1850, which admitted California into the Union as a free state and banned the slave trade in Washington, DC, in exchange for allowing most of the remaining territory captured from Mexico to decide the issue of slavery locally and passing a federal fugitive slave law requiring state authorities to assist federal marshals in capturing and detaining escaped slaves. However, Taylor died in office before he could veto the bill, leading to its successful passage under his successor Millard Fillmore. After his death, there were rumors that slavery advocates had poisoned him; tests of his body over 100 years later have been inconclusive. Taylor did not free any of his slaves in his will.

Millard Fillmore—13th President: Did not own slaves but only became President when Zachary Taylor died during his term in office.

Franklin Pierce—14th President: Did not own slaves but supported the expansion of slavery

James Buchanan—15th President: James bought two women, freed them, and then employed them as servants. Depending where one searches, one will find that 4 of the first 18 Presidents did not own slaves or 6 of the first 18 Presidents did not own slaves. One of the controversial ones.

Abraham Lincoln—16th President: Never owned slaves. He issued the Emancipation Proclamation on January 1st, 1863, which stated all slaves in the Confederate States of America would be free. Somehow he was convinced by Andrew Johnson, who was military governor of Tennessee at the time, to omit Tennessee from the Emancipation Proclamation.

Andrew Johnson—17th President: Johnson owned a few slaves and was supportive of James K. Polk's slavery policies. As military governor of Tennessee, he convinced Abraham Lincoln to exempt that area from the Emancipation Proclamation. Johnson went on to free all his personal slaves on August 8, 1863.[19] On October 24, 1864, Johnson officially freed all slaves in Tennessee.

Ulysses S. Grant—18th President: Although he later served as a general in the Union Army, his wife, Julia, had control of four slaves during the American Civil War, given to her by her father. It is unclear if she actually was granted legal ownership of them or merely temporary custody.[22] All would be freed along with those freed by the Emancipation Proclamation of 1863, although by Julia's choice, as the proclamation did not apply to her state of Missouri.[22] Grant was given a slave, William Jones, from his father-in-law. Even though he was not an abolitionist at this time, he didn't like the idea of slavery, and could not bring himself to make Jones work as a slave, nor sell Jones. So, Grant's holding was brief and he freed William Jones on March 29, 1859.

No President from the 19th to the current 47th owned slaves.

56 men signed the Declaration of Independence with the language "All men are created equal." It is estimated 40% of them owned slaves.

Just for fun I did a Google search with this question: Was phrase "all men are created equal" meant to include women?

Answer copied verbatim:

> No, the phrase "all men are created equal" in the Declaration of Independence was not intended to include women. At the time of its writing, the phrase was primarily understood to mean that all white, male landowners were equal in the eyes of the law, effectively excluding women, African Americans, and Native Americans from its scope.

CHAPTER 404:
Tribalism

Tribalism is one of my favorite observations. Tribalism is in our DNA. 10,000 years ago when we were running from saber toothed tigers, we needed to be part of a pack. There is safety in numbers. I'll watch the camp whilst you sleep and you watch the camp whilst I sleep. You go looking for food to the east and I'll go looking for food to the west. Regardless of who has the successful hunt, we will split our bounties and we will both survive…OR…I saw large game to the north, if we join forces we can bring down this larger game. One kill will feed the tribe for longer periods of time. Ok, let's go together and it will benefit us all. We developed the understanding that teaming up equals survival.

Ancillary benefits (of being able to feed the tribe) are it will bring more women to our tribe. More women in the tribe means more babies to add to our tribe. Not only does having a larger tribe increase the likelihood of survival but it also increases security. Also, a larger tribe is the makings of our own kingdom. A pack mentality arose. Filling the needs for significance, connection, certainty and love through tribalism, became forged in our brains.

Smaller tribes formed within the larger tribe. Maybe because people looked more alike, had similar interests, beliefs, or abilities. Some of those smaller tribes may have broken away and moved to different areas. As we began to separate and settle new places we adapted to different climates, which cemented the separation. We brought to this new place our original language, let's use Latin as an example and (as we discussed in Communication) it slowly, over time, began to change. This furthered the separation because "they don't sound like us." As people, isolated from other people, began to use slang, have dialects and add new words, language evolved differently than within other tribes. Language changed until it became an unrecognizable version of itself. In fact, the original Latin isn't currently spoken at all! It is considered a dead language! How is that possible that NO ONE speaks Latin anymore? I get it that some people speak it for events and ceremonies but I am talking about a commonly accepted daily language. Latin evolved into what is commonly called "romance languages." French, Italian, Portuguese, and Spanish, to name a few. Even English has romance and Latinate sources.

Today thankfully we are no longer running from tigers. Our ability to create and build has made us, for now, the dominant species on this planet. Yet for some reason as smart as we think we are, we still share Tribalism (and some other) instincts with our ancestors. We exude them on a daily basis. We just do it in a modern way.

Modern Tribalism is:

Rooting for a specific sports team and wearing around your jersey

University Alumni—wearing your Penn State hoodie (as an example.) Especially if you give an endowment to your university. Let me break this down further in case you are not aware. There are people, who graduate from a university and go out into the workforce. They have their degree and are completely done with the university. Then they voluntarily give money back to their university for years and decades, after graduation. Some people give generously and I mean generously. Check some of these numbers out:

Harvard endowment in 2024: over 50 BILLION dollars (I had to check that 3 different ways because I didn't believe it)

Yale endowment in 2024: over 40 BILLION dollars

MIT endowment in 2024: over 24 BILLION dollars

In fact, the average endowment for a Top 20 school, in the US, is over 18 BILLION dollars. Average! Per year!

If they make that much money, WHY do they still charge new students a tuition? WHY isn't college free in the US? Hmmm, a mind bender there.

So, Rob, let me get this straight. Alumni from universities give money back to their university? Yes. WHY? Because they want to. Does the college pay taxes on this money? Nope! It's tax free.
Alumni love their tribes!

Let's explore more Tribalism…

Belonging to a church—especially if you give tithes (their version of an endowment) to your church

Believing in a particular religion

Supporting a political party

Belonging to a group or club

Gangs—WHY would one join a gang? A replacement of family which can fill one's need for connection. Also, the need for significance while sporting your "colors." Strength in numbers, just like our ancestors. The need for certainty because I know I am going to feel this way. The need for uncertainty because I don't know what is going to happen next! The need for love because members support each other the way loving family members do/should. Remember in the Six Basic Human Needs chapter when I wrote that if one behavior fills three or more needs, it will become a habit? This is WHY gangs are so popular. Tribalism in raw form, just like our ancestors.

What about other "show of force" organizations? What was the motto of The Musketeers in France hundreds of years ago? "All for one and one for all!" Today the US Marines are often referred to as a "Brotherhood." I have heard a Marine say, "If you are/were a Marine, then every Marine past and present is your brother." Tribalism in raw form just like our ancestors.

More Tribalism examples...

Being from a particular area (people may wear shirts or hats with their phone area code to signify they are from that area. 405 = Oklahoma, 305 = Miami etc. Today I saw a guy with "215" tattooed on his body, in very plain site. I don't mean on his upper arm and he was wearing short sleeves. This was a tattoo that can't be covered up easily. A tattoo! That guy is very proud of where he is from!

What solidifies our Tribalism? One way is physical reminders of our tribe.

Flags—WHY do you think we have flags? Physical symbols of countries and states which are meant to invoke feelings of pride, which entices Tribalism.

Mascots—same as flags. Physical symbols meant to invoke emotions to entice Tribalism. How does an American feel when they see their national symbol, a soaring bald eagle? How does a French feel when they see the cock? That is not a joke, the French national symbol is a rooster but they call it "le cock." Have you ever seen a mascot and associated feelings toward what it represents?

Logos—again physical symbols meant to remind us of a company, organization or club. Trivia question: today, what is the number one most recognizable logo in the world? What logo is second? Answer at the bottom of this chapter.

We have a need to be a part of a group and to show/flaunt/exude that we are part of that group. So much that we will even defend the group, it's mission, it's goals or it's outcomes.

This is WHY sports teams have strong names and mascots. To invoke pride and emotion towards that team. For example, in the NFL we have Chicago Bears, Philadelphia Eagles, Detroit Lions.

I would be afraid if I encountered a bear, or a lion, and maybe even a really mad eagle, but WHY these names? Maybe these names are supposed to intimidate players from the other team, but that doesn't work.

Chicago is not known for its bear population. In 1922, the owner renamed the team by saying "Football players are bigger than baseball players, and since the Chicago baseball team are the Chicago Cubs we will call our team the Bears." Hmmm, ok…

Philadelphia is not known for its eagle population. How did the team get its name? In 1933 Bert Bell, the owner of the team, named the team after he was inspired by the eagle in the NRA logo. 2nd Amendment anyone?

How about the Lions? In 1934, the owner was inspired by the Detroit Tigers baseball team and named his football team the Detroit Lions because he wanted them to be king of the NFL, like a lion is "king of the jungle." I can offer some kudos for this one even though Lions have nothing to do with Detroit.

I'm not hating on anyone. You can name your team whatever you want. I just want to know WHY. The bottom line is none of those team names coincide with the cities they represent. These team names and mascots, embodied in strength, are supposed to ignite emotion within a fan. Team owners are hoping this emotion turns into loyalty towards the team.

You don't know any teams called the ants, the mosquitoes, the gnats, nor the lazy bums, do you? Of course not, what person would want to root for a team with that name? Even the Ducks are called the Mighty Ducks (NHL), so they sound stronger. Named by team owner Walt Disney. Maybe Donald and Daffy played a hand in that. Does the team name make them any better or worse? Of course not. The stronger team names are playing on our need for Tribalism.

Another popular option is to name a team after something significant within the city they represent. For example:

Pittsburgh Steelers—Pittsburgh is known for its steel workers. The Steelers logo even mimics the American Iron and Steel Institute (AISI) so proud steel workers link associations towards the team.

Houston Oilers—Texas is known for its oil and probably proud of it.

New England Patriots—New England was the birthplace of the American revolution. Let's associate this significance with our team and we will gain fans by playing on their emotions. Note: they were previously known as the "Boston Patriots." Talk about a good way to expand one's tribe. Instead of having one city root for us, let's expand the team name to encompass 6 states!

A really fun part of Tribalism is band wagon people. One day they are wearing this team's jersey in support of them and as soon as they lose, that same person is wearing the jersey of the winning team. WHY do you think that is? It's because they are filling their need for significance by wearing the team colors of the team what is doing well. They get to rub it in other fans' faces by saying "my team is doing better than yours." When they see people with the same team jersey, they are filing their need for connection because they both get to revel in their team's success and validate one another.

Anything that people flaunt in support of, or are a part of, is Tribalism.

WHY do you think teams come from a particular city or state? Because of Tribalism. The local people will root for the local sports team. Let's pick on the Dallas Cowboys since they are one of the most expensive franchises in the world. Originally called the Dallas Steers (yes it's true, I am not making that up) then changed to the Dallas Rangers. This was a genius idea (not really) because they ran into problems with the already existing Dallas Rangers baseball team. People got confused as to which Dallas Rangers everyone was talking about. They were later renamed the Dallas Cowboys because it resonated with Texas' culture.

All of these teams have a huge following spanning decades. The reason many of the fans are fans is because their parents were fans, and they grew up that way. Generational Tribalism! The truth is, the players are not from your city, the coaches are not from your city, and even the trainers are not from your city. They never were (maybe a few but this is a small minority and strictly coincidence.) Chances are they didn't even go to college in your city. So WHY does one root for their local sports team other than Tribalism?

Do you own any sports jerseys? Do you have a favorite sports team? I grew up watching and favoring a particular sports team. WHY? Because some of my family members were fanatics and had me watch the team when I was young. I saw how excited my family got when "their team" won and I wanted to participate. When they bought me my own jersey, I felt like I was a part of something. It was a connection we all shared. Fun emotions when they win, commiserating when they lose, passionately talking about the game before, during, and after the event, while looking forward to the next event. Assembling to watch the game whether at the field or at one of our homes.

I have had times when people came up to me and said "I saw your team won last night, congratulations!" After receiving this statement I'm thinking, "ya know I didn't actually do anything to contribute to that win, right?" When the star player scored, I was two knuckles deep in the nacho cheese. I am going to go out on a limb and say my nachos did not contribute to the win. I don't say any of that, I just simply reply "thanks!" Have you ever paid five times the value for a t-shirt just because it had the logo of a team, club, company, or group? Having that little (or large) logo on your shirt inspired you to pay so much more than what the actual shirt, without the logo, was worth. Tribalism is big and profitable business!

If you want to create Tribalism, then you need a rival. Yeah!

We love to hate rivals. When we are against our rival, it is a much bigger deal. Tickets are more expensive, pride comes out, arguments happen, fights happen, emotions run high, and Tribalism is making someone more money.

I remember when the Cleveland Browns moved to Baltimore in 1996. The owner renamed the team the Baltimore Ravens. They are/were in the Steelers' division. The Steelers have a HUGE fan base dating all the way back to 1933. What better way to create a fan base and invoke Tribalism than by starting a rivalry with the Steelers? So that is what they tried to do. The upstart team beat the Steelers one time in their first season and tried to create a rivalry. The Steelers simply replied, "it's not a rivalry until we say it is." The Ravens kept at it and today they are considered rivals.

What happened to the Browns? Well, the NFL wanted to add another team to their league and what better way to gain instant fan base than to give Cleveland back their Browns in 1999. Instant Tribalism from the yearning Cleveland fans who went without a team for three years. WHY are they called the Browns? The original team owner, Paul Brown, named the team after himself. Hmmm… ok…it's hard to leave me at a loss for words. Maybe I should buy a sports franchise and change their name to "The Robs." When we win, we can all yell, "you got Robbed!" LOL

What about Chevrolet vs Ford? OMG. Chevy and Ford fans can be obsessed and borderline crazy. You drive a Ford? Those are junk! You know that means "Found On Road Dead," right? OR "you like Chevy? WHY? Ford is so much better!" I think the Ford people are still trying to turn Chevrolet into a negative acronym, but haven't done it yet. The point is, people love to choose sides, love to argue those sides and love to defend their decision (discussed more in the chapter Good Pride vs Bad Pride.) So having a rival invokes Tribalism and is good for business. If you are smart you might even let that rival win once in a while so they don't go away and it builds more tension.

Maybe I should have put these paragraphs in the chapter "Are you smart enough to feel stupid" because they are literally playing with your emotions, to create associations, and invoke your need for Tribalism.

Where else can we find Tribalism?

- national pride
- state pride
- regional pride
- town pride
- community pride

Notice I did not say worldwide pride. WHY is that? Some people may have a t shirt from their favorite place or country; however, I ask you, when is the last time you saw someone wearing a shirt that reads "EARTH"? LOL. Ever heard anyone say, "Yes I am from Earth"? That would be weird, right? WHY? Because Earth has no rivals! WHY do we feel the need to separate ourselves?

Unfortunately, at this time, there is only one way the whole world would instantly unite. Can you guess what it is? The answer will be at the end of this chapter.

Family, community, town, region, state, or country. I am a part of these, when it suits me, and I will defend my tribe! WHY? Because it gives us an identity! A significance or perhaps a connection with others in that same tribe. WHY not enjoy a sports team, a group, an event or activity for the pure enjoyment of the experience? One should use caution and recognize if one has the ulterior motive of Tribalism. Tribalism is a form of exterior validation and not a feeling of being whole.

Bottom line is we currently still have a strong desire for Tribalism. One will be a part of a tribe. It is in our nature. What we have to watch is when we don't feel like we are part of a tribe at home, or at least a good enough tribe, for we will venture out to fill our need for Tribalism. Hopefully what we find is positive but we might find negative. Negative behavior like joining a gang or cult (if they do bad things) can result, if no positive path is found first. As I will explain in the upcoming chapter, The Negative Wave, negative is quicker, easier, faster and more seductive, than positive. Right Yoda?

Go through your closet and see what tribes you support…

Tribalism plays into Pride, which is the chapter coming up.

Trivia question answers:

Number one most recognizable logo: Coca-Cola, aka Coke. It is estimated 94% of the entire world can recognize this logo.

Number two? Ferrari. The yellow shield with the prancing horse. In fact, I was speaking to the manager of a Ferrari dealership one day and he told me "Ferrari made 300 million dollars last year selling cars and 2.7 billion (yes that was a "B") dollars licensing their logo. Remember when I asked you if you have ever paid five times what a shirt is worth because of the logo on the shirt? Well Ferrari is not a car company. It is a licensing company that sells cars. Tribalism at its finest.

How do we get the world to instantly unite? If the world was attacked by aliens. Sadly that may be the only way human beings could set our differences aside and unite. Again, that is Tribalism dating back to our ancestors. If we join forces we can bring down larger game and survive.

CHAPTER 405:
Good Pride vs. Bad Pride

GOOD PRIDE

What is Good Pride? Good Pride is a healthy internal feeling of accomplishment, self-worth, perusing goals, perseverance, creativity, confidence, contribution, overcoming adversity, starting something positive or beneficial, building something positive, and satisfaction from helping people and society.

Good Pride is:

- Being proud of your accomplishments
- Being part of, or contributing to, something positive
- Making the world a better place
- Personal growth
- Helping others
- Realizing when not getting the results you want and making adjustments without being deliberate
- Feeling positive and good feelings
- Healthy passion
- Strong connection
- Good connection

Admit when you do not know something and ask to be taught. Understand that ignorance is not stupidity.

Healthy Tribalism: When you are an active, and contributing, part of a healthy team, group, or society. The sense of accomplishment you feel when your team does well or has properly prepared to do well. Watching a team on tv and then saying "we won" is not what I am talking about.

BAD PRIDE

What is Bad Pride? Bad Pride is self-obsession, arrogance, unwillingness to ask for help, not accepting help nor feedback, when we force a bad position, inability to admit mistakes, holding grudges, choosing isolation over communication, defending something we said because we don't want to be wrong or embarrassed, limiting personal growth because you think you are fine the way you are, and oppressing someone else (or a group.)

Bad Pride is:

- Making excuses for your lack of results

- Wanting to be right instead of having the right answer

- Being deliberate

- Defending failure

- Seeing the good parts of something you are interested in and not being able to see the bad

- Blindly believing in something

- Lack of accountability

- Inability to sincerely apologize

- Feeling you don't owe someone an explanation, if you do

- Defending failure
- Competition through envy or jealousy
- Refusing to congratulate someone who beat or outperformed you
- Refusing to surrender to minimize your losses
- Bringing others down to make yourself feel better or equal
- Not challenging your belief system. Remember beliefs are rarely formed by logic and they typically cannot be reversed through logic. Scary and Unevolved (more on this in the chapter "Evolution")

Pride is expensive. Don't let it affect your ability to be a good human.

SECTION 500:
YOUR WHY NURTURE

Growing from what we now know

CHAPTER 501:
Being in the Right Environment

Chris had always wanted to move to "the big city." When he was 18, he thought to himself "I am going to move this year" but it didn't happen. He stayed in the small town in which he grew up. It's important to know Chris has strong needs for significance, connection, uncertainty, and love. He has moderate need levels for certainty and growth/contribution. Living in a small town gave him lots of close friends since everyone knew everyone. He had grown fond of most of the people in the town, which fulfilled his need for connection and love. Since the town had a very slow pace, things didn't change that much. He knew the church would have a yard sale every Wednesday, and every Friday night the town hall would host a square dance. His need for connection and love were being fulfilled at the expense of his need for uncertainty. He was mostly happy, or at least he thought he was. His strong need for significance and moderate need for growth/contribution were rarely met. The guy who ran the general store called him Mr. Chris, but that's about it. His best friend had zero need for significance, a low need for growth/contribution and always seemed to talk Chris through the times when Chris felt out of balance in his need levels. This made it a little easier not to have those areas fulfilled.

Twenty years slipped away. Chris was so far out of balance

from years of certainty, lack of significance, and too little growth/contribution that he decided to take action. Diving head first into uncertainty, he moved to the big city. Since he always had a love for journalism, he applied to get a job at a weekly paper. He got a job as an editor.

He started on Monday morning. Twenty minutes into his first day Chris's boss dropped a ton of papers on his desk, and gave him instructions to have all that prepared by Wednesday. To Chris it looked like two weeks' worth of work. Chris decided he wanted to make a good impression, so he worked day and night. When deadline Wednesday came, the boss came to Chris's desk and asked for the finished work. When Chris handed it to his boss, the boss had a surprised look on his face. "It's all done?" asked the boss. "Yes sir!" Chris replied. Impressed by this the boss enthusiastically told Chris "Good job!"

Chris liked the compliment. It made him feel significant. It also made him feel like he had a strong connection with his boss. Doing well at work also made him feel a connection with the city he had decided to move to. Things were going well. On Thursday Chris's boss placed five times as much work on Chris's desk and demanded it by the following Wednesday. Chris was driven by his need for significance and connection, so he worked day and night once again. He had everything done by Wednesday. The boss showered Chris with praise again. The next Thursday he got the same workload, plus a little more. Then his boss started adding "rush work" into Chris's week. Chris ate it up.

Three months later Chris was called into the boss's office. He was told that he was doing an outstanding job and was being promoted to Senior Editor! He was given a raise and the responsibility of overseeing five people, in addition to his regular work. Chris was excited since this was the first time his need for growth was being fulfilled. Two months into his new position he went to his boss and suggested the paper do more local stories. The boss liked this small-town approach to the big city paper. Soon stories came across Chris's desk just like they would have if he had never left home. The paper's revenue doubled, and Chris was given another big raise. Chris was feeling an even stronger connection to the big city by contributing this small-town feel. He was a significant part of the company, he connected with people at work, he was growing personally and professionally, he was contributing to his city, contributing to his company, the uncertainty of every week being different was exciting, he was certain he was good at his job, and with all these compliments and praise he was feeling the love. Life had gone from "I think I am happy" to having an intensity toward living.

Question for you:

Did you keep waiting for a turning point in the story where something "bad" happened to Chris? If you did, the WHY is because our brains are wired for safety and security, not happiness. If you had a problem with reading a happy story and kept waiting for it to turn from happy, to having a problem with safety/security, watch your EBR.

Then Chris died. I'm kidding! I'm literally laughing out loud again. Chris is fine. What a fun story. The point of the story? Remember the glass of water we talked about in the chapter "Balance"? Chris's WHY NATURE was born into an environment that filled some of his need levels. The relentless environment of the small town changed Chris. He made do with it and tried to be happy. During the first 38 years of his life, he was generally a happy person, but the second half of his life was outstanding. When Chris's WHY NATURE was put into the WHY NURTURE where his need levels flourished, he loved it.

What would have happened if Chris had moved to the big city when he was 18? More importantly, what would have happened if Chris had never moved to the city? Wow. That's a thought, huh?

Try different environments and enhance your versatility. You never know what may come of it.

The part of the story I didn't tell you was that when Chris was promoted to Senior Editor, he asked his best friend to move to the city with him. Since they both enjoyed journalism, he gave his friend his old job as editor. Unfortunately, his friend didn't like it at all. He thought the city pace was way too fast. The pressure of weekly deadlines was way too much and felt he disconnected from everyone in that "rat race." Since his friend had zero need for significance he didn't care when people told him "good job." He wasn't interested in being "Employee of the month" because that significance was embarrassing to him. When Chris asked his friend if he was willing to do what it took to be promoted, the friend barely responded. His friend had no need for growth. His strong need for connection made him want to go back home. He didn't understand WHY Chris liked the city so much. The friend moved back to his small town and they stayed in touch.

What is the other take-away from this chapter? Everyone is different and that's ok. Embrace your family and friends for who they are, who they want to be and (most importantly) who they are not. You may have a lot of versatility which means you may have friends you do one activity with, and you may have other friends you do different activities with. They may not cross over. That's perfectly fine. Understand their WHY NATURE and accept them for who they are. Before you turn the page stop and think about each one's WHY NATURE. Once you think you have it, turn the page for the answers.

BONUS SECTION

Chris's WHY NATURE and what were the clues I gave you:

Primary Driver—because he loved accomplishing all the tasks at the paper

Secondary Analytical—he was in his own head a lot thinking about what if

Sigma—had a Lone Wolf kind of attitude with seemingly few friends. I didn't make this one very obvious but nothing indicated he was and Alpha, Gamma, nor Omega, so if you guess one of those read the story again. If you guessed Beta or Delta, those guesses are acceptable.

MT—he created his own motivation once he wanted the prize of filling his need levels

6 BHN—those were in the story

Capacity—C3. I mentioned he kept taking on more and more work, including intermittent rush work, and ate it up. A C1 or C2 couldn't handle this.

5 LL—WOA is his primary love language as indicated by how happy he was when his boss told him he was doing a good job as well as the compliments and praise were making him feel the love.

The Best Friend's WHY NATURE and what were the clues I gave you:

Primary Amiable—he wanted Chris to be happy so he kept talking him off the ledge and moved to the big city when Chris asked him to

Secondary Analytical—he was low on emotion and had a lot of reasons WHY Chris should just be happy where he was

Beta—he was a nice person with unclear boundaries, laid back and Amiable. Agreed with something he didn't want to do: move to the big city. He is a loyal friend. Even though Betas crave external validation, his need for significance was zero which is WHY he didn't want to be employee of the month.

Nothing in the story indicated he had a dominant personality, which rules out Alpha and Sigma. If you guessed Delta, I will take that answer. Nothing indicated he was a Gamma nor Omega.

MA—he wasn't motivated by prizes, promotions, money, nor recognition. When Chris asked his friend if he was willing to do what it took to be promoted, the friend barely responded

6 BHN—those were in the story

Capacity—C1 or C2. The pressure of weekly deadlines was way too much for him.

5LL—Unknown. He didn't receive the praise that Chris received so we don't really know.

CHAPTER 502:
Winning

Many have a point of view that in order for one to win, another must lose. I want to give a different viewpoint.

When I was a child, I played baseball. At the end of the baseball game, one team scored more runs than the other and was declared the winner. The other team was the loser. Since we were children, the childlike behavior ensued which included rubbing someone's face it. This typically included language like "we won," "you lost," and "you guys are terrible," etc…" Oh and let's not forget my personal favorite:

There is no "i" in T.E.A.M. but there is a "u" in S.U.C.K.!

For those who have a strong Need For Significance and Bad Pride, these sayings really resonate with you and you will probably reject this chapter. At least initially anyway.

I remember listening to an interview with an NFL Quarterback when he said "I have never lost a football game. I have been on a team that had less points when time ran out, but I have never lost." I love that.

To me this also means when we engage in sport and I scored more runs than you, I was better skilled (or maybe just luckier) than you, on that day. Key phrase: on that day. It means if you scored more runs than me on that day I got the opportunity to understand WHY, on this day, I could not prevail. Bad pride, or the Need for Significance, might make us throw a world class hissy fit but the adult in you learned what we need to work on, where our team's weaknesses are, and how we can be better prepared the next time we play. So they "won" the game and we "won" the knowledge we needed. Not to mention we had fun playing the game we love, which is a win in itself.

I remember when my son was 8 years old and he played travel baseball. We had a new team of 8-year-olds, which were just assembled. For our first game we played another 8-year-old team, who had been playing together for quite some time. They beat us so badly it felt like we owed them tuition. I mean, I wanted to apologize for wasting their time. When we were at practice the next day I was speaking with the other coaches and said "well now we know what we have to do in order to be competitive." We won knowledge that day. This builds character.

When we agree to participate in win/lose situations like play a game, have a match, or have a race, we are agreeing to have a clear winner of the contest. I scored more runs or points than you, so I won the game. If we both agreed to line up at the starting line and race, then we want to have a clear winner at the finish line. In these situations, we both want to know who won the contest and who won the experience they needed to improve.

If we are competing for the same job (submitting your resume is agreeing to compete), role in a play, or position of significance then only one of us can get it. In these situations, the person who got the job, role or position won the contest and the other people won the experience of now knowing how unprepared they were. They may not want to hear it, but it's the truth.

Kobe Bryant used to say, "I am going to play so well that my goal is to make you rethink your life's choices." Were you prepared for an opponent like that? Maybe Kobe had a strong need for significance. I heard a basketball player say he went to the arena to warm up and saw Kobe Bryant, who was on the opposing team, already there working out. The player worked out as long as he normally would and even a bit longer because Kobe was there. When the other player left, he saw Kobe hadn't stopped working out. After losing the game to Kobe's team, the player went over to Kobe and asked him WHY he worked out so long. To which Kobe replied "Because I wanted to show you no matter how hard you try, I am willing to outwork you." Now I ask you, was there a loser in that game? Absolutely not. Kobe won the game and the other player won the valuable lesson of what it takes to compete at the highest level. RIP Kobe.

Let's reframe winning shall we? We can have a win-win in any situation.

Because many people reading this book grew up playing sports or watching sports we have the preconceived notion that one has to lose, in order for another to win. That is not the case. Especially in life outside of sports.

Let's take the art of selling as an example. First of all, a professional salesperson, with proper integrity, knows that they should never sell something unless the product or service has more value to the buyer than the price. That salesperson is happy to charge their price as long as they know the value of what they are selling means more to you (key phrase) than the price you are paying. This is a win-win.

In relationships a win-win situation involves communication and compromise. In relationships you don't have a problem, and I don't have a problem; however, we might have a problem we need to discuss. The problem is the problem even if one person's behavior is clearly the reason. Again, we don't have to have a winner and loser. When making an agreement with someone, look for ways both of you can win.

CHAPTER 503:
Character

Character is revealed in your moments of action when no one is looking.

Are you an upstanding person, or are your morals, values, and Character for sale?

What would you do if you were sitting on a bench and saw someone drop money out of their pocket? What if you knew you were the only one who saw it? What would you do? Stop right here and answer these questions honestly.

1. What is the first thing that came to your mind when I asked you that question?

2. Are you asking how much money?

3. Do you consider your financial situation before you take action? By the way, telling them they dropped it, going to pick it up yourself, or even making the conscious decision to leave it there are all actions. You can't avoid taking action.

4. Are you asking who dropped it? If it was an old man who looked like it was his last buck, would you return it? What if it was a $100 bill dropped by a very well dressed middle aged person walking towards their very expensive car? Would your action change? If you said yes, you justified your action.

If you returned it, would you expect an award? People with good Character know honesty is its own reward.

If you decided to return the money, when would you give up trying to return it? If the person was several steps away and didn't hear you calling them, would you get up off the bench? Would you walk after them? If you knew you couldn't catch up to them by walking would you run after them? Are you considering what you are wearing right now in order to decide if you would run after them? Would you continue trying to get their attention after they got into their car? Would you get into your car and drive after them if they had driven away before you got their attention? How hard would you try? The point of this exercise is to see how far you would go to do what you know is right. Would you only do the right thing if it were easy for you to do it? The faster you gave up, the more we may have to reflect on our Character.

If you kept the money without trying to return it to its owner, how would that make you feel? Does your answer include justification of your actions? Does it include a description of the person? If yes, then you have Character issues. I will take this one step further and guess many of your behaviors are Category 2 (good for you and not good for others.) Actually, you think they are Category 2 behaviors when in reality, they are Category 4 behaviors (not good for you and not good for others.) You know what is right yet you are trying to accept and validate your actions through justification. This is a flaw in your Character. Example of justification: "That rich guy didn't need that $20 bill. He is probably a criminal anyway. That is WHY he is losing his money. He makes it too easily he loses it too easily. It's just Karma."

PRO TIP: Karma is a bitch when you are a bitch!

Justification cannot replace good Character

If you kept the money after trying to tell the person they dropped it, but they left without hearing you, how would that make you feel? Would you be able to justify it to yourself then? What would you do with the money at that point? Would you donate the money to a charity or keep it for yourself? Would you spend it on a good deed for someone else or spend it on yourself?

Character builds upon itself. If you stole something (I'm not talking about the money the person dropped) what happens when you are caught? Will you add to your bad Character by not telling the truth, in order to try and avoid the consequences? Avoiding the consequences of your actions is also bad Character. Stealing something (bad Character), leads to lying (bad Character) to try to avoid the consequences (bad Character) of your actions. See the snowball effect bad Character has?

Good Character builds upon itself as well. If you tell someone they gave you too much change, they will think you are an honest person. Having those expectations on you will make you want to live up to them and you are more likely to do honest things and things of good Character. The day will come when having the reputation of being an honest person and a good human, will come in handy. When you have built your Character to the point where people take your word at face value it will validate your actions of good character and reinforce your behavior.

If I tell you not to run any red lights on the way home, so you don't, and you made it home safely, was I right? We don't know because we cannot quantify it. This is the same with good Character. When one has bad Character they don't know how many opportunities they missed, times they didn't get invited, or how many times they were passed up for promotion, because of their bad Character. If you have good Character you were given the opportunity, got the invitation, and were considered for the promotion. Each of those opportunities, invitations, and promotions will change the course of your life by one degree. Raise the course of an airplane by one degree and over the course of 10 or 20 years that airplane is significantly hire than the one that was flat. This is a metaphor for your life.

Look at these words for a minute and realize how they make you feel:

- Honesty
- Integrity
- Honor
- Dignity
- Trustworthy

- Truth
- Respect
- Responsible
- Caring
- Discipline

- Patience
- Morals
- Ethical
- Virtuous

Some of you are reading this chapter right now thinking "oh crap, I'm about to be called out."

Some of you are thinking "yeah I've got some of that."

Others are thinking "yeah I've got most of that."

If one of the last three sentences describes the way you feel then please keep reading, because I am most certainly writing this for you. Oh, and you're welcome.

If you are thinking "yeah, I've got all of that, without question." Then here is your reminder that you are the quality human that makes the world a better place.

Let me properly introduce you to those words. I am sure you have heard all of these words before but we should revisit them. Please read and understand them thoroughly as defined by Webster.

Honesty

2 a : fairness and straightforwardness of conduct **b :** adherence to the facts **:** SINCERITY

synonyms HONESTY, HONOR, INTEGRITY, PROBITY mean uprightness of character or action. HONESTY implies a refusal to lie, steal, or deceive in any way. HONOR suggests an active or anxious regard for the standards of one's profession, calling, or position. INTEGRITY implies trustworthiness and incorruptibility to a degree that one is incapable of being false to a trust, responsibility, or pledge. PROBITY implies tried and proven honesty or integrity.

Integrity

1 : firm adherence to a code of especially moral or artistic values : INCORRUPTIBILITY
2 : an unimpaired condition : SOUNDNESS
3 : the quality or state of being complete or undivided : COMPLETENESS
synonym see HONESTY

Honor

1 a : good name or public esteem : REPUTATION
b : a showing of usually merited respect :
8 a : a keen sense of ethical conduct : INTEGRITY <wouldn't do it as a matter of *honor*> **b** : one's word given as a guarantee of performance <on my *honor*, I will be there>

Dignity

1 : the quality or state of being worthy, honored, or esteemed
4 : formal reserve or seriousness of manner, appearance, or language

Trustworthy

: worthy of confidence : **DEPENDABLE** <a *trustworthy* guide> <*trustworthy* information>

Truth (truthful)

1b : sincerity in action, Character, and utterance
(telling your version or part of the truth is not the same as telling the truth)

Respect

2 : an act of giving particular attention : <u>CONSIDERATION</u>
3 a : high or special regard : <u>ESTEEM</u>   **b :** the quality or state of being esteemed   **c** *plural* **:** expressions of respect or deference <paid our *respects*>

Responsible

1 a : liable to be called on to answer
2 a : able to answer for one's conduct and obligations : <u>TRUSTWORTHY</u>
b : able to choose for oneself between right and wrong

Caring

1 a : to feel trouble or anxiety   **b :** to feel interest or concern <*care* about freedom>
2 : to give care <*care* for the sick>
3 a : to have a liking, fondness, or taste <don't *care* for your attitude>
1 : to be concerned about or to the extent of <don't *care* what they say> <doesn't *care* a damn>

Discipline

4 : training that corrects, molds, or perfects the mental faculties or moral character
5 a : control gained by enforcing obedience or order   **b :** orderly or prescribed conduct or pattern of behavior   **c :** <u>SELF-CONTROL</u>
6 : a rule or system of rules governing conduct or activity

Patience

Etymology: Middle English *pacient,* from Anglo-French, from Latin *patient-, patiens,* from present participle of *pati* to suffer; perhaps akin to Greek *pEma* suffering

1 : bearing pains or trials calmly or without complaint
2 : manifesting forbearance under provocation or strain
3 : not hasty or impetuous
4 : steadfast despite opposition, difficulty, or adversity
5 a : able or willing to bear

Morals

: of or relating to principles of right and wrong in behavior : <u>ethical</u>
moral judgments
: expressing or teaching a <u>conception</u> of right behavior
a *moral* poem
: conforming to a standard of right behavior
took a *moral* position on the issue though it cost him the nomination
: sanctioned by or <u>operative</u> on one's conscience or ethical judgment
a *moral* obligation
: capable of right and wrong action

Virtuous

Having or showing high moral standards

These words are some of the pillars of good Character. These are some of the traits and actions a person with good Character displays on a daily basis:

1. fairness and straightforwardness of conduct

2. uprightness of character or action. <u>HONESTY</u> implies a <u>refusal</u> to lie, steal, or deceive in any way

3. firm adherence to a code of especially moral or artistic values : <u>INCORRUPTIBILITY</u>

4. good name or public esteem

5. a person of superior standing
6. one whose worth brings respect
7. a gesture of deference
8. a keen sense of ethical conduct
9. one's word given as a guarantee of performance
10. the quality or state of being worthy, honored, or esteemed
11. formal reserve or seriousness of manner, appearance, or language
12. worthy of confidence
13. sincerity in action, character, and utterance
14. the property (as of a statement) of being in accord with fact or reality
15. an act of giving particular attention
16. able to answer for one's conduct and obligations
17. able to choose for oneself between right and wrong
18. to feel interest or concern
19. a rule or system of rules governing conduct or activity
20. bearing pains or trials calmly or without complaint
21. not hasty or impetuous
22. steadfast despite opposition, difficulty, or adversity
23. We do not lead with prejudice
24. We do not make someone guilty without a trial (simply asking what happened is a start)

Do these traits and actions describe you? Hopefully you answered "yes." If not, we should think about our Character because the farther off the mark these traits are to describing you, the worse our Character is. The actions you take are windows into your soul. The actions you take reflect your values. You will know if you are displaying good Character when you do not have to justify your actions and you know you have not violated your values.

Doing the right thing means playing by the rules. Keeping your word. Telling the truth. I am fascinated by the Knights in medieval times. In order to be a knight you must take an oath to always tell the truth. Always, even if it means your own death. Can you do that? Can you tell the truth even if you knew the consequences were that you would be killed? Well, that is the highest level of Character so let's work backwards from there. If that is the standard for good Character then where, if any, do you violate the standard? It is ironic that this seems to be an old fashioned word because the speed in which information travels now would seem to make people want to have good Character. If they do or don't display good Character the information is going to travel much faster than it used to.

When you agree to do a job, make sure you do the best job that you can do. Don't be lazy. Don't do the least you can do or just the minimum of what is expected of you. The desire to do a good job shows good Character. When you do a good job, go above and beyond or do more than what is expected of you. You will get referrals, good testimony, or other job offers. This will provide opportunity in your life. Employers always keep an eye out for overachievers. Because overachievers overachieve. Overachievers require less management. When you do a good job or go above and beyond the task, people notice. When the right person notices your Character, you may benefit from it. When your boss knows you have good Character, the company will do more to keep you. You may get larger raises than others. You may get promoted faster than others. Employers want people with good Character in important positions. Be one of them and opportunity will present itself. If you always do the least you could to get by, or do a half ass job, and you can't get ahead well now you know WHY.

Character test

Here is an excellent example: If you could do something or sell something that would make you rich but would damage society or people's lives, would you do it? Some people are asking "How rich?" and "How much damage are we talking about?" Let's say the level of rich you would achieve would be directly related to the amount of damage you would do. Very rich would do a lot of damage, rich would do damage, and a little rich would do a little bit of damage. Some people are knowingly selling a product that actually damages people's health in the pursuit of monetary gain. They are providing a product that is bad for people (even worse if it's addictive) and has been shown to reduce the life expectancy of the person who uses their product.

If you said you would do it then you have Character issues. If you even thought about it or was one of those people who asked "How rich?" or "How much damage?" you may want to consider taking a strong look at your Character. It means you would violate your principles for money. In short, your actions, and your morals, are for sale. Not good.

If you can do something you know is wrong, or doesn't serve the greater good, and be happy with what you see when you look into the mirror then you should rethink your life. I am sorry if I am not being politically correct here, but this point needs to get across so people can learn to live together. Have you ever heard the question asked "Can't we all just get along?" If everyone had good Character the answer would be "Yes!" Now do you see WHY good Character is so important? If everyone was respectful of one another, gave as much as they took, and did the right thing, the world would be a much better place for everyone. Do your part.

To the people that think "no one does the right thing." If you think this way, then you are misguided. There are plenty of good and selfless people in the world. You need to read the chapter "Expectations, Beliefs, and Rules" repeatedly until you change your point of view. WHY is this so important? Because the more people that have good Character, the better our world will be. Do your part.

Want another test of Character? When you leave a room is it in the same or better condition than when you entered it? If you said "yes" then you are exhibiting good Character. The world is a better place with you in it. If you don't know what I am talking about simply because you have never considered this (sorry for the cold water) it means you are selfish and your parents have more work to do.

If you knock over a glass (breaking it) and spill something on the floor, make an effort to clean it up. If you can't clean it up, or it is not appropriate for you to do so, then at least own up to it. Apologize to the person who is responsible for the room or who owns/manages the property for leaving the room in a worse condition than when you entered it. Offer to pay for the glass you broke. People will accept your apology. You will have a clean conscience. If you can't afford what you broke, then at least offer that explanation (and an apology) to the person it belonged to. Communicate, communicate, communicate! Tell the person you would love to replace what you damaged, broke, or devalued but it is not within your means to do so and convey your apologies. People will admire your Character for it. Having good Character will benefit you in your personal and professional life. It will provide opportunity. It goes the same both ways. If you are the one responsible for the room, then allow the other person to apologize. Allow the other person to concede that they made a mistake and keep their dignity. Can't we all get along?

Use manners, say please, thank you, excuse me and look people in the eye. Let people who got there before you go first. Respect others. My Father once said: "Everyone is just trying to make it through the day. Be respectful of that and don't make their day more difficult unnecessarily." Be a good sport. Remember, the choices you make should display good ethics and represent your values.

Another good Character test: What if the hero in a movie did what you just did? What would you think about their actions?

> *"You become a good person by doing good things."*
> ~ARISTOTLE

It is ok to have fears and insecurities. These do not determine Character. Actions do. Your actions will dictate your Character. Don't act on your insecurities and do damage to people out of fear because you think they may do damage to you. Communicate. Find out the facts. Tell the truth. If you are guessing, or assuming, while you are taking action then you should communicate more.

Would you buy stolen property? If you just asked "What if you didn't know it was stolen?" You are probably trying to justify your actions (and you are probably an Analytical) and have the ability lie to yourself. You usually know or suspect because your gut will tell you. The question actually was "Would you buy stolen property?" This denotes that you know (or at least suspect) it is stolen. If you would buy stolen property then you have bad character. Imagine that the item was stolen from you. How would you feel about that? Have you ever heard the phrase "Do unto others as you would have them do unto you?" Imagine if no one would buy stolen property. What would the person do with the stolen item? Since they couldn't get any monetary benefit from stealing it, they probably wouldn't steal anymore. Wouldn't that make the world a better place?

What are our "standards?" What are your moral values?" After reading this do you think we need to "raise the bar" a little? If you said "no" then hopefully you have great Character. We are only as good as the moral standards we set and the actions we take to enforce them.

WALK A MILE IN THEIR SHOES

In order to have high quality good Character, one must have the ability to do this. How do I walk a mile in someone's shoes? Before you pass judgment on someone or think you know WHY they did something, make it a practice to really imagine their situation. If you were really in their situation, what would you do? Consider everything. All the circumstances. Put yourself in that situation with all the circumstances, abilities, and lack of abilities they have. The resources, and lack of resources, they have and then really imagine if the choice was yours. Mentally walk a mile in their shoes. Really immerse yourself in that thought. If you don't do that, then you cannot truly pass judgment. After all of that you may decide their choice wasn't far from yours after all. This is much more than appreciation. It is understanding their situation exactly. Learn not to be prejudice.

GRATITUDE

Lastly, we should be grateful. Gratitude shows good Character. Happiness is wanting what you have, not having what you want. Take some time every day to be grateful for the people and things you have in your life. You may not have them tomorrow. One day that tomorrow will come.

Here is the good news! You don't have to live with your choices forever. If you have done something you are not proud of, or regret, you have time to make it right. As long as there is breath in your lungs it is not too late. Like Bob Marley said, "Only you can redeem yourself."

Do your part and sweep your doorstep before you try to clean up the neighborhood.

BE A WOW!

What is a WOW!?

A WOW! is when you are done completing the task, the person following up comes to see your work and all they can say is "WOW!"

It's when you did more than what was expected of you and the person seeing your results says "WOW!"

It's when someone is describing the quality of your work to someone, your precision, completeness, competence, knowledge, and the quality of work and all the other person can say is "WOW!"

It's when someone finds out you are the one in charge, the record holder, or the one who calls the shots, but you didn't introduce yourself that way and when they find out they say "WOW!"

It's when someone describes your character, they say how truthful, honest, and forthcoming you are and tells the other person you are like no other and the listener can only say "WOW!"

WHY be a WOW? Because everything you have ever wanted will be at your fingertips. Whether you want significance, connection, opportunity, options, advancement, stability, growth, contribution, love, or just simply to live a life you are proud of.

Being a WOW means people want you on their team or want to be on your team, will do everything they can to retain you, want you to mentor/teach them, you will get the opportunities, invitations, promotions, advancements, people want to be your friend, and people want to be romantic partner.

Be a WOW!

Your personal and professional life will change drastically for the better.

Remember when you are good, you tell everyone. When you are great, people tell you.

CHAPTER 504:
Evolution

What is Evolution? For WHY purposes it is the change in one's behavior from Unevolved to Evolved.

Unevolved behaviors are raw, unfiltered, instinctual, and selfish.

Evolved behaviors are refined, filtered, calculated, and a balance of selfish/selfless.

Let's dive in!

THE UNEVOLVED

We are born childlike, selfish, self-centered, and without manners. Ever heard a child yell "mine, mine, mine!?" This is what is naturally inside us. Few children have the natural instinct to share. They also are selfish and prefer instant gratification. Try this test with a child: offer them two cookies now OR three cookies tomorrow. When I saw this test performed, every child took the "2 cookies now" option. WHY? Instant gratification is a characteristic of the Unevolved. Even though the child will be happier tomorrow with three cookies, they can't bring them self to look past instant gratification.

Characteristics of the unevolved (in no particular order):

- childish behavior
- name calling
- immature
- irresponsible

- inappropriate
- emotional slave, emotionally unstable, avoids or deflects emotions
- defensive
- impulsive
- manipulative
- attention seeking (inappropriate or unsolicited)
- inability to compromise or share
- unsophisticated
- bratty
- lacks boundaries (or can't enforce them)
- intolerant
- unaccepting
- chaotic
- racist
- judgmental
- comparing yourself to others
- selfish
- self-centered
- angry
- quick to snap
- short temper
- appears out of control
- resorts to physical action (or confrontation) too quickly
- anxious
- yells / cannot control tone especially when they don't understand
- quick to correct people when they are wrong (especially when one has a strong need for significance)
- lacks capacity and needs help
- puts others down in an effort to make themself look or feel better
- blames others or blames the world when they don't have success
- have an ongoing "hurt" or a story they carry along with them as to WHY they cannot get ahead or move on

- is in competition with others (not realizing you are only competing against yourself)
- not accountable for their actions
- thinks the world owes them something
- speaks poorly of others
- victim mentality
- unreliable
- exhibits bad Pride
- low emotional EQ
- poor speech and use of their language
- tribalistic
- uses a room (enters any room and leaves it in worse condition than when they entered it. has little to no regard for the next person who needs it)
- bad character
- prefers dopamine hits over peace
- confuses pleasure with happiness

Definition per Google:

Low emotional intelligence (EQ) is the inability to recognize, understand, and manage your own emotions and those of others, leading to poor social skills, damaged relationships, and difficulties with self-regulation. Common signs include lacking empathy, becoming defensive when given feedback, struggling to control emotional outbursts, blaming others for problems, having trouble taking responsibility, and making conversations about oneself.

Children are naturally Unevolved. Children have childlike behavior that is pure, beautiful, and positive. They also have childish behavior that is selfish, instinctual, and self-centered.

PRO TIP: Some people never grow up. AKA children can have gray hair.

If I can change your state of mind, then you are my slave because I can control you. If I cannot make you upset, happy or otherwise change your state, then you are in control of yourself. You don't get to change my mood. I will not give you that power over me. If you think I'm awesome, that's great. If you don't think much of me, that's great too. It's ok. As long as my behavior (or your behavior) isn't hurting anyone, then live and let live. We understand we are not fans of one another. Through understanding we can have tolerance. Through tolerance we can have acceptance. Through acceptance we can have peace. You do you and I'll do me.

Just like we talked about in the chapter "Being a Good Human": if I give you a gift that you do not want, who has the gift. You, right? If I try to give you a gift, but you refuse the gift, who has the gift? Me, right? Well if I try to give you unhappiness, unpleasantness, and rudeness yet you don't accept the gift, who has the gift? Me right? WHY would you accept that gift, take it home to your family and open the gift? Simply refuse the gift. "I can see you are in a bad place, or negative space, right now and thank you for trying to give it to me, but I refuse to accept it. You can keep it."

Did you know that positivity is more powerful than negativity? Wait a minute Rob, I read the chapter "The Negative Wave" where you said it takes several positive things to equal one negative thing. Yes that is correct, for the Unevolved! If someone says you are ugly and you yell back at them "you are double ugly," who is going to win the yelling contest? No one right? Negative only feeds negative. If someone tells you that you are ugly and (you don't accept that gift) you look at them and say "you are so smart and attractive, I bet you are even more attractive when you smile." Maybe they can resist you once, but each time they come back with something negative just say that over and over and eventually they will smile. Then you can say "see you are more attractive when you smile!" Positivity will always win. Evolved people understand hurt people, hurt people. Those people need love and light, not more negativity.

Being low on Capacity can make Evolved people slip back into

Unevolved behavior. During these capacity drains we revert back to Unevolved behavior. Remember we were born Unevolved, with Unevolved behaviors, so sometimes the brain may find comfort "running back there." Realize when Capacity is being drained. When are those times? Multiple things going on, frustration about something not working (Drivers especially), ideas spinning without solutions, being pulled in multiple directions, being short on money, being short on time, and trying to rush. Know when this is happening and get ahead of it, keep your composure, watch strong, foul or abusive language, take deep breaths, try to eliminate what are multiple drains on capacity, ask for help, divide and conquer, or simply try to accomplish the task at a different time.

The Unevolved are a slave to Associations, Triggers, and Demons. Described in that chapter.

Unevolved people react when they are feeling emotional. Evolved people identify the signal, thank the signal for its message, then respond accordingly, and move on with Equanimity. Equanimity is the practice of mental calmness, composure, and evenness of temper, especially in a difficult situation.

> *"Worrying is about as effective as chewing bubble gum to solve an algebra equation."*
>
> ~Baz Luhrmann (Sunscreen song)

The Unevolved cannot uphold their promises, control their urges, nor keep their commitments. Watch out for the Unevolved because they may also be unfaithful to their romantic partners. If the Unevolved also have bad pride, they will justify and rationalize their behavior.

The Unevolved crave material things. Review Lifestyle Creep that we discussed in the chapter "Balance." I want to be clear here. Having material things is ok. Wanting material things is ok. Craving what you cannot afford or being stressed in order to afford the lifestyle you want, is for the Unevolved. Wanting what you don't have more than wanting what you do have, is for the Unevolved.

> *"Possessions make you rich? I don't have that kind of richness. My richness is life, forever."*
> ~Bob Marley

UNEVOLVED PERSONALITY TYPES

Here is where the rubber meets the road. Remember children are Unevolved so each personality type, and social hierarchy, begins Unevolved. Females Evolve quicker than males. Sometimes a lot quicker.

PRO TIP: Boys are dumb. Like really dumb. Maybe there are a few exceptions, but don't get excited because odds are it isn't your son. I assure you it wasn't my mother's son (and I don't have a brother.) Boys want to climb things, test the physical limits of an object until it breaks, and they have loads (and loads) of energy they need to get out. This makes them not want to stop and listen. If your son is an Expressive, this is multiplied. The sooner you grasp this concept the sooner you will understand your son, and both of you will have an easier time during his childhood. Want to test it? Look a boy right in the face and tell him what you would like him to do. He will say "Ok." Then ask him to repeat what you just said and he will say "What?" because he can't repeat it. I'm literally laughing out loud right now. One of the funniest things to witness is a mom, who only has daughters, in a room full of boys. Their eyes are as wide as saucers because they have never witnessed such chaos. Remember it this way and your life will be easier: boys are tougher on things (the house, the walls, the lamp, their toys, the dog, etc.) and girls are tougher on you (emotions, they try to outsmart you, hormones, etc.) Boys are like having little out of control buddies whereas girls are actual parenting.

This is WHY all personality types begin Unevolved. Let's get into it…

Unevolved Amiables

These poor people. They are fantastic, caring, giving, and loving people who are their own worst enemy. They don't have boundaries; therefore they do not enforce any boundaries and cannot say no. They get walked on and used in one-sided relationships, from people who are capacity suckers. They are Einstein's definition of crazy: "doing the same thing over and over again and expecting a different result." They think if they keep giving, even when they are out of capacity and are giving from an empty cup, the person they are giving to will one day wake up and be grateful. They give without even letting the recipient know how much they are sacrificing in order to fulfill the request. They assume other people are mind readers. They will remain Unevolved until they grasp this one concept: "it doesn't work, it doesn't work, it doesn't work! You have to, have to, have to, have and enforce boundaries." Unfortunately, you can scream this in their face and nothing will change, until one day they decide to help themselves. Some people wake up and make this change. For some that change takes a lifetime and for others, a little longer. They are such good people they don't deserve this, but they won't help themselves.

Unevolved Analyticals

Overthinkers. Paralysis from analysis. May misdiagnose themselves as Drivers. WHY? For no reason other than they don't want to be labeled as Analyticals. Most likely to have anxiety issues. Can't hold a conversation because they overthink what you are saying. Low on emotion, which may take a toll on their relationship because they are likely to approach their partner from a logical point of view rather than sympathetic, empathetic, loving, and romantic. May be rigid, have an inability to see other perspectives, inability to compromise and likely to be deliberate to force an outcome. Intelligent Unevolved Analyticals have figured out the best way to accomplish something. Because of this they may be intolerant of people who have other points of view, or are lagging behind in their ability to come to the same conclusion. They need, and crave, information and they mistakenly think everyone else does too. This is most likely to conflict with Unevolved Drivers who are probably saying "get to the point," "shut up already," "we don't care anymore," or "WHY do you talk so much?" Unevolved Expressives have already cut them off and turned the attention back on themselves, which upset the Unevolved Analytical. Unevolved Analyticals are voted most likely to say, "Excuse me, I was talking." Unevolved Amiables are still listening to them talk because they don't have the boundaries to say they are bored out of their mind, and they think continuing to listen makes you happy. Unevolved Analyticals can't "read the room."

Unevolved Drivers

Unevolved Drivers want the task to be done above all else. They can be forceful, rude, demeaning, short, and inconsiderate of other people's feelings (including rude or abusive language.) If you inhibit their ability to accomplish the task, you are going to hear about it. If you purposely inhibit their ability to accomplish the task, be ready to fight. Unevolved Drivers subscribe to the philosophy "WHY use 10 words when 2 will do." This can be off-putting to people who are trying to connect with them. Especially off-putting to Unevolved Analyticals who want information. Ask an Unevolved Driver what happened at the game, and you will hear "we won." That's it! In their mind that is all you need to know. Ask them for more details and you will hear "I scored twice." Again, that's all you need to know. They really don't understand WHY you need to know more than this and get frustrated when asked for details. Since they don't care about the details, they may not even remember.

How the Driver reacts to not being able to accomplish the task, especially if the Driver is being inhibited, determines their level of Evolution. Not being able to accomplish the task is frustrating, not having the proper tools is more frustrating, and if you took one of their "tools" and didn't return it, once again be ready to fight. Being inhibited by someone or something is their highest level of frustration. An Unevolved Driver would much rather use force, than logic. Voted least likely to read the directions.

Unevolved Expressives

Jeez where do I start? They can be loud, obnoxious, and highly insistent on being the center of attention. When they are not the center of attention they will ramp up their behavior more and more and more, until the are. They will be relentless which may include negative, class 4 (not good for me and not good for others), or destructive behaviors. They think to themselves "if the only way to get attention is to shock everyone, then let's do it!" If you have ever seen an athlete score a goal, a point, a run, or a touchdown and there is a teammate who does something loud, surprising, inappropriate, or even unsportsmanlike (shock value) to take the focus off of the accomplishment and put it onto themselves, the other teammate is the Unevolved Expressive. They really can't help themselves. It's in their DNA. If you have one as a child, good luck. If you have two or more children who are Unevolved Expressives, you are really feeling the pain. Your house is chaos because the children keep increasing their Unevolved behavior to one up the other, in a never ending effort to gain the spotlight.

In their mind, WHY would they change? They are popular. They know a lot of people (99% shallow relationships) and everyone knows them. They think everyone likes them because they are too self-centered to realize all these shallow relationships just use them for entertainment value. People can only handle Unevolved Expressives for limited amounts of time. When the Unevolved

Expressive leaves the room, the people left in the room are saying to one another "OMG now we can finally have some peace and quiet." I feel like I need to give the parent of the Unevolved Expressive some advice. I have never tried to Evolve an Unevolved Expressive; however, I think the only way to do it is through understanding. The parent needs to understand their behavior and their WHY. The child needs to understand themselves, WHY they are doing what they are doing, and understand the impact it actually has on others. From this understanding, there can be tolerance, acceptance, and peace. Realize what you are saying to them though. You are saying: I'll give you three cookies tomorrow, or you can have two cookies today. The Unevolved will continue to choose the two cookies today.

Now it is a good time to revisit the chapter "Personality Types" so you can better identify your primary and secondary. Your primary may be an Evolved Driver (which slips into Unevolved Driver under certain conditions), with a secondary Evolved Analytical. Remember there are eight options for your primary and eight options for your secondary.

Do you see WHY it is difficult for humans to get along? Do you see how everyone is violating everyone else's EBR? Rodney King said "can't we all just get along?" Yes Rodney we can but it takes people doing their part and it starts with understanding YOUR WHY NATURE. Unevolved personality types are more likely to violate another person's EBR and now we are going to add to this…

UNEVOLVED SOCIAL HIERARCHIES

This means the person does not identify with their true self, does not accentuate the strengths of their hierarchy, focuses on their weaknesses, or is envious/jealous of other hierarchies. They have misdiagnosed themselves, want to be something they are not, or otherwise do not accept themselves.

Unevolved Alphas

Alphas won't have a problem identifying they are Alphas. The only time they may lose perspective is if they are put in an environment where their dominance is beaten out of them. If (especially when the Alpha is young) people in their environment say "WHY do you have to try to take over all the time?," or "can't you let someone else do it?," followed with "what is wrong with you?" This is only temporary though. Eventually the Alpha will move away, push through, or otherwise take charge. It may not be pretty when they do. Unevolved Alphas are likely to exert their dominance in "less than pleasant" ways. They may get aggressive, physical, threatening, invade your space, verbally assertive, or otherwise force you to submit. Have you ever seen a Silverback Gorilla get super aggressive on another animal? A Silverback Gorilla is an Unevolved Alpha. Literally.

PRO TIP: Never raise a child and try to control their behavior through fear. One day you will get old and the child will grow up to be stronger than you. Once you cannot intimidate them anymore, their resentful behavior will turn assertive or aggressive. WHY? Because this is the Nurture they learned from you. This is not good for anyone involved. This applies to all personality types and hierarchies.

Unevolved Alpha females are their own worst enemy. Voted most likely to be called a "bitch." She will exert her dominance in loud (figuratively and literally) and forceful ways. She doesn't care who she offends because she is not here to make friends. She has plenty of submissive females who want to be her friend because they want to ride her social coat tails. Romantically she is her own worst enemy. She seems to "chew men up and spit them out." She gets tired of making men fold but sometimes she does it for sport. She has no time for weakness and she will test the fences of a man's dominance. If she gets involved with an Unevolved Alpha male, the relationship will be a toxic, explosive, and a constant power struggle. Both are trying to make the other submit, but neither will. If she can make him submit, she will no longer respect him so it's a lose-lose situation. If she chooses a Sigma male, he will quickly discard her because he won't tolerate her behavior. She may think "he is the one who got away" or may accuse him of "being afraid of commitment." If she chooses a Beta, she will get frustrated because he won't take charge. When he tries to take charge, it is awkward and doesn't feel natural to either of them. If she constantly has to be in charge, she won't respect him. She may verbally and emotionally abuse him, even publicly. "Don't you have a spine?" and "be a man" may be things she is tired of saying. If she chooses a Delta male, she will be frustrated with his lack of ambition. If she chooses a Gamma male, misunderstanding him for an Alpha or Sigma, she will get frustrated with him when she finds the cracks in the armor (and she will because women always uncover the truth.) She won't be interested in an Omega male. Unevolved Alpha females will have to settle in their relationship one way or another. Again, she is her own worst enemy.

If she ever becomes an Evolved Alpha female, she will get rid of the man she chose when she was Unevolved, because she was settling for that relationship. The new Evolved Alpha female will have to find balance in her life. She will need to channel her dominance into her work, or other areas. When she is home, she should submit to an Evolved Alpha male whom she respects. More on this when we discuss Evolved Alpha males. The other option is an Evolved Sigma male. His quiet and passively dominant nature will intrigue her. He will set boundaries about her behavior and if she abides by them, the relationship will work. When her behavior violates his boundaries, and occasionally it will, he will calmly sit her down, remind her of his boundaries and explain how her behavior was unacceptable. Remember female energy is beautiful, but also chaotic. She won't like being "spoken to" because no one ever has done this with her. The only time a male spoke to her about her behavior was the Unevolved Alpha male, but he was yelling at her, so she wasn't listening. When the Evolved Sigma male unemotionally sits her down to "speak with her," she will be impressed that she cannot push back his boundaries (she also will respect him for it.) She will be impressed by his technique in comparison to Unevolved Alphas (soon she will also notice a pattern that both males were saying the same thing and will begin to realize the problem is her) and the relationship will work.

PRO TIP: If "she should submit" bothered you, you are Unevolved. You're welcome.

Unevolved Sigmas

An Unevolved Sigma is typically a Sigma who has misunderstood themselves to be an Alpha. Since both are dominant hierarchies, it is easy to do so. The reason is the Sigma never felt they met the definition of an Alpha, yet people mistakenly called them an Alpha. It just never "felt right" to them. They didn't understand WHY they wanted to be off the beaten path and their dominance was more passive than that of an Alpha. They see an Unevolved Alpha beating on his chest and realize they don't want to behave that way. Once a Sigma understands they are a Sigma, everything quickly falls into place. It's like a weight lifted off their shoulders.

Unevolved Sigma females can have the same romantic problems that Unevolved Alpha females have. One caveat being her dominance and lone wolf personality may make her think "I don't need a man." She will be much quicker to dismiss a potential romantic partner. In contrast to the Unevolved Alpha female who "chews men up and spits them out," the Unevolved Sigma female is much quicker to dismiss potential suitors. She constantly hears (from her friends) "WHY didn't you even give him a chance? He seemed nice." Once she becomes Evolved, she has to follow the same path as the Evolved Alpha female.

Unevolved Betas

They want to be Alphas. They have a hard time accepting their hierarchy. They sit in the background watching the Alpha males get the spotlight and the Unevolved Beta male doesn't like it. They want to be in charge but others don't see them as a natural leader. Unevolved Betas will focus more on their weaknesses, than their strengths. Mainly because they don't understand that their positive traits are actually valuable to potential romantic partners. They just don't sell themselves correctly and are most likely to end up in "the friend zone."

Unevolved Deltas

Deltas are less likely to misdiagnose themselves, which makes their understanding of themselves pretty seamless. Describe a Delta hierarchy to a Delta and they may say "yep, that's me!" Deltas will Evolve quickly because of their realistic outlook.

Unevolved Gammas

Here is where it gets a little dicey. They are the most likely to misdiagnose themselves and are delusional enough to think they are an Alpha above other Alphas. Gammas don't want to accept they are Gammas. They have actually convinced themselves they are not Gammas. Their rebellious nature can make them off-putting. Their independent nature can make them seem aloof and is one of the reasons people misdiagnose them as Sigmas. Gammas are actually called "fake Sigmas" for this reason. They lack social skills and as I mentioned before, they are most likely to "poke the (Alpha) bear." Alphas and Sigmas will find them annoying because they will know right away, this person (the Unevolved Gamma who mistakes himself for being above an Alpha) is not what they think they are. When the onion is peeled back, they will be envious and jealous, yet they won't understand WHY because they still delusionally think they are Alphas (or above.) They can end up having several, very short relationships because they are most likely to get into a relationship with this false diagnosis. They aren't doing it on purpose, they really do think they are Alphas and they obsess over the opposite sex. A handsome and outgoing Gamma, who thinks they are dominant, may appear to be the dominant personality a romantic partner is looking for; however, the truth always comes out.

Unevolved Omegas

Unevolved Omegas are also less likely to misdiagnose themselves. They really don't care what people think so the Unevolved Omega is very unfiltered. They may tell you the truth not realizing what they said was socially unacceptable. Voted most likely to be a fashion disaster. They can act and appear nerdy. They are not likely to change it because they simply don't care.

THE EVOLVED

Evolved people understand the distance between where you are now and who you want to be, is simply the way you think. The quicker you grasp that, the happier you will be. Evolved people have an ability to see things wholistically. Your diet, your sleep, your choices, and your behaviors are all connected and affect each other. Evolved people see both, or all, sides of a story objectively.

Look at the list of Unevolved traits and realize an Evolved person is the opposite of all of those. Here is a partial list:

- practices etiquette
- manners, including proper usage of cutlery
- good judgment
- good character
- self-control
- understands discretion
- boundaries

- discipline
- in control of their actions
- in control of their reactions
- controls emotions—practices equanimity or stoicism
- ability to act and execute, not just plan
- overrides primal thoughts
- controls urges (sexual and non-sexual)
- diplomatic
- self-awareness
- self-respect
- self-esteem
- empathy
- compassion
- sympathy
- desire for personal growth
- versatility through new experiences
- understands balance between short term goals and long term effects
- embraces change
- detachment from external opinions
- understanding not everyone is like they are
- polished
- confident
- patient
- forgiving
- has their "act together"
- master of capacity, has a full cup and has enough capacity to help others
- nice to other people and animals
- leaves a room in same, or better condition, than when they entered it
- can "take the high road" or "be the better person"
- understanding, tolerating, and accepting who you are and who you are not, in order to have peace within yourself
- understanding, tolerating, and accepting who you are and who you are not, in

- order to have peace with others
- understands and practices "live and let live" mentality
- accepting of others: do you think a billionaire cares about the skin color of another billionaire? Not at all. Let that soak in.

Self Confidence

Evolved people are self-confident. Here is the WHY of self-confidence. If you want to build more self-confidence, master these things:

- Internal validation: don't rely on other people's opinions otherwise your confidence will be an emotional roller coaster. Trust yourself and believe in yourself.
- Self-awareness: understand your strengths and weaknesses so you can set realistic goals and expectations.
- Self-efficacy: your belief in your own ability to accomplish new tasks
- Self-esteem: a positive view of yourself
- Emotional regulation: your ability to manage your emotions

Evolved people understand 20% of people aren't going to like you, for one reason or another. That's ok. Your job is to be a good person and not get that number over 20%. Haters are going to hate. Not everyone is Evolved.

Evolution is cutting relationships out of your life that are one sided, or that do not serve your happiness. Cutting it out may just mean putting it on hold or it may be just keeping it in the manner it is good for. Meaning: if you have a good friend at book club and you enjoy their company and perspective on books; however, they otherwise don't align with your morals, values, or you just simply don't get along too well then keep the relationship solely at book club. Know who your friends are and accept them for who they are (and who they are not.)

As we Evolve we learn Emotions are nothing more than signals or instructions. The same way we are learning a language in which to communicate who we are to ourselves, and other people, we need to learn the language of Emotions. Here are some examples:

- Happiness or Joy: My EBR has been met or my need levels have been met

- Upset or Sadness: experiencing loss or EBR has been violated

- Anger = my boundaries have been violated on purpose

- Fear: time to prepare

- Shame: violated EBR or boundaries of yourself or another person

- Jealousy: feeling of inadequacy. It's time to get better or it's time to lower expectations.

- Frustration: there is something violating your EBR or need levels but you haven't figured out what it is yet

- Disappointment: EBR were not met

- Nervous: time to prepare

- Anxious: living in the future and not the present, overanalyzing outcomes

- Elation: I finished reading WHY and finally know who I am (had to throw a fun one in there)

When you have an emotion, thank the emotion for the signal or instruction it gave you, act on the signal if needed, then continue on your path of equanimity.

Don't be deliberate. Hello Analyticals. Insisting on a certain outcome to where you cannot compromise, are blinded to anything else in front of you, and are inflexible to other options is an unhealthy EBR.

You cannot convince a loser, that you are not a loser. The loser has a Belief and, as we discussed in the chapter "Expectations, Beliefs, and Rules," you cannot talk someone out of a Belief, using logic.

Look at the results of the person giving you advice, before you follow that advice. If an inmate is telling you "go ahead, you probably won't get caught," maybe we shouldn't follow that advice because we don't want their results. Also, Category 4 behaviors are not where we should be.

I mentioned this in Capacity: The highest level of Capacity is an Evolved Capacity 3. Evolved 3's do all of the things I described except they know when it is time to ask for help. What Sally has to understand is if Sally never asks for help, she is robbing her friends and loved ones of their opportunity to give back to her. This is unfair and unbalanced. Give people the opportunity to help you and it will strengthen the relationship. Don't have bad pride.

The Evolved understand the golden rules:

1. Put your mask on before helping others (getting on a plane will remind you)

2. One should only give from a full cup

EVOLVED PERSONALITY TYPES

The common theme you will recognize is they all understand who they are, have accepted who they are, and have made peace with it. Every personality type has pros and cons. Embrace what is special about you!

PRO TIP: Evolved personality types can identify Unevolved personality types easily.

Evolved Amiables

Evolved Amiables are fantastic fantastic people. Remember Amiables want other people to be happy. Once they establish, and enforce, boundaries, they learn not to drain their capacity in order to make people happy. They learn to tell people "no." They cut one-sided relationships out of their life and focus on healthy relationships. They become less gullible and less manipulated. Their capacity levels increase and they give more of that capacity to healthy and positive things. They start to put themselves first (golden rule.) Evolved Amiables understand self-care and supporting yourself expand capacity levels, which you can give to those you really care about. It's self-fulfilling.

Evolved Analyticals

Evolved Analyticals learn:

- to read the room
- not everyone needs the level of information they do
- to get to the point without boring everyone with details
- the value of emotions and expressing themselves more, which helps their need for connection
- to identify the personality type of the person they are talking to, so they can curb their responses to that personality type
- to be more fluid in conversations—it's ok to make some assumptions about what someone is talking about
- not to be deliberate

- not everyone figures out the best way to do something—live and let live
- to control their anxiety and overthinking to how to stop spiraling
- not to get paralysis from analysis—they learn to take action. Note: if they are a secondary Driver, then the Driver already balanced them out.
- to make decisions faster

Evolved Drivers

All Drivers develop skills to help them better accomplish tasks. I know a Driver who can type 55 words per minute, using only four fingers. WHY four fingers? Because they never took a typing class and they taught themselves how. Evolved Drivers learn they need their team and realize the techniques they use (sometimes self-taught) don't make people happy. They understand that if they make everyone mad while accomplishing the task, they won't have a team tomorrow. They start working well with others, have more patience, and control their frustration. Evolved Drivers use more words than they need to, including pleasantries. Learning to tell a story and give more details makes them more engaging, which helps their need for connection. They will type an email by being frank and getting to the point, then alter it.

Example of an Evolved Driver typing you a message:

> Original message: *I need that book I gave you*
>
> Retyped as:
>
> *Hello Sally,*
> *What did you think of the book I loaned you? I would really like to have it back, please. Can I pick it up today?*

The Evolved Driver literally types out the message first (remnants of Unevolved behavior) and then goes back to add the pleasantries. Note: this was painful for them because it is against their natural behavior. They might have rolled their eyes while they retyped the email and said to themselves "WHY do people need all this fluff?" but they did it because they know they need to Evolve.

Evolved Expressives

Evolved Expressives? Talk about a unicorn! You have a better chance of seeing Jesus! Kidding! Mostly because there is truth in every joke. Evolved Expressives have learned they don't always have to be the center of attention. WHY? Because not everyone likes that. They learn to read the room and dial down their behavior when people are not happy with them. Balancing being the life of the party with connecting with people is their new skill. They realize having more connection (actual deep connections) in their lives is a good thing and interacting with people doesn't mean them looking at you right after you say "hey watch this!"

EVOLVED SOCIAL HIERARCHIES

Evolved Alphas

I went to Google to search for movies that have Alpha males to see if I could give you some examples. What I found is a lot of characters people think are Alphas, are actually Sigmas. This is how easy it is to misdiagnose.

Evolved Alphas are the guys at or near the top of the corporate ladder with the very, very expensive suits. WHY? Because they can afford them. They handle conflict and confrontation well because they are not afraid of either. Conflict and confrontation are handled with some level of restraint even when they are about to highly dominate the person they are conflicting with.

Evolved top Alpha tip: if you are the person in charge, the head cheese, the one who calls the shots or the person where "the buck stops here," then don't say it. There is an old saying "when you are good, you tell everyone. When you are great, people tell you." The times I have been the most impressed is when I was speaking with someone, who just introduced themselves by their first name, to later find out they were the owner, or the president or the person who calls the shots. When people find out later you are "the person" and you didn't introduce yourself that way, it is much more impactful.

So how do multiple Alphas coexist while the individual maintains control of their environment? Alphas begin to Evolve when they understand they cannot do everything. The self-confident and dominant Evolved Alpha does not have a problem with a person more qualified for the situation, in charge of that situation. If they determine they have to step in and take charge, they will. How the Alpha takes over depends on how Evolved they are, and whether or not there is a need for force. As long as the appointed person is doing a good job (irrelevant to personality type) they will let them do their job.

How does an Evolved Alpha (or Sigma) male handle an Evolved Alpha (or Sigma) female? The first thing to understand is, she is willing to submit to you because she trusts your judgment. So don't screw that up or the relationship will be short lived. Understand she either hasn't done this before or if she has, it didn't work out. Either way, this is new for her. Give her leeway while she is trying to balance this new life. Encourage her to be herself. To dominate where she wants to dominate, be a fan of her successes, do not be intimidated by her (if you are a true Evolved Alpha, or Sigma, I didn't have to tell you that), and let her know that there will be many times where she will take charge in the relationship. Reassure her that you also trust her judgment and you are fine with her being in control, when she should be.

Do not try to outwardly dominate her because her Unevolved

side may come out. If the relationship is going to last, sit down and have a conversation to discuss the tough topics: kids, religion, politics, and finances. Agree on how those topics will be handled in your relationship. When (not if) her behavior becomes chaotic, do not lose your cool or she won't respect you. Remember "I messages" and communicate "I would like you to stop now." Talk about this when cooler heads prevail or at your next strategy session.

PRO TIP: Do not ever, and I mean *ever,* let a potential romantic partner compare you to anyone else. Remember, being Evolved means self-confidence, self-esteem, and self-worth. In any relationship one has to bring value. Understand what value you bring to the table and accentuate your strengths. If their last romantic partner was a fitness model and you aren't, so what. If they miss the fitness model, tell them to go find what makes them happy and move on. There are over 8 billion people on this planet. If someone is not a match for you, it's ok. Does that mean there is anything wrong with you? No, as long as you are a good human. Does that mean there is anything wrong with them? No, as long as they are a good human. It just means there wasn't a connection. The asterisk is: if you keep losing romantic relationships due to the same issue, then you may want to take a good look at that issue.

Evolved Sigmas

Are a quiet force to be reckoned with. Their speech is eloquent and they doesn't mince words. When an Evolved Sigma walks into a room, he (or she) does it like they own the place. Not in a loud or obnoxious way, but more in a "passive dominance" way. Voted most likely to say, "You heard what I said." The mood of the room has changed and everyone knows they are there. Submissive males look at him to access what's going on, then they look down. Other Evolved Alphas and Sigmas will simply nod, acknowledging one other. Unevolved and challenging males will stare too long, but the Evolved Sigma will simply look away (never down) and give indifference to those people.

As I mentioned in Unevolved Sigmas. Once a Sigma understands they are a Sigma, and not an Alpha, everything falls into place quickly. The Sigma will slide into their hierarchy like a pair of old shoes. It fits just right! Once this happens, they will become even more dominant. They will better understand and will embrace their lone wolf behavior and accept themselves. WHY? Because now they finally understand their behavior and WHY the Alpha role never seemed to fit them.

Evolved Betas

Betas will Evolve when they understand who they are and accept their hierarchy. By the way, are we seeing a pattern here? I keep saying over and over understanding brings tolerance, tolerance brings acceptance, and acceptance brings peace. In order to Evolve one has to make peace with themself! Back to Evolved Betas.

Evolved Betas understand they can bring themselves from the background to the foreground by learning management techniques and through assertiveness training. They have to work on their techniques because this is not natural for them. If a female asks, "If this doesn't work romantically, maybe we can still be friends?" the Evolved Beta has to take a deep breath, go against their instinct, and reply, "I'm sorry but no. I have enough friends. This is either romantic, or it's not." Whereas these words would flow effortlessly off the lips of an Alpha or Sigma, a Beta has to override the "nice guy" mentality and stick to his boundaries.

Evolved Betas are great people. They are nice, easy going, are great friends, and are very loyal people. Everyone should know who they are and play to their strengths. When an Evolved Beta is courting a female, he needs to tell her who he is and who he is not. The female will recognize he is Evolved and will admire his confidence.

Writing about the Betas in the friend zone made me think of this...

PRO TIP: Men and women can be friends. However!, and this is a huge however, once one of them has crossed the romantic line, the friendship is over. Period!

Let me clarify:

No person in your life is more important than your life partner. The only caveat to this is if you have a "marriage of convenience," then these boundaries don't apply to you.

X's are nothing but trouble for your relationship with our life partner. Once they are an X, move on. Many times, there is that one X who "just wants to check in every few years to see how you are doing." Here is the answer "I am fine, I will always be fine, thank you for your concern but let's move on with our lives and sorry but now I am going to block you." Again, struggling with boundaries only causes problems.

If you don't currently have a life partner and are looking for one: you have to create a safe space for that person to come into your life. Nothing will make a quality person (male or female) runaway faster than a person who has X's lingering around. Remember the movie "Field of Dreams" and the famous line "build it and they will come?" Imagine if Kevin Costner never built the baseball field! They never would have come, and the movie would have been over in 5 minutes. This is the same for your life. You have to build a safe space so when this person does come into your life, they feel comfortable and want to stay. If you are a woman wondering WHY you are not attracting the quality man you want, it's because you are not acting like a wife. A quality man doesn't want a girl they have to change into wife material. Dress the way a quality man thinks a quality woman would dress, behave in a quality way, and prepare the safe space for him to enter your life. He is looking for you, like a hawk. Once he sees what he is looking for, he will approach you.

These boundaries apply to any friend where your gender is their sexual preference. Meaning: if a man is homosexual and has a female friend, this doesn't apply. If a woman is homosexual and has a female friend, these rules apply. If a heterosexual man and a heterosexual woman are friends, these rules apply. You get the point, I don't need to list all the variables here.

Here are the boundaries:

If both of you went on a few dates and decided you weren't a match yet there was some romantic activity, move on.

If you met on a dating site and during the initial meeting you decided there is nothing there romantically, but you have a lot in common and can be friends, then be friends.

If you have a friend who you have been romantic with, move on.

If you have a friend who asks for you to sleep with them, to go on a date, or if they "see us getting together in the future," move on. This is crossing the line. Secretly, they are what is called "a hopeful." They are only hanging around in the hopes that one day something romantic will happen. Do them a favor and don't continue to lead them on.

If someone "hits on you" and asks you out on a date, you cannot be friends. WHY? Because one, or both, of you have had an action which has crossed the line.

I have a friend named Greg. We have met for coffee and chatted for hours, we have been to Vegas together and had hotel rooms next to one another, we have been intoxicated at the same time and through all of that we have never, ever, once even been confused about our friendship. This is the definition of a friend. If the person you are concerned about in your life doesn't meet the same description as this, move on.

You cannot move forward with a rear-view mirror in your face! This is WHY the windshield is larger than the rear-view mirror, in your car! If your romantic partner tells you they don't agree with me, it's because they want to keep their options open and (sorry for the cold water) you are not the one they think is their forever. Listen to Uncle Rob, it's true. I promise. Evolved people live by these boundaries.

Submissive hierarchies and Amiables read that part again! Do not allow people to cross these boundaries.

Males who have "friends" who meet the descriptions above, and are not willing to cut them off, have only one reason: because you are not worth cutting them off for. Sorry (not sorry) for the cold water.

Females with "friends," who meet the descriptions above, have ulterior motives and may shame males by saying "are you insecure?" and "WHY can't I have male friends, don't you trust me?" These manipulative females will gaslight their male and make them think they are not a man because they are acting insecure. Don't fall for it. Males (especially Sigma males) know when another man has ulterior motives. Listen to your gut because it is correct.

If you are the true friend of a person of the opposite sex (or same sex that is your sexual preference) and you meet your true friend's current romantic partner, go out of your way to offer them a safe space. Be transparent, explain your relationship, and offer for them to ask questions about it. Show them you have nothing to hide. If you want to stay friends with your true friend, you will do it for everyone's benefit.

PRO TIP: Don't ever talk about your exes to your current romantic partner unless (and this is the only exception to this rule) you are explaining to your current that the previous relationship created a trigger and you need them to be aware of it to help you clear it. Other than this, if you have to talk about your exes, this is what your friends are for.

I warned you will not like everything I have to say, but it will be the truth. You can either learn this now, or you can learn this the hard way. Unfortunately, too many people like to learn the hard way.

I told my girlfriend, "The password for my phone is your birthday so you won't forget it. If you ever need a safe space, grab my phone and go through it. I never need a warning nor notice. WHY? Because you are the one I want to be with and nothing is worth messing this up, so there isn't anything in that phone I am ashamed of. Also, I expect the same in return. This is non-negotiable." What did I just do here? I established my future boundary as a rule as we discussed in EBR. Oh, and what happened to that girlfriend? I married her and I still treat my wife with the same respect.

Evolved Deltas

Evolved Deltas are confident people because they have their act together. They have been in their jobs for a long time, they can do their job with their eyes closed or in less time than they used to, they are getting paid well for their time, they are solid people, they acknowledge and pride themselves on their competence, and their realistic view of life has given them a good handle on things. They have probably been promoted to "supervisor" or "manager." The Evolved Delta, who is an MT personality, understands when he is not happy in his environment, and when his hard work is not being recognized nor rewarded. In contrast, the MA personality has used his competence and knowledge from being the backbone of the company, to get everyone else to do his work so they can "just supervise." Evolved Deltas have increased their capacity because they have a good work/life balance. Evolved Deltas are attractive mates due to their strong foundation and competence, and if they present themselves this way their relationships have a greater chance of success.

Evolved Gammas

Evolved Gammas dial down their rebellious and independent nature, focusing more on their strengths. Including: self-awareness, caring and sensitivity. They understand social norms and don't feel as if that have to be so vocal about being a contrarian. Evolved Gammas use their self-awareness to understand how their behavior is affecting their relationships, including their romantic partner. They let their romantic partners know, up front, they don't like taking risks, they are very romantic, and love making big romantic gestures. And WHY wouldn't they? Those last two are great selling points!

Evolved Gammas finally don't have a false perception of themselves and no longer blame the world for their lack of results. They have put away their ego, have embraced their "nice guy" side and use this to be mediators, helpers and to give people comfort. They may even use this peacemaker persona to fill their need for connection, and to fit in, so they don't feel like an outcast. Evolved Gammas understand they don't really like the stress of managing people and have shied away from leading any groups. They understand confrontation can be a part of life and have learned how to be confrontational, when needed. This includes no longer being passive aggressive.

Evolved Omegas

Evolved Omegas are good people. They really aren't going to change that much when they Evolve, if they ever do. Genuine and probably honest to a fault. They know who they are and still don't care what you think. Maybe they have increased their filter, so they add some level of diplomacy when they tell you the truth. Evolved Omegas have realized the value of social graces. Maybe they worked with a stylist on how to dress while they were single and looking for a life partner.

CHAPTER 505:
Get a Glass of Cold Water Before You Read This

Do you have your glass of cold water? If not, put the book down and go get one.

I'll wait...

Seriously...

Don't proceed until you have a glass of cold water. You will need it for the exercise. This means you.

Got it? If not, the only one you are cheating is yourself!

Now try this test

Do each part before you read the next task or you will lose the experience and the benefits it will bring.

Grab your glass of cold water. It will aid you in the exercise. Do not read on until you have a glass of cold water in your hand.

Now pick up the glass and take a drink to prepare your throat for the next exercise. You should do this before reading any further. Are you really doing this before you read on? If not, put the book down and go do it. It's important!

Drink.

If you took a drink, turn the page to complete the exercise...

That was it! That was the experience: to take a drink of water. If you did as you were asked, then you were probably so interested in the glass of water being a preparatory devise that you did not experience it fully. Now try it again knowing what the outcome should be. Take that same cold glass of water in your hand or hands. Feel the surface of the glass. It is smooth. Feel how the glass is ergonomically correct to fit in your hand.

In a minute try it again with your eyes closed. When your sense of sight is not there it will heighten the other senses. I want you to feel the temperature. It is cool and pleasing to the touch, like the cold side of the pillow. Take a drink and feel the water touching your lips and entering your mouth. Really concentrate on the experience uninterrupted by anything or being anxious for the next experience. Feel how it leaves your mouth cooler than it was when you started. Let the taste "finish" in your mouth. Letting the taste finish is especially important when drinking wine. It makes a big difference. Ok close your eyes and take a drink of cold water. Once you open your eyes hold the glass up to the sunlight and see how beautiful the water is when the sunlight goes through it (if you can't do this because you have a solid cup, please note the instructions that you didn't follow, were to get a glass. I suggest a heart felt apology letter to your third grade teacher letting her know you still aren't taking her advice to follow instructions; however, as we already established in "Are you smart enough to feel stupid" you can't remember her name anyway so just forget it. OMG I am the biggest fan of my own jokes.)

Now that is the full experience of taking a drink of water! See the difference in the experience? If you go through life like the first time you drank the water, you will simply go through the motions. Embrace each experience uninterrupted. Don't rush the experience and don't try to move on to the next experience so quickly. Experience life like you drank the water with your eyes closed. Literally stop and smell the roses. There is a difference between living your life and waiting to die. Experiencing things in this manner is living your life.

Apply this to everything you do. Getting in the car, sitting at your desk, and of course drinking a fine wine should all become totally new experiences now. Enter each experience without any pre-conceived notions and a clear mind, so the world can open up to you. You may discover something so simple as you do not like the brand of socks that you have been wearing for years or something more complex which may improve your life. Enjoy!

CHAPTER 506:
Being a Good Human

"To know thyself is the beginning of wisdom."
~Socrates

Know your WHY NATURE and be fluent in understanding other people's WHY NATURE. Once you understand, you will have tolerance, acceptance, and peace within yourself. More importantly, this is what will spill out when life bumps your cup.

"Do the work" on yourself so you can be a Good Human with good character:

- Emotional completeness: Identifying emotions as signals to prepare. Emotional intelligence (EQ).

- Telling the Little Runner Man what files you want to see more of and reprimanding him when he brings you files you no longer want to see.

- Having C3 capacity and using some to help others—this can become addictive because it fills your needs

- Practicing Equanimity: you will have a calmness about you. You understand that your first reaction may not be the best one.

- Being whole: accepting yourself, having balance in your life, self-esteem, self-respect

- Clearing Associations, Triggers, and Demons
- Having good self-talk and speaking to others well
- Greet others with a certain level of respect. They can earn more, or lose more, from there.
- Be someone you respect, which means Category 1 behaviors
- Be polite
- Have manners
- Have social graces (also means you respect other cultures)
- Practice etiquette
- Give people the benefit of the doubt (or at least offer someone a trial before you make them guilty)

You don't live a double life. You won't have one façade of you that you show the world, to be respected or to be liked, and then when no one is looking, you do things that you are ashamed of. When people get to know you, they will see the congruency and consistency. You will be proud of you in public and private.

Treat other people's property the same or better than they treat it.

Through this you will have healthy boundaries, healthy relationships, reciprocal respect for your close friends and inner circle.

Through understanding who you are you can explore that more and really get to know yourself. I mean the real you, what is on the inside. You can let it all come out and explore all of you through a healthy lens of understanding. Not the lens of how others see you nor what other people think you are or should be.

Through this understanding comes self-control, good decisions, and healthy habits. These self-reinforce into more love, respect, and being able to enforce boundaries.

It does not mean you give from an empty cup or when you are low on capacity. This is where healthy boundaries come in.

You prioritize your health, fulfillment, and happiness. You should have so much fulfillment overflowing from your cup, that it is spilling over into the world. You become a beacon of light people gravitate towards. This is very different than being a manipulated Amiable that people take advantage of.

Through this you will find happiness. You understand mean, rude, and intolerant people need extra love, patience and understanding while being mindful of your boundaries.

Through these actions and beliefs your needs for significance, connection, certainty, love, growth and contribution will be filled and overflowing.

Remember when I said whenever one action satisfies three or more needs, it will become a habit? Self-reinforcing behaviors.

In this state you will have gratitude and appreciation for yourself, your life, your connection with family, friends and loved ones.

You will have your finances in order.

Through this strong foundation you will have the confidence to grow into the highest level of yourself. Self-actualization on Maslow's Hierarchy of Needs.

You will be a good person, a mentor to people, an example that other people strive to be.

And most importantly…

Be mindful of the cup you carry around. When life bumps into you, what spills out? If peace, love, prosperity, and connection spill out, then you are carrying around Good Human traits in your cup. If ugliness, rudeness, and hostility spill out of your cup, this is your signal that you have work to do. This is the cup we discussed in EBR.

Do you know what I just described? Enlightenment and being whole.

BRING THE LIGHT

Sometimes people are having a bad day, a bad week, a bad year, or even a bad lifetime. These people can be negative, angry, hateful, sadistic, pushy, rude, nasty, and/or downright evil. What is their WHY? WHY are they like this? We may not ever know but we need to understand, in their mind they have a reason. The problem with darkness and negativity is, it is usually met with darkness and negativity.

Rivers of blood cannot bring peace, only obedience. Obedient people do not stay obedient unless they are afraid. They have to be afraid of consequences from a governing authority, or stronger entity, or pandemonium and lawlessness will begin.

Let's say someone cuts you off in traffic and gives you the finger. What does that mean? Before you read this book it might have meant that someone has violated your expectations, and we should retaliate. Maybe our need for significance has been undermined. Perhaps we should show them how significant we are by blowing our horn and flipping them off with both hands! Maybe we just let it go and go about our day. Maybe we call a friend to commiserate how horrible people are. What does it mean and what should we do?

I'll tell you what it means so we can reframe this experience. First of all, we have to remember the immortal words of George Carlin who said, "Everyone that drives slower than me is an idiot and everyone who drives faster than me is an asshole!" I'm kidding, but many feel this is true. Focus, Rob! Ok, sorry. Here is what it means: it means your life is better than theirs. Congratulations, you have already won. They are upset and you are happy. Their life isn't going well right now, but yours is. Someone trying to give you negativity is a reminder we should be grateful. They don't know you, which means it is not personal. Remember when someone tries to give you a gift (in this example it's their middle finger) and you don't accept the gift, they still own it. If you accept the gift, try to give them a gift back (your middle finger), and if you internalize their gift who really wins? I mean have you ever said to yourself "OMG their middle finger is bigger than mine, so they win?" Of course not.

Think of the person who would do such a thing. Are they having a good day or a bad day? Are they happy in that moment, that day, or maybe even with their life? No, they aren't. If we retaliate in some hateful way, does spreading more hatred solve anything? No. This person needs love, they need perspective, they need understanding, they have issues, they have problems, and they need help. I am not suggesting you pull over and try to have a therapy session in the moment. What I am suggesting is they need your light. A smile, a friendly wave, making a heart with your hands (if it's safe to take both hands off the wheel) or even yelling to them "someone loves you and I hope you have a better day." Give your light and your capacity to them. They don't need more negativity. Remember what we discussed in the chapter "Evolution," positivity always wins.

What do I mean when I say "bring the light?" The sun is our source of light in the solar system. Without it we would have cold, darkness, and the inability to live. Darkness is never better than light and warmth. Light and warmth brings life. People who have this darkness inside them (whether they are having a bad day or a bad lifetime) need light, love, and positivity.

If someone is mean, or negative, they need your light to help them. If someone calls you a bad name, rather than calling them one back just turn to them and say, "I love you" and start smiling. They will probably break their negative behavior and laugh. If someone is acting angry with you and you turn to them and say "You seem angry and this doesn't seem to be the way you usually are. Are you ok?" Also remember the one we talked about before "you are such an attractive person but I bet you are even more attractive when you smile."

What if you said in an argument "I agree with this part of what you said and that was really smart!" While the person it totally disarmed you follow up with "Do you mind if we discuss this other part more? Because I am still trying to understand your point of view." Validating someone, even if it is a small validation, makes them feel heard and disarms them. It starts a level of connection which leads to understanding and compromise. Negativity will not survive unless we feed it.

What if we had a "jail" where we had psychologists to talk to the inmates to figure out WHY they committed their crime? What if inmates had meditation classes, were bombarded with positive music, positive movies, loving themes, bright colors, smiling faces, and themes of connection and love. What if their "penalty" for doing something bad was to have a life of good servitude? What if when they did enough good in the world, that was when they had "paid their debt to society?" What if inmates were trained to be the psychologists to help the new inmates who came to the prison? So when an inmate was released they had a skill they could take out into the world to support themselves financially and continue bringing help, positivity, and light to the world? Like Bob Marley said, "only you can redeem yourself." Maybe this is a better idea than when someone does something negative and we just retaliate with something negative.

Good Humans (hopefully) wear their bracelet!

CHAPTER 507:
The WHY Bracelet

What's with the bracelet? One of the things I have noticed about people is when people sit near one another, get in an elevator together, or are otherwise in close proximity, they don't talk. WHY? 99% of people are good people!

When I am in proximity to strangers I will find something in which to compliment them. I say something simple (and polite) like "hey, I like your shoes," "you look so pretty today," "hey man, tell me about that gorgeous watch you have on" or the one I did the other day when there was a guy collecting parking money at the stadium I rolled up in my car and said "hey handsome, how is your day?" That guy smiled so big, it looked like I made his day! Every time I have done this, maybe with one exception, people have been nice and receptive. WHY not make it a habit?

So, what's with the bracelet?

Wearing your WHY bracelet tells others "I'm approachable," "I'm a nice person," "I'm a good human," "I have good character," and "I am committed to doing my part to make the world a better place." The best way to start a conversation with someone is to ask them what they liked most about this book. "What did the book do for you?," "How did WHY change your life?" or "What epiphanies did you have while you read WHY?"

When we build this society, the world will open up to us. We will realize how many people are good humans who want the world to be a better place. Our need for connection is going to be filled off the charts! Bracelet wearers have committed to sweeping their own doorstep, like you have. If there is a time, or a day, where you don't feel approachable (maybe you are temporarily low on capacity), simply put your bracelet in your pocket. I want to offer the silicone ones which are simple to wear as well as nicer, or fancier, ones which may just have the letter "Y" on them (I have to think of my fashionista friends too.)

When I see someone wearing a WHY (or simply the letter "Y") bracelet my goal is to out MMFI (Make Me Feel Important) you. I told you in the chapter "Relationships" that you will not out relationship me. I imagine someone has the letters "MMFI" written on their forehead and I will make you feel important. If I can give you a smile that you can wear for the rest of the day, then my day will be even more complete. I feel so happy when I do it that it's almost selfish. I can tell you it's addictive though! It will fill all your need levels with one simple action.

**Order bracelets on our website:
www.iWantToKnowWHY.com**

SECTION 600:
YOUR WHY NURTURE

Summary

CHAPTER 601:
Bringing It All Together

DO NOT read this chapter first! This is not a "who done it" novel. I know there are some of you, like my sister, who skip to the last chapter and read it first. This chapter will not make sense unless you read it last. Once you are done reading this chapter, go right back to the beginning and read the book again. Each time you read the book you will gain more insight and deeper understanding.

WHY'S WHY

I am continuing Bob Marley's message for all of us to live in peace, love, and unity. I don't think it's a coincidence Bob's first name was Robert, and so is mine.

OK ROB, SO WHAT'S WITH THESE WHY FOCUS GROUPS?

The goal is we should be able to explain our WHY. Hi, my name is Sally and my WHY is:

- Primary Personality: Evolved Driver
- Secondary Personality: Unevolved Analytical
- Hierarchy: Evolved Sigma

- MT or MA: MT
- 6 BHN (Six Basic Human Needs):
  - Need for Significance = 9
  - Need for Connection = 5
  - Need for Certainty = 6
  - Need for Uncertainty = 8
  - Need for Love = 9
  - Need for Growth/Contribution = 9
- Capacity = C3
- Primary love language: Words of affirmation
- Secondary love language: Physical touch

Even throw in a Birth Order to round things out:

- Generational Only Child

If you can explain YOUR WHY like this, the world will be a better place. When someone else can explain themselves to you this way, you will understand their WHY instantly. How amazing!

Let me ask you…

What do you think Sally (above) does for a living?

What if I told you she is a Trial Attorney who is a partner in a small law firm? Would that make sense? When she goes to court the silently dominant Sigma (small law firm) wants to win (MT and Need for Significance.) The Driver loves that each case seems like a task and her C3 Capacity can handle a lot of pressure. She is Contributing to people who were wronged and is Growing as a better Trial Attorney, learning from each case. The Analytical loved all the information that studying law provided. She loves Words of Affirmation which makes her really good at word choice and conveying what she wants to say, which also makes her a more effective

Trial Attorney. She is a Generational Only Child which made her independent, so she loves to be on her own winning these cases and the autonomy it brings.

So, did she choose to be a Trial Attorney or did the job choose her? The most important thing to understand is that when she got into that position, it felt right. She knew in her gut she was in the right place. If she couldn't find the right firm, she may have started her own.

Remember Chris and his best friend from the chapter "Being in the right environment?" Chris wasted years of his life not being in the right environment because he didn't fully understand himself. He also didn't understand his best friend because he asked him to move to the big city. If he understood the best friend's WHY NATURE, he would have known his friend wouldn't flourish in the editor job.

Once you can articulate YOUR WHY the way we did for Sally, what you should do for a living and where you should be, will seem obvious. If not for you, it will to your WHY Focus Group.

WHY FOCUS GROUPS ARE

People who have read the book and understand WHY NATURE and WHY NURTURE

People who wear their bracelet and have the desire to make the world a better place

Agree to meet weekly, bi-monthly, or (at a minimum) monthly

A group can be 3 people, 30 people, or 300 people. Video calls or in person meetings.

The group helps one another understand themselves so they don't waste years of their life in the wrong environment or with a romantic partner they don't fully understand. Put away the pride, put away the ego, no judging, there should just be understanding, clarity, and epiphanies.

The goal is to learn what is special about you! Understand which traits can be changed and which cannot. Change the ones you want to change and Evolve the ones you cannot change. Learn the positive traits of your personality types and hierarchy.

HOW TO IDENTIFY PERSONALITY TYPES AT A GLANCE

Amiable: probably very nice, attentive, maybe a bit wishy-washy (if they don't yet know what you want) and is somehow asking what would make you happy.

Analytical: low on emotion, asking a lot of questions, and needs more information.

Driver: trying to get the task done. Uses very few words. Gets to the point. Doesn't really care how it makes you feel.

Expressive: loud, drawing attention to themselves, life of the party, or otherwise trying to get everyone's attention.

Once you distinguish these traits, identifying personality types will come naturally to you. Once you identify someone's personality, then you will see when they are acting differently and have toggled into a different personality type. If you truly never see them toggle, then both primary and secondary are the same, although one may be evolved and the other unevolved.

HIERARCHY TYPING

We can't just say I want to be an Alpha or my need for significance won't let me self-identify. I want to be the top of the social hierarchy so I am just going to call myself an Alpha. This won't work for your life and for those you want to be in a relationship with. Identify your Hierarchy, learn what is special about you, and accept yourself.

PRO TIP: Whatever you focus on determines your life. If you constantly focus on your negative traits, it will adversely affect your life. If you focus on your positive traits and know who you are and who you are not, it will have a profound, uplifting, and positive affect on your life.

RANDOM TAKE AWAYS:

Your EBR spills out of your cup when life bumps you. Pay attention to what spills out of your cup and out of other people's cup. It will give great insight.

Ask any coach, of any sport, and they will tell you the same thing "the best players do the basics well." WHY? Because if you don't do the basics well, then you can't build from there. Understanding YOUR WHY is one of those basics. Repetitious boredom is one of the basic skills which must be mastered. I described it in the chapter "Bringing your WHY NATURE all together." We must have a good foundation before you can build!

Remember there are 7 billion people on this planet. Not everyone is going to like you and that's ok as long as we are all good humans. Wish them well with their life and move on. There is someone out there for everyone. Read the section on being a good human and embrace it. Learn it, live it, love it!

Do what you can to raise your Capacity and give the extra Capacity to positive things. Remember what I said in Balance? What do you think would happen if you cut the people out of your life who were capacity suckers? You know who I am talking about. The people you have an unBalanced relationship with. You only speak to them when you call them. They only call you when they need something. That person. How much more time would you have without that person in your life? How many more well rested nights would that bring you? This will increase your Capacity to have more Balance in the relationships you should be focusing on.

Create Balance in your life so you work "on your life" as much as you are "in your life." Have a life by design and don't wish your life away

Have regular strategy sessions in your important relationships.

Remember to speak clearly, enunciate your words, have a command of your language, and use "I messages." In fact, just revisit the chapter "Communication" often and it will provide many benefits in your life.

What category is your behavior in? If you are slipping out of Category 1, WHY? Which needs are you trying to fulfill with Category 2, 3, or 4 behaviors and WHY?

The mind is wired for safety and security, not happiness. This is WHY The Negative Wave affects us. This is also WHY when you are with someone you deeply trust, your body releases oxytocin, the love hormone, which lowers stress, promotes relaxation, and makes you sleepy. It literally signals your nervous system that it is ok to rest. We have to override our brains wiring and change it to be programmed for happiness.

Whenever we have something that separates people, it breeds resentment, jealousy, and problems. Separation is not unity.

The biggest **PRO TIP** is about the Need for Significance: Evolved people know not to fill their Need for Significance externally. It doesn't work. What do I mean by that? Creating actions to feel Significant, or simply telling people you are Significant, is a hole you can never fill. WHY? Because no one cares and consequently, no one really thinks you are Significant. Trust me on this. When you are good, you tell everyone. When you are great, everyone tells you. When people start telling you how good you are, only then are you truly Significant in the eyes of others. Filling your Need for Significance internally means you know you are special to your life partner, your family, and your friends. You are Significant in their eyes and in their lives.

Don't believe me? Ok fine, one more test:

Name all the Presidents of the United States (if you live in a different country, name all the Presidents in the last 250 years). Unless you work in politics, you can't do it. Maybe you named 10 of them, or 20 if you paid attention in history class, but there have been almost 50 US Presidents to date. A 20% or even a 40% grade on this test is still a failing grade.

Want to try an easier test?

What did your great-great grandfather do for a living? What was his middle name? What was his favorite hobby? If you are a 5th generation family business or have the same name as him then answer the question on the other side of your family. Can't do it? Do you even know his name? Probably not. WHY? Because he has been forgotten, as you will be.

Let me say this another way: over 5 billion people have been born in the United States since 1776, and less than 50 people have been President. We just showed you can't name the people who have been some of the most significant people in the United States. To drive my point home, you don't even know the details about your own family member from a few generations ago. What makes you think anyone is going to remember you? I'm sorry for the cold water but this is the truth.

I told you that you won't like everything I have to say but once you realize this truth then you will realize you should just live your life for yourself and life is not that serious. In these truths there is freedom. Be Significant to your family and your loved ones. If you are Significant in another way, people will tell you.

So if I don't focus on my Need for Significance, what should I focus on? Raise your Need for Connection! This is the key to living a fulfilled life. Let connection, love, and unity spill out of your cup every day and your life will be Significant. Let me tell you something, when I pass away I don't want to be remembered for how Significant I was, but for how much I brought the world together, just like Bob Marley.

What do you want to be remembered for? How you looked? The company you built that made a lot of money for you? The perfectly straight teeth you had? These don't seem to be so important now, do they?

Make a difference in the world
Start by sweeping your own doorstep
Then give back and help others
Start by wearing your bracelet

*"First we must have Understanding
From Understanding we can have Tolerance
From Tolerance we can have Acceptance
From Acceptance we can have Peace"*
~Rob Abel

"One Love. One heart. Let's get together and feel all right."
~Bob Marley

www.iWantToKnowWHY.com

www.RobAbel.com

THE END

www.ingramcontent.com/pod-product-compliance
Lightning Source LLC
Chambersburg PA
CBHW060450030426
42337CB00015B/1534